Personnel
Psychology

Personnel Psychology

John B. Miner

Professor, University of Maryland
Consultant to the Firm, McKinsey & Company, Inc.

THE MACMILLAN COMPANY
COLLIER-MACMILLAN LIMITED, London

To Barbara, Cynthia, David,
Frances, Jillian,
John

Materials reprinted from *Personnel and Industrial Relations: A Managerial Approach,* by John B. Miner, © copyright 1969 by The Macmillan Company.

Library of Congress catalog card number: 69–14270

THE MACMILLAN COMPANY
COLLIER-MACMILLAN CANADA, LTD., TORONTO, ONTARIO

Printed in the United States of America

Preface

It is often as important to specify what a book is not as to specify what it is. Titles can be misleading. Definition by both inclusion and exclusion becomes particularly desirable amid the shifting emphases and concerns of modern-day industrial psychology.

This book is about the personnel process and psychology's contribution to our understanding of it. As such, it deals with what traditionally has been the core of industrial psychology. There is very little discussion of organizational behavior, employee motivation, and leadership, which are the major topics of organizational psychology; even less of human engineering and conditions of work; and practically no consideration of the various aspects of consumer psychology.

For those who may wish to concentrate on personnel psychology alone, this book should provide a rather comprehensive coverage. For those who are concerned with industrial psychology as a whole, it should be read in conjunction with other material. In recent years, a number of relatively small volumes have been published dealing with organizational psychology, engineering psychology, consumer psychology, industrial clinical psychology, psychological testing, the psychology of labor-management relations, and other topics. These might well be read along with *Personnel Psychology* to provide an extension, in depth or breadth, of knowledge within the total field of industrial psychology. Or some of the more comprehensive readings books in industrial psychology might be utilized for the same purpose.

The selection of subject matter to be included was strongly influenced by the theoretical framework that underlies the presentation. The various aspects of personnel psychology are considered in terms of an explicit theory of industrial organization. This approach has the distinct advantage of providing specific guidelines as to what is and is not part of the personnel process. It also places primary stress on problem-solving and the selection of personnel strategies, rather than on description of existing practice. In the author's opinion, such a problem-oriented, as opposed to a technique-oriented, approach to the field is absolutely essential to its further development.

The theory is developed on a piecemeal basis as appropriate to the topic under discussion. Chapter 14 then contains a complete statement. There is no reason why this theoretical part cannot be covered earlier, right after Chapter 1, and in fact, many may wish to take up the material in that order.

As with most volumes of this kind, assistance has come from many sources. I particularly want to express thanks to Abraham K. Korman, who is currently on the faculty of New York University, for the work he did in connection with Chapters 1, 2, and 3, and to my wife, Mary Green Miner, for her efforts in connection with Chapters 12 and 13. Also my appreciation to Lyman Porter and Edwin Ghiselli for providing an opportunity to try out this material with psychology students during a visiting year on the Berkeley campus of the University of California.

This book and *Personnel and Industrial Relations* are published as parallel volumes to satisfy particular course needs and disciplinary interests. Their content is frequently overlapping. *Personnel and Industrial Relations* is the more general, dealing with the personnel process broadly defined. *Personnel Psychology* is more specific, covering those topics within the larger volume that are primarily of psychological concern.

J. B. M.

Contents

5
Employee Evaluation: Rating Systems and Attitude Surveys   **104**

6
Selection: Validation Models and Nontest Techniques   **128**

7
Selection: Psychological Testing   **159**

8
Management Development   **183**

1

Personnel Psychology and the Industrial Organization

Personnel psychology, in the simplest terms, is the application of psychological research and theory to the problems of organizational human resource utilization. People are the essential ingredient in all organizations—be they business, educational, governmental, or religious—and the ways people are recruited and utilized by the leadership largely determine whether the organization will survive and achieve its objectives. Thus, company managers are constantly concerned with human resources—with the way these resources are developed and utilized, with the assumptions made about them, with the formulation of personnel policy, and with the methods and procedures used in dealing with the work force.

Developing, applying, and evaluating policies, procedures, methods, and programs relating to the individual in the organization is generally designated as the personnel function. This function may be carried out by a personnel department or it may be dispersed widely throughout a firm, among managers who have numerous nonpersonnel responsibilities as well. Personnel management is defined in terms of a specific set of activities, and not with reference to the organizational loci where the work is performed.

PERSONNEL PSYCHOLOGY
AND PERSONNEL MANAGEMENT

Knowledge in the field of personnel management derives from a host of disciplines: sociology, economics, engineering, law, medicine, and, of course, psychology. Colleges and universities offer courses in Industrial Sociology, Labor Economics, Industrial Engineering, Labor Law, Industrial Medicine, and Industrial Psychology; all these cover topics related to one aspect or another of personnel management.

Personnel psychology is, thus, the area of overlap between psychology and personnel management. Psychologists have contributed a great deal to the personnel field; in some areas, almost all that is known derives from their work. In addition, the contributions of psychology are largely responsible for original scientific research in personnel management. Industrial and personnel psychologists are particularly likely to be employed in an organization's personnel research unit.

This book deals only with those aspects of the personnel field that concern psychologists. A model, or theory, of the personnel function will be developed, but those segments of the theory that bear on matters currently outside the rubric of psychology will be given very little attention. Thus, such major concerns of personnel management as industry differences, labor law, employment law, organization planning, industrial medicine, governmental manpower programs, labor relations, employee benefits and services, and wage and salary administration will be mentioned briefly, if at all. These areas to date have been influenced more by other disciplines than by psychology.

PERSONNEL PSYCHOLOGY
AND INDUSTRIAL PSYCHOLOGY

Although psychologists have been interested in the personnel function for a longer period of time than in other aspects of business organization, and have done more research and made a greater contribution to existing industrial practice in this area, they also have been concerned with other aspects. Marketing and production have achieved particular attention, to the extent that there now are fully developed subfields within industrial psychology: consumer and engineering psychology, respectively. In addition, psychologists have recently become concerned with accounting and finance, dealing with such matters as the prediction of credit risks and the extension of accounting practice to include human assets. It seems likely that psychologists soon will be conducting research related to all the major processes and functions of business organizations.

Another subfield within industrial psychology, closely related to personnel psychology, but not part of it, has emerged with considerable vigor in recent years. Organizational psychology deals with the total functioning of a company, or any type of organization for that matter. In practice, it has been particularly concerned with such topics as leadership, employee motivation, work-group dynamics, and communication patterns, but matters related to organizational design and effectiveness are receiving increasing attention. The model for human resources utilization that provides the framework for this book was generated out of certain concepts originally evolved within organizational psychology.

Thus, personnel psychology must be viewed as a subfield within industrial psychology, as well as a subfield within personnel management. Historically it antedates most other subfields; in fact, for a number of years it was practically coterminous with industrial psychology as a whole. Yet today, with the tremendous growth of industrial psychology in a variety of directions, personnel is appropriately considered as only one of the numerous organizational functions to which industrial psychologists have turned their attention.

The relationships that we have been considering are pictured in Figure 1–1.

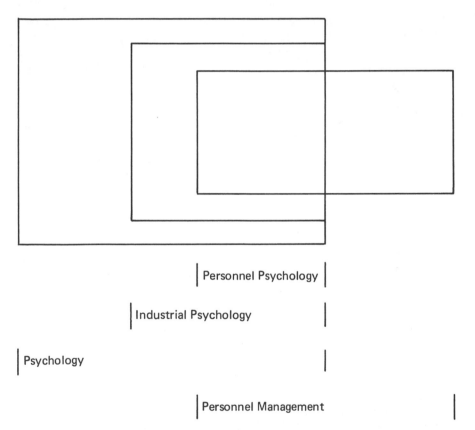

Personnel Psychology

Industrial Psychology

Psychology

Personnel Management

Figure 1–1. A Definition of Personnel Psychology

PERSONNEL PSYCHOLOGY
AND ORGANIZATIONAL GOALS

As an applied discipline, personnel psychology is basically concerned with achieving concrete results within an organizational context. In the applied areas of psychology, it is not sufficient to accumulate knowledge regarding human behavior and thus increase our total understanding; one is also concerned with such matters as prediction, change, and control. The primary objectives of personnel psychology are to make business organizations, which are its major concern, more effective and more satisfying as places to work.

Although the methods used to achieve them are different, the goals that the personnel function seeks to achieve within the organization are the same as for the company as a whole. Those working in personnel carry out a unique set of activities having to do with the utilization of human resources, activities that are not duplicated in other components of the organization. But this work is done with a view to accomplishing exactly the same objectives as is the work of others.

There appear to be two interrelated, but distinct categories or types of organizational goals involved here. The first of these is to maximize the productivity of the organization. This is, of course, no new concept. Some organizations, in fact, have considered it the only goal worth mentioning. In the business world, productivity must be considered in relation to earnings and long-term, net profit. In its most general sense, this objective refers to the entire gamut of procedures and activities that management carries out to maximize the attainment of the stated functional purpose of the organization. This purpose may be to manufacture and sell automobiles, to provide a valuable stock market investment-counseling service, or to produce missiles for the national defense effort. Some larger corporations have become so complex, and their product lines so diversified, that a full statement of this productivity objective can become quite lengthy. Yet, in all instances, a company produces something that has value and that, therefore, has prospects of yielding a profit. In this sense, there is always a task objective.

The procedures used to compute or identify the extent to which this goal attainment has actually occurred vary considerably. Thus, in manufacturing, it is not uncommon for management to determine productivity by computing the number of units produced per man-hour worked. This figure may be modified to account for the quality factor by dividing the percentage of all units produced that meet previously established standards of excellence by the number of man-hours. A department store, on the other hand, may establish productivity in terms of the dollar volume of sales divided by the man-hours worked, or perhaps the dollar value of goods returned per man-hour, or over a given time period. Sometimes, much more complex procedures are introduced that take into account investments, depreciation allowances, share-of-the-market factors, and company growth curves of one sort or another. Whichever method is used, the assumption behind it is that a major goal is to maximize the attainment of the stated functional purposes of the organization.

The second organizational goal is related to the first, but can be distinguished quite clearly from it. It has been recognized much more recently, and is probably still not nearly so likely to be given explicit statement as that of organizational productivity. It is, nevertheless, of equal, and perhaps even greater, importance. Stated most simply, this objective is to maintain the organization as an ongoing unit in the face of internal and external pressures and stress. The term *organizational maintenance* is often used to refer to this goal.

The importance of organizational maintenance began to be appreciated in the period following World War II when manpower shortages developed and there was strong competition for the available talent. During this period, management started to realize that, if it was to maintain a loyal work force, an effort would have to be made to establish working conditions that would contribute to job satisfaction and thus facilitate talent retention.

Recently, management has become much more aware that increased effort must be devoted to problems of organizational maintenance if the company is to remain intact under the stresses of a changing labor force, automation, and technological innovation. These factors have brought about sizable alterations in many firms, and, in the process, their organizational structures have often been strained to the breaking point. New occupational groups have appeared from nowhere to demand a position, often of considerable importance, within the existing hierarchy. At the same time, other groups have been striving to maintain their traditional status.

Management has also come to realize that practices developed during a period when large numbers of relatively poorly educated employees made up the work force are no longer suitable when a sizable percentage of the employees are as well educated as the top management group. But this realization has on occasion lagged well behind the actual changes in the composition of the labor force, and major problems of organizational maintenance have resulted. Situations such as these place an enormous strain on any social group and may create so much tension that the productivity goal is almost entirely forgotten for long periods of time.

As we will see in subsequent chapters, major contributions in the area of organizational maintenance have been made by the basic behavioral sciences of psychology and sociology. Research and theory derived from these fields have been extremely helpful to personnel management in that they have provided a variety of procedures for measuring and quantifying such concepts as job satisfaction, organizational commitment, and morale. In addition, these disciplines have contributed to a much greater understanding of how group and organizational dynamics may be modified so as to foster stability and continued existence. Just as economics and political science have made their greatest contributions in providing a knowledge of the ways in which *external* stresses have an influence on a company's capacity for survival, psychology and sociology have been particularly valuable as sources of information regarding the nature of *internal* pressures and stresses.

THE CONCERNS OF PERSONNEL PSYCHOLOGY

Let us now turn to the actual content of the work—what things personnel psychologists do for an organization and the major topics of research interest. At this point, only a brief preview is possible. But it is important at the outset to get a general feeling for the subject matter and to gain some appreciation of the more important functions.

1. *Organization Planning and Job Analysis.* One major activity is the study and analysis of jobs throughout the company in terms of the various tasks and duties required, as well as the personal characteristics needed for effective performance. This involves an initial analysis of each position. These separate studies are combined and compared so as to provide information regarding job interrelationships. Groupings are developed on various bases: in terms of the difficulty of the work, the specific tasks performed, and the characteristics required for successful performance. In this way, it is possible to use job analysis data in establishing wage and salary scales, as a guide when transferring employees, in promoting employee health and safety, and for many other purposes.

Organization planning and job analysis have much in common, since both are concerned with establishing what a person is expected to do. Organization planning, however, focuses specifically on managerial activities. It provides a structure for the company by identifying the various subgroupings headed by individuals in managerial jobs. Thus, whereas organization planning defines what is expected at the upper levels of the hierarchy, job analysis carries the process down through the organization.

2. *Appraisal and Evaluation.* Once a job has been established and some definition of what the incumbent is expected to do developed, it is possible to evaluate the performance of an individual. A great variety of measurement techniques have been invented for this purpose, and not all of these are normally administered by personnel specialists. Industrial engineers, for instance, are likely to be responsible for developing measures of output, waste, and so on for production employees; accountants set up systems for determining profitability that are used to evaluate department managers. However, many techniques, especially those involving some type of rating, are clearly of major concern to psychologists working in the personnel area.

It is characteristic for management appraisal programs to be administered separately from procedures applied at lower levels. This is, in part, because of differing requirements. A major approach in management appraisal is to evaluate the manager in terms of the productivity and the attitudes of his group. To what extent is the particular function supervised contributing to the goals of the organization? Nonmanagerial employees, on the other hand, are evaluated directly, rather than by the performance of others.

Whatever the level and technique, the purposes of appraisal and evaluation procedures remain much the same. The resulting information is used to establish pay, to make personnel placement decisions, to determine the degree to which training is needed, and for a number of other purposes. In recent years, there has been considerable interest in the values and problems associated with feeding back appraisal information to the employee with a view to stimulating greater effort and helping him to perform more effectively.

3. *Selection.* Among the most important responsibilities of personnel psychologists are those relating to the selection of future employees from the usually much larger number of applicants. There is reason to believe that more problems of human resource utilization have their origins in the initial selection than in any other area (1). Thus, the selection policies and procedures utilized by an organization are of major importance, and since the personnel department has the technical skills needed to deal with this problem, it is usually assigned responsibility not only for developing recruiting procedures that will ensure an adequate supply of applicants, but for developing techniques to choose among applicants as well.

In developing such a selection system, it is necessary to keep the company goals of productivity and organizational maintenance in mind. It is not enough merely to determine whether an individual can perform the work effectively; there are also the questions of whether he will remain sufficiently satisfied in his new position so that he will stay with the company, whether he will work effectively with others or be a source of dissension, and whether he is likely to do anything dishonest or disloyal that might serve to undermine the firm's very existence. These are important questions for any organization, and it is impossible to dismiss them as merely reflecting an excessive concern with matters of conformity.

There are some types of selection procedures that are used almost exclusively to identify those individuals who will be most productive. Other techniques are characteristically used to select those who will not threaten the organization in any way or leave it before a reasonable period of time has elapsed. Although some of these latter procedures, such as the employment interview, are not widely recognized as performing this function, they remain important to the total selection process. Subsequent discussions will cover the entire range of techniques and procedures in this area, while, at the same time, attempting to specify exactly what objectives are achieved by each approach.

4. *Training and Development.* Personnel psychologists also are a source of specialized information in the area of employee and manage-

ment training and development. On occasion, this involves actually teaching various courses for company personnel. In order to carry out their responsibilities in this area, irrespective of the specific nature, personnel psychologists must be thoroughly informed regarding relevant research findings in the fields of education and psychology, as well as those developed in the industrial training field itself. Often considerable knowledge of various fields of business study such as accounting, management, and marketing may be required as well.

The specific nature of the training programs developed will, of course, depend on the organizational objective. Training may be used to increase directly the job skills of a group of individuals by teaching them how to perform their tasks more effectively. Thus, production workers may learn to operate new equipment or new supervisors to handle bookkeeping details associated with their work. It is clear that training primarily contributes to the productivity goal. However, the educational process also is used in connection with the organization maintenance function, as when production foremen are taught how to handle various types of labor relations problems or when a number of managers participate in a sensitivity training laboratory in order to increase their ability to work cooperatively.

5. *Safety*. The objective here is to keep employees in physical shape to continue working. American industry has been very successful in this regard, to the point where many factories are in fact safer than the employees' homes. Yet, this result is achieved only at the expense of a continuing effort involving physicians, safety engineers, and personnel managers, as well as psychologists.

The approaches used are varied. They include safety training, posters and contests, and equipment design. In addition, psychologists have been concerned with the accident-prone employee. These individuals have repeated accidents, presumably as a result of certain personality predispositions. In fact, much psychological research in the safety area has been devoted to this problem.

6. *Industrial Clinical Psychology*. When a man is not doing well on his job, something must be done to change the situation. Of course, he may be fired and that, like hiring, is basically a personnel function, but there are a number of alternatives.

Some kind of counseling may be introduced in the hope that the man can come to understand the source of his difficulties and correct them. This is a costly approach from a company viewpoint, and as a result it is now usually restricted to highly trained employees, such as those in research and development groups and legal departments. In these cases, the demand for manpower of a.kind that is in short supply makes replacement difficult, and thus investment in such retention procedures as counseling is deemed worthwhile.

Discipline and job change are additional procedures for improving unsatisfactory employees. Discipline may take the form of a warning or of suspension without pay, or in extreme cases, of discharge. The specific approaches are usually spelled out in considerable detail in the union contract, and the procedures involved tend to be rather legalistic. Transfer, on the other hand, at least as it relates to ineffective performance, primarily attempts to overcome the errors of initial placement. Thus, an effort is made to shift the man to a type of job where the expectations are more consistent with his capabilities and desires.

7. *Communications.* Communications procedures are used primarily for purposes of organizational maintenance. In many instances, they play a major role in labor-management relationships, communicating the company viewpoint on issues that are in dispute. Even where this is not the case, the goal is to create a sense of belonging in relation to the firm, to pull the total organization together as a cohesive unit. Downward communication programs of this kind can include the use of company magazines and newspapers, bulletin boards, meetings, and handbooks.

But organizational maintenance is not most effectively fostered by a total emphasis on downward communication. In addition, procedures are needed that will permit dissatisfactions, questions, and ideas to flow upward. This is one objective of attitude surveys, counseling, grievance procedures, and suggestion systems. Unfortunately, techniques of this latter kind, which will provide valid feedback to management on the consequences of its policies and decisions, have not been developed to the same degree as have downward communication mechanisms.

8. *Payment and Labor Relations.* Although wage and salary administration, employee benefits, and labor relations traditionally have been a concern of economists, psychologists have taken an increasing interest in these matters. Central to the operation of any organized group activity is the existence of some type of reward structure that will be viewed by the members as fair and equitable and that is sufficient to induce individuals to contribute their efforts toward the common goals. Although, in recent years, there has been some tendency to place increasing stress on nonmonetary considerations, the major formalized reward system used by business organizations remains the wage and salary structure. Since matters of motivation and reward traditionally have been a primary focus of psychological theory and research, it is not surprising that industrial psychologists have become interested in the payment process as it operates within ongoing organizations.

Another area of increasing psychological concern involves the labor union, or unions, that represent the company's employees. This concern is not entirely restricted to those firms that have been unionized, for in those instances where a union is not present, there is always the prospect that the situation may change at some later date. The personnel department may devote considerable effort to developing strategies designed to forestall such an event and to conducting attitude surveys to determine whether it might be imminent. Where a union does represent a sizable segment of the company's labor force, collective bargaining, grievance procedures, arbitration, court cases, and other such activities may absorb much of the time of all those working in personnel.

In order to carry out the necessary planning and minimize errors in decision-making, it is essential for a sizable proportion of the company's total management to be involved in the various aspects of labor relations. Yet, it is also true that those with specialized knowledge in the area of human resource utilization will almost invariably have a central position in labor relations. In most companies, the primary responsibility for advising on labor-management problems is allocated either to an industrial relations specialist or to someone trained in the intricacies of labor law. In many instances, these two are actually the same person. In any case, the function performed is basically a component of the personnel activity, and psychologists may well be involved.

Since the ultimate goal of management with respect to labor relations is the minimization of internal conflict without sacrificing profit and productivity, labor relations activities can be viewed as serving a primarily organizational maintenance function. A number of firms have completely disappeared under the pressure of extreme labor-management stress. In these instances, the organizational maintenance goal of the personnel component clearly failed.

These, then, are the aspects of the personnel function with which psychologists have become particularly concerned. Certainly, there is much in the field of personnel management that has not as yet been an object of psychological research; yet, in recent years, psychologists have extended their vistas considerably. As we shall see in the chapters that follow, psychology has made a very important contribution to our knowledge of human resources utilization.

REFERENCE

1. Miner, J. B. *The Management of Ineffective Performance*. New York: McGraw-Hill, 1963.

QUESTIONS

1. How does personnel psychology relate to personnel management; to industrial psychology? What other disciplines and areas of specialization are included in each?
2. What are the goals of industrial organizations; of personnel management; of personnel psychology? Do you see any conflict between the role of the psychologist as a scientist and his role as a professional within the personnel department of a business organization?

2

Constraints on Personnel Decisions: Individual and Cultural Differences

People differ from one another. They differ in an almost infinite number of respects, including intelligence, personality, and physical make-up. We tend to take the fact of difference for granted; yet personnel decisions are influenced as much by this diversity of human characteristics as by any other factor.

At any given point, the action that may be taken in an effort to maximize the attainment of productivity and organizational maintenance goals is restricted severely by the nature of the available human resources. Any manager has at his disposal a limited set of abilities, specialized knowledges, motives, muscular skills, and so on. His freedom to make and carry out decisions, to initiate programs, and to implement policies is confined by the existing potentialities. Thus, a major scientific research effort cannot be begun by a firm devoid of employees with advanced training in the sciences, and an effective office machine unit cannot be achieved within an organization that lacks people with sufficiently high levels of work motivation or industriousness to operate the machines (36,37). It is in this sense that individual differences constrain personnel decisions.

Constraints of this kind are not so rigid as to preclude the possibility of modification. At a given point in time, with one's perspective limited to a specific organization and the individuals constituting it, these constraints do appear insurmountable. But, given an expanded time span and the possibility of utilizing human resources outside the existing firm, many constraints can be made to disappear. Thus, it is important to know not only how people differ in those characteristics that are related to the attainment of organizational goals, but also how various types of individuals may be changed, at what cost, under what circumstances, and in how short a period of time. Which constraints are for all practical purposes absolute, because no matter where one searches in the national labor force or what type of change procedure is introduced, the restrictions imposed are not likely to be overcome? Which internal constraints are relatively resilient, given the opportunity to go outside the confines of the existing organization and to extend the change process into the future?

This chapter attempts to answer these questions. Some of what is currently known about the differences that exist between various major groups in our society is reviewed. In the process, the reader should gain an understanding of many human factors that play an important role in determining whether an organization will survive and attain high levels of productivity. In addition, an attempt will be made to indicate which factors are susceptible to change, and to at least note in passing how these modifications may be brought about. Subsequent chapters, however, discuss the personnel psychologist's role as a change agent in much greater detail. The primary emphasis here must be on the *degree* to which internal constraints of the kind represented by individual differences, in view of the present state of our knowledge, are subject to alteration and circumvention.

In this review, no effort will be made to cover the entire field of differential psychology, the scientific specialty that deals with individual and group variability, since the area is far too large and complex (2,51). An attempt will be made, however, to discuss those factors that are of primary significance for personnel decisions.

INDIVIDUAL AND GROUP DIFFERENCES

Because the major problem is to determine where within the labor force as a whole a given level of ability or a given characteristic is most likely to be found, the discussions that follow deal primarily with group differences. If a department within the company contains individuals of a particular age, sex, occupational group, social class, and so on, it is important to know which human characteristics might be expected to predominate in such a group. Similarly, if one wants to overcome a constraint imposed as a result of these characteristics, by recruiting individuals from the outside, it is desirable to know in which groups the required characteristics are most likely to be found.

This type of analysis is limited, however, in that groups are generally described in terms of some average value, usually the *mean*. Thus, we will be concerned primarily with differences between group means and with contrasting trends between groups. This is not the same as talking about individuals. Not all members of a group are likely to be at the average; rather they will be distributed above and below the mean, often in a pattern similar to the bell-shaped *normal distribution*. Thus, generalizing from knowledge about a group to specific individuals within the group can be rather hazardous. And it is not necessarily true that, because two groups have distinctly different means, two members of the respective groups will invariably differ in the same manner.

Anastasi (2) makes this point clear in discussing a research study that required that a test of arithmetic reasoning ability be administered to 189 boys and 206 girls in the third and fourth grades. It was found that the boys had a mean score on this particular test of 40.39, whereas the girls had a mean score of 35.81. The difference between the two groups appeared to be substantial. (It was significant at the .01 level, and thus would be expected to occur less than once in a hundred times, if a mere chance fluctuation rather than a real and basic difference between boys and girls were responsible for the result.) However, the author goes on to emphasize that even in this instance of a highly reliable group difference, 28 per cent of the girls reached or exceeded the median score for the boys. The significance of this is that, if these differences are retained into adulthood (and other evidence would indicate that they are), there will be a greater concentration of high levels of arithmetic ability among males. But many females may also possess comparable ability. In times of talent shortage, this source might be well worth investigating; previously male jobs might be staffed with individuals of both sexes. Furthermore, it is clear that one cannot classify an individual in terms of arithmetic reasoning competence merely on the basis of knowledge regarding his or her sex. Many of the girls scored higher than a number of the boys. Apparently, therefore, in this area at least, group differences cannot be translated directly into individual differences.

This point emerges even more clearly from a study made by the U.S. Army Personnel Research Office (13). The researchers knew that on a number of the aptitude tests used for assigning army recruits to occupational specialties, males performed significantly better than females in terms of average scores. The problem posed was, given this fact of a clearcut sex difference, how many females would be able to meet various required minimum acceptable levels of test performance (cut-off scores) in times of talent shortages. The results of the study are presented in Table 2–1.

It is apparent that there are a number of female recruits who could qualify for work in the areas represented, especially electronics, without time-consuming and costly training. Yet it is also clear that under normal conditions of manpower availability, males are most likely to be equipped to perform effectively in the type of position under study. One would have to search much less widely among male recruits to find a specified number of acceptable workers.

TABLE 2–1. Sex Differences in Qualifications for Three Aptitude Areas

Aptitude area	Per cent qualifying for aptitude area with cut-off score of 90		Per cent qualifying for aptitude area with cut-off score of 100	
	Females	Males	Females	Males
Electronics	55	93	19	76
General maintenance	27	88	5	70
Motor maintenance	14	85	2	52

Source: E. F. Fuchs and C. H. Hammer, "A Survey of Women's Aptitudes for Army Jobs," *Personnel Psychology*, Vol. 16 (1963), p. 153.

Differences Between the Sexes

In view of the major differences in the upbringing of members of the two sexes, and in the roles they play in adult life, it seems important to extend our discussion of the relative positions of males and females, especially in those areas that are closely related to the goals of business organizations. This field has received considerable attention from researchers, and, consequently, a good deal of information is available.

DIFFERENCES IN ABILITIES

The sexes do not appear to differ very much, if at all, in terms of the most important type of mental ability in our society, verbal ability. In a nationwide survey of intelligence, using a short vocabulary test that is apparently very similar to most measures of general intelligence, the mean score for the 721 males was 10.75 and for the 779 females 10.78 (35). The difference is of no significance and is typical of most that have been obtained, although another national survey did produce a somewhat larger discrepancy in favor of the female sex (52). In any event, such differences as may exist in verbal ability do not appear to be sufficient to influence personnel decisions.

There are other abilities, however, in which important differences do exist (2). In the area of manipulative abilities, for example, there is evidence that women are clearly superior, both in the speed of their movements and in their accuracy. Females consistently score higher on the standard measures in this area, such as the O'Connor Finger Dexterity Test, the O'Connor Tweezer Dexterity Test, and the Purdue Pegboard. In addition, women generally excel in tasks relating to the rapid perception of details. On the Minnesota Clerical Aptitude Test, which requires the checking of similarities and differences between lists of names and numbers, only 16 per cent of the male working population scored above the level attained by the average female.

However, the ability to pay visual attention to some specific object without being disturbed by the surrounding context, an occupational skill of some importance in these days of dial-watching and automated equipment, is much more pronounced among males. In fact, men generally do somewhat better than women on tasks related to the spatial and mechanical abilities, apparently because of the differences in what society expects of the two sexes. As indicated previously, men tend to be rather markedly superior in activities involving the use of numbers, and arithmetic or mathematical reasoning.

Finally, the average female is superior insofar as abilities related to artistic and musical performance are concerned, although the predominance of males at the very top levels in these fields suggests that the amount of time and effort devoted to learning is an important consideration. When an individual man or woman is willing to break through the sex role constraints, he or she may well achieve a great deal. Yet, in an over-all sense, it seems generally true that men are more skillful in those areas that have traditionally been defined as masculine in nature, and women exhibit greater competence in tasks that society considers essentially feminine. It appears likely, therefore, that the differences noted will remain, as long as there is no major change in the way children are raised in this country, and in the things they are taught.

DIFFERENCES IN PERSONALITY

Among the many differences that have been found between men and women, a pattern that is manifested again and again is the generally much stronger social orientation of members of the female sex. This greater concern with and for other people begins early and continues throughout life. It is evident both within and outside the work situation.

Two examples illustrate the relevance of this difference for personnel. The first derives from a research study dealing with the introduction of automated office equipment in an insurance company (23). It was apparent that the female employees developed highly negative attitudes toward the change because they were afraid that social relationships in the office would be upset. In another study (32), females were found to be much more oriented toward attempting to gain high scores on a specially constructed test when their superior performance might lead to social, rather than intellectual, acceptability. Men, on the other hand, were much more strongly oriented toward achievement and advancement in an intellectual sense.

The pattern of social orientation paramount among women and achievement orientation more pronounced among men is further substantiated by research that has been done with a variety of psychological measures. On the Kuder Preference Record, men tend to obtain higher scores on the mechanical, persuasive, computational, and scientific scales, whereas women do better in the literary, musical, clerical, social service, and artistic areas (2). Similarily, with the Study of Values, men score higher on the Theoretical, Economic, and Political indexes and women on the Aesthetic, Social, and Religious ones (1). In general, the evidence from a number of studies indicates that women are more concerned with such matters as spiritual values, the enjoyment of artistic experience, and a concern for the welfare of others. In contrast, men tend to have a greater desire for prestige and power, as well as a greater appreciation of abstract knowledge and understanding. There is, however, considerable overlapping on all of these characteristics. Thus, it is not uncommon to find a number of success-oriented women in a group of reasonable size. In such fields as retail sales, where women have considerable opportunity to advance, the incidence would appear to be quite high (39).

Another important difference that probably has both biological and cultural origins is the greater aggressiveness of the masculine sex (2). This trend manifests itself in a variety of ways, suggesting that internal stresses tending to divert a company from its maintenance goal will be at a maximum in the primarily male organization or department. On personality inventories, this factor apparently accounts for males usually scoring higher on scales measuring ascendance and dominance, traits that appear to have much in common with aggression (15,16).

Finally, a very important difference between the sexes occurs in the area of emotional adjustment. There is good reason to believe that many more women than men experience emotional distress and that symptoms of an emotional nature are also more prevalent among women (17). Although a greater sensitivity to internal feelings generally and a greater willingness to report such feelings to others may account in part for these findings, the evidence suggests that women are actually less well adjusted as a group in our society than are men. The implications of this difference for employment are discussed at some length toward the end of this chapter.

THE PROSPECTS FOR REMOVING CONSTRAINTS

It appears, then, that there are certain types of work for which women are much less likely to be qualified than men, and other types where the reverse is true. This fact may well serve to limit the alternatives open to a personnel manager or psychologist as he attempts to solve the problems facing him. Thus, if a company employing primarily semiskilled female workers engaged in individual manual assembly tasks wishes to move to an automated production process requiring primarily spatial and mechanical skills of the operators, the existing work force could constitute a major problem. There is every reason to believe that the abilities required for the change would not be available in sufficient quantity among the present employee group. In order to circumvent this constraint, it would be necessary either to go outside the company, presumably among the male population so as to keep recruiting costs at a minimum, to find the skills now required, or perhaps something could be done to overcome the barrier imposed by the existing characteristics of the present employee group. Perhaps the abilities of the women could be changed.

What are the chances that constraints of this kind can be removed by changing people? In general, the prospects, insofar as various intellectual abilities are concerned, do not appear to be very good. Although learning is clearly involved here, this learning tends to occur at the most rapid rate during the formative years, when the individual is devoting his energies almost entirely to his education. Probably, if a similar amount of time were allocated to the learning process in adult life, similar changes could be produced then, and many women could develop their mechanical, spatial, and numerical abilities to a much higher level. This assumes, however, that they would also *want* to learn in these areas. As our society is now structured, the time involved and the problem of motivation present almost insurmountable barriers in adult life.

Unfortunately for any attempt at change, most differences between the sexes are firmly embedded in the culture. In spite of some recent changes, we still have deeply rooted concepts of the male and female role, of the things men and women should be good at. Since the members of the two sexes want to meet these role prescriptions, it is difficult to induce a sizable number of males to develop skills and personality characteristics that they consider basically feminine, and it is equally difficult to get women to acquire behavior patterns that are generally designated as masculine.

It is also true, of course, that certain of the abilities we have discussed may well be determined in large part by sex-linked biological factors. This would seem to be particularly true in the physical area, insofar as such things as physical strength and manipulative skills are concerned. Here the chances for major change would seem to be small, although training can make some difference.

The prospects for removing internal constraints by changing members of the existing work force are not quite all bleak. There is reason to believe, for instance, that the relative lack of success and achievement motivation among women can be overcome to some degree. One way this may be accomplished is to open up to women some of the more challenging high-level positions that previously have been denied to them. The increase in level of expectations resulting should contribute to an over-all rise in achievement motivation throughout the female work force. In addition, the greater opportunity will attract to the firm women who want to attain occupational success.

If this greater opportunity within the company can be coupled with attendance at adult education or university courses, the prospects for change would seem to be even better. A number of university programs designed to facilitate the return of married women to the labor force have been developed in recent years. Psychologists can help to bring these programs to the attention of employees and, in the process, contribute to a much more pronounced success orientation.

The degree to which women can be changed in this respect is best illustrated by reference to a specific study (39). Forty-one college women moved from an initial mean score of 1.59 to a score of 4.24 on a measure of motivation to assume management responsibilities and exercise power, after completing a course specifically designed to produce this type of change. The increase is highly reliable and thus cannot be attributed to chance. The women clearly did change, even though, as might be expected, they held rather unfavorable attitudes toward managerial work at the outset and were still somewhat negative after the training. Other evidence indicates that these changes can be retained over a considerable period of time.

Age Differences

Among the group differences that are of significance for personnel processes, those related to age rank toward the very top. Pension plans and retirement policies must be formulated with specific reference to variations in the degree to which older and younger workers can contribute to company objectives. In addition, replacement planning should be carried out with a view to constraints imposed by differences between age groups. If, for instance, younger workers can generally contribute most effectively in certain areas, it is important that whenever possible they be brought into the company to fill vacancies that occur because of retirement or other reasons. Without this precaution, the average age of the work force may creep up to the point where only the skills of older employees are available. Eventually a time will come when practically all employees are eligible for retirement, and the company will lack adequately trained replacements.

DIFFERENCES IN ABILITIES

For many years, psychologists and educators in this country believed that general intelligence (primarily verbal ability) showed a steady rise until the late teens and then began a decline that continued throughout the rest of life. Recent advances in research methodology and a greater sophistication in the use of research tools, however, have led to a drastic revision of this belief. It is now recognized that the studies that demonstrated a decrease in intelligence with increasing age may have turned out as they did largely because older people in our society have had less education. When the older and younger groups are equal in terms of education, no evidence of decline can be found (35). In fact, it appears that, at least among those with high school or college training, there is actually a slight tendency for intelligence to rise throughout adult life. Many people apparently have greater ability toward the end of their occupational careers than at the beginning. These findings have received support from other studies in which the same individuals were tested at various times (3,42).

Thus, at present, there seems little reason to expect any decline in general intelligence or verbal ability with age, and, in fact, at the higher occupational, educational, and intellectual levels, there should be an increase. On the other hand, it is true that, because of their somewhat lower average educational level, older people generally do score below the peak age group: the late thirties and early forties.

Other abilities do not follow quite the same pattern; there does seem to be a decline in many cases. In most areas other than the verbal, people tend to become somewhat less competent after their mid-twenties, although in individual cases where the skills are continually practiced this drop off may well not occur. A rather pronounced lessening of ability with age is particularly likely on tasks that emphasize speed. There seems little doubt that significant decreases do occur; partly as a consequence of reduced efficiency in visual perception, partly as a result of a fall off in the rapidity with which muscular responses can be carried out.

None of this implies that older workers cannot be taught new skills. Such problems as do arise in this regard appear to be primarily attributable to inappropriate motivation rather than to a lack of the ability required for learning. Older people have had an opportunity to develop rather definite attitudes as a result of their extensive work experience. Over the years, beliefs regarding the correct way to do things have been reinforced again and again, to the point where they become firmly entrenched in the personality. For this reason, individuals who have been in the labor force for a considerable period often fail to appreciate the value of new techniques and procedures. They fail to learn new skills largely because they do not believe such learning is desirable, rather than because of lack of ability. This is an important point to keep in mind during this particular period in our history when, because of technological change and the introduction of automated equipment, retraining is a constant fact of life.

Insofar as work performance is concerned, it seems clear that problems are most likely to arise when an older worker is employed in a job that requires extensive physical activity. After about forty-five, it becomes very difficult to carry out repetitive physical activities at a rapid pace (53). Thus, the quality of work may be maintained at a high level, but the quantity of output is likely to fall off. In office jobs, however, and in managerial or professional positions, where intellectual and particularly verbal abilities take on more significance, performance should not decline with age. In fact, in many managerial positions there may be a steady improvement, as a result of increased verbal competence and experience.

DIFFERENCES IN PERSONALITY

We have already noted that there is a tendency for older people to maintain previously established attitudes and to oppose the introduction of new work procedures. This pattern of resistance against the unfamiliar, the unforeseen, and the novel is not, however, restricted to the occupational sphere. It appears to be true generally (49) and may take on a uniquely personal tone, so that an experienced employee can stand out as being somewhat obstructionist even when almost everyone else favors a new approach.

Research has revealed a number of additional changes that tend to occur with age (50). The work motivation of the average person in the United States, for instance, rises during the teens and reaches a high point in the early twenties. After that there is a decline, at first precipitous and then more gradual, that continues throughout the years of employment. Thus, people tend to be most devoted to their work and presumably most interested in accomplishment shortly after entering the labor force. The average person, however, becomes less and less industrious as he continues in his occupation.

Interest in people and thus the desire to be with other human beings follows just the opposite course. It rises from a low point in the early twenties to a maximum just prior to the time of retirement. As people decline in work orientation, they seem, in a great many instances, to shift toward a much more pronounced social orientation. This is not to say that they conform more to social pressures, however. In general, the tendency to follow the lead of the group, to go along with what is socially accepted and think like other people, is most characteristic in the early years. Sometime around thirty, or shortly thereafter, a decline in conformity sets in that continues uninterrupted throughout the remaining years of employment. Thus, individualism is most likely to emerge later in life, when a man's station has become reasonably well established and when he has less to lose by repudiating social norms.

Taken as a whole, these data seem to imply that the commitment to the company's productivity goal will be greatest among younger employees and considerably less in the older age groups. Perhaps this accounts in part for the resistance to innovation we have noted in this latter group. Work, productivity, and profit are not considered important enough to warrant all the effort involved in learning and becoming accustomed to the new procedures.

The commitment to organizational maintenance, on the other hand, would seem to be less directly related to age, although a change in the basis for this commitment may well occur over time. In the early years, an individual avoids behavior that would produce conflict and dissension within the organization, not because he likes the people around him, but because he feels a need to conform to socially accepted behavior patterns. Later on, intracompany stress may be minimized by the positive feelings toward one another that people develop with increasing age. Many older employees may care very little about conforming, but still not want to do anything to disrupt their extensive network of friendships in the work situation.

REMOVING CONSTRAINTS

In general, the constraints imposed on personnel decisions as a result of age differences can be overcome either by going outside the firm to hire new employees, thus maintaining a balanced work force appropriate to the tasks to be performed, or by carrying out various changes within the company.

The decline in visual perception that usually comes with age need not result in a major decline in performance on the part of the worker. To a considerable extent, job restructuring and redesign can mitigate the effects of these losses in perceptual abilities. Such restructuring now appears to be possible in many cases where it was not considered feasible previously. For example, an individual required to react to various dials on a dashboard may have difficulty doing so accurately and quickly. A simple repainting of the dashboard may make the dials stand out more vividly and thus reduce the effects of poor visual perception.

Similarly, the decline in muscular speed among older employees may be compensated for by emphasizing the penchant for accuracy that also appears to develop with age. In many instances, a reduced quantity of output per individual becomes acceptable if waste and breakage are almost completely avoided and errors are rare. Often a separate inspection job can be eliminated entirely when older workers are engaged in the production process; the duties of the inspector are taken over by the production workers themselves, thus reducing the need for extremely high output rates.

Even the resistance to change and novelty that seems to characterize many older employees at all levels within a company can be overcome under appropriate circumstances. There is a growing body of research dealing with procedures for inducing attitude change, and if the personnel psychologist keeps himself informed regarding this work, there is every reason to believe he will find considerable opportunity to put his knowledge to good use. Although Chapters 8 and 9 treat this area much more thoroughly, it is important to note here that some general principles beginning to emerge from the research can be put to use by practitioners, not only in the personnel field, but in such areas as advertising, sales promotion, and public relations.

Geographical and Racial Differences

Another set of constraints on personnel decisions arises because of the specific location of the company installation. If a plant is located in a rural area, the employees are likely to possess the characteristics of the rural population; if it is located on the West Coast, anything that is distinctive among residents of this region can be expected to emerge in the employee group as well. The resulting homogeneity may act to make certain alternative courses of action impossible, at least without some change in the composition of the work force.

Since in the United States the major racial differences significant for the personnel process involve Negroes and whites, and since the Negro population still tends to be clustered on a largely geographical basis (in the South and in the large cities), it seems appropriate to take up racial variations in conjunction with those related to location.

DIFFERENCES IN ABILITIES

There can be little disagreement, among those conversant with the research literature, that major differences along geographical and racial lines do exist in the United States. The differences in mental abilities seem to be narrowing in practically all areas, but true equalization has not yet occurred. Changes over the past thirty years or so have been sufficient to produce a sizable overlap, however. Even the most deprived geographical area can now be presumed to possess many individuals who are intellectually superior to the national average. The same pattern emerges from the numerous studies in which Negro and white groups have been compared.

Geographical Area. One significant finding involves differences in general ability between the various major regions of the United States. Although there are sizable variations among areas within each region, it is still true that when these internal fluctuations are averaged out regional differences do remain (35). The highest level of ability has consistently been found in the three West Coast states. Other areas of the country do not appear to differ a great deal, except for the Deep South, where studies have repeatedly indicated that the general level of intelligence is well below the national average. Interestingly, this tendency to low scores does not seem to extend to the Border South: Virginia, North Carolina, Kentucky, Tennessee, Oklahoma, Texas, and Florida.

When the country is cut up on the basis of the population of the area, i.e., when rural-urban differences are studied, significant findings again emerge. In general, lower average scores are found in the rural areas, in farming country and in towns with a population under 2,500 (34,35). The highest levels of ability are found in the suburban areas around the largest cities. With the demise of the one-room schoolhouse and the general improvement of education throughout the less populated parts of the country, this difference, however, seems to be decreasing.

There has, in the past, been a tendency for individuals of higher intelligence to migrate from rural areas where opportunity was at a minimum to the cities, and this trend is probably still continuing to some degree.

Yet it is also true that with the advent of large-scale farming in the West and Midwest, there has been a major increase in opportunity within the rural areas. The rewards for those intellectually and educationally qualified to engage in large-scale farming have become sizable. Thus, in many areas, the drain off of the upper levels of talent now is probably minimal, if it exists at all.

On the whole, it is probably true that differences associated with specific localities are larger and more important insofar as personnel decisions are concerned than those found when the major regions of the country or various groupings based on population density are compared. Local circumstances affecting the caliber of education and the patterns of migration, either in or out of an area, seem to be the really crucial factors insofar as geographical differences are concerned.

Negro-White Differences. There can be little doubt that there does exist a significant difference on general ability tests between Negroes and whites in the United States today. Typical of the many studies reporting such a result is one based on the short vocabulary test mentioned previously. Samples of 1,347 whites and 153 Negroes, both selected as typical of the two racial groups throughout the United States, yielded mean scores of 11.06 and 8.08 respectively (35). The difference is large enough so that there is little possibility that a chance fluctuation associated with these specific samples could account for the result.

In part, however, findings of this kind reflect the influence of regional factors. Negroes on the West Coast score well above those in the Deep South. Since many more Negroes reside in the South, where the whites also appear to be somewhat less intelligent on the average, comparisons based on samples drawn to represent the country as a whole tend to over-emphasize Negro deficiencies. A much greater proportion of low ability Southern Negroes is included than would be appropriate if an estimate of racial differences within a local labor market were desired. In a given area, the Negro population can be expected to score somewhat below the white, but the difference may not be very large. Usually it is this local situation that matters most.

Also, these racial differences have apparently been decreasing in recent years as more and more Negroes emigrate to the cities of the South and North from the rural South (26). In the cities, their children have characteristically received somewhat better schooling, and, as a result, intelligence levels have improved (29). Thus, there is reason to believe that despite the existing Negro-white differential, the future may see a narrowing, perhaps even an elimination, of the gap. Even at the present time there is reason to believe that a large percentage of the Negroes employed in any given company are, at least intellectually, capable of higher level positions, just as many whites are (35).

DIFFERENCES IN PERSONALITY

Geographical Area. Relatively little is known about regional and rural-urban differences in personality characteristics. There is some basis for concluding that such differences do exist, but their nature has not been established with any certainty. One of the few studies bearing on this problem was carried out in the warehouse installations of the McKesson and Robbins Company throughout the United States (25). The findings indicate that both the over-all level of employee satisfaction and the quantity of work produced were higher in small-town locations than in larger cities. It would appear that the commitment to the goals of organizational maintenance and productivity may well be greater in rural locations.

This conclusion is supported by the history of unionization in the United States. It seems clear that the union movement has had its greatest successes in the large metropolitan areas. In the rural parts of the country, especially in the South, the unions have had much more difficulty, and many workers in these areas are still not represented by any organized labor group. It would appear, therefore, that there must be geographical differences in those personality characteristics that contribute to labor-management conflict within an organization, and thus to deviation from the maintenance goal.

Negro-White Differences. Racial differences in personality characteristics, on the other hand, have been studied rather extensively and, in at least one instance, have been tied in with the geographical factor as well. It seems clear that there are few real differences between Negroes and whites insofar as attitudes and values are concerned. The major factor that differentiates the groups is that being a Negro is of much greater relevance and importance to the Negro than being white is to the white person. The Negro tends to be more conscious of his specific group membership and to view events within this particular focus (8,43).

Probably the most comprehensive piece of research in this area was carried out with a view to identifying personality differences between whites and Negroes, and within the Negro population between Northern and Southern Negroes (24). One of the most striking findings was that the differences that emerged when Northern whites and Southern Negroes were compared also appeared when the Southern Negroes were compared with Northern Negroes. Thus, in the North the evidence seemed to indicate that racial differences were minimal. On the other hand, the traits identified as typical of Southern Negroes seemed to suggest considerable personality disorganization. Most pronounced was a tendency to pretend that feelings of aggression and the aggressive acts of others did not really exist, to blot out and deny anger and hatred as if it did not occur. This characteristic appears to be so pervasive among Negroes in the rural South that almost all emotion is restricted and inhibited. The fear of the consequences of aggression is so pronounced that it has spread into other areas as well, and all emotional expression tends to be held in check. In the urban South, this suppression of emotion seems to be less drastic. Although anger is held back, it does tend to emerge eventually, sometimes long after the event that provoked it and often toward someone who was not originally involved. Only the Northern Negro appears to feel sufficiently free to express his emotions in a manner comparable to whites.

As might be expected from these findings, the incidence of emotional disorder among Negroes does appear to be considerably higher than for whites. Even more important from the personnel viewpoint, a great many more cases go untreated and remain in the labor force. Yet even here the influence of regional differentials is evident. It appears that although Northern Negroes are more likely to require hospitalization for emotional illness than Northern whites, this difference is entirely attributable to the Negroes who have migrated to the North from the South. Negroes born in the North are not particularly prone to disorders of this kind (24).

REMOVING CONSTRAINTS

Little need be said here about removing constraints imposed by geographical differentials. When freedom of action is restricted because of characteristics of the work force that are indigenous to the area, it is not possible to circumvent these constraints by recruiting new employees from the local labor market. The same limitations will be found outside the company as within. Geographical differences of the kind discussed are, in fact, as much external constraints as internal.

Racial differences, too, may not be subject to elimination by the simple expedient of going outside the company. Increasingly, external constraints are being imposed by society, which for all practical purposes require companies to include Negroes as part of their potential labor force. A firm that seeks to overcome any limitations imposed as a result of the presence of a primarily Negro work force by hiring whites only is likely to run into considerable difficulty on legal grounds and in other respects as well. These external pressures will be noted again in the chapters that follow, but their consequence is that personnel practitioners would do well to go outside the company to seek out those Negroes who have the abilities and personality characteristics that are in short supply.

The alternative is to attempt some change in the existing employee group. In a sense, the differences between the Southern and Northern Negro can serve as a model. Outside the South, in those areas where the fear of emotional expression has been removed, the level of emotional adjustment is considerably higher. Outside the South, in those areas where educational opportunities are better, the level of intelligence is higher also. This would suggest that a company can improve the caliber of its Negro work force, if this appears necessary, by reducing those conditions that arouse anger, while at the same time serving to suppress emotional expression, and by providing extensive training in areas where knowledge is lacking.

Occupational Differences

A final area of major concern involves the differences in abilities and personality that exist among the various occupational groups within a company. This, of course, is relevant in reaching decisions with regard to the selection and placement of employees at all levels of the organization. It is crucial to have people working in jobs where their abilities and personality characteristics will contribute to success.

In this instance, the primary concern is with the way in which an existing employee group may limit the freedom of personnel action because only a specific set of occupations are represented and these occupations characteristically attract individuals with particular skills and talents. Thus, the emphasis is on the factors that discriminate *between* occupational groups, rather than between successful and unsuccessful employees *within* occupational groups. If, for instance, a company wishes to expand rapidly, it will need large numbers of new managers. Is it likely, in view of what is known regarding the characteristics of employees working below the managerial level, that the needed talent can be found within the present nonmanagerial work force? Will the abilities and personality traits prevailing in existing occupational groups constrain the expansion decision?

DIFFERENCES IN ABILITIES

Perhaps the most striking ability difference between occupations involves the association between the level of the job and general intelligence. There is no question that intelligence test scores are much higher among those in the more skilled occupations, in the professions and in management. Table 2–2 illustrates this point. The test scores are those obtained when these individuals were inducted into the armed forces.

A similar pattern is found when occupations are grouped according to the classification system used by the Bureau of the Census. Table 2–3 contains the results obtained when the short vocabulary test was administered to a nationwide sample of 745 individuals. This sample may be considered typical of the national labor force.

In general, a similar pattern has been found for the other intellectual abilities—numerical, spatial, mechanical, and so on. This does not mean, however, that there is not a very sizable overlap. There are many individuals in lower level jobs who possess the abilities required for performance much further up in the hierarchy. Whether these people can be expected to possess the other characteristics required for effective performance at higher levels in the organization, however, is another

TABLE 2–2. Army General Classification Test Scores Classified by Civilian Occupation

Civilian occupation	Number of cases	Mean score
Accountant	172	128.1
Lawyer	94	127.6
Public relations	42	126.0
Auditor	62	125.9
Draftsman	153	122.0
Pharmacist	58	120.5
Sales manager	42	119.0
Manager	234	116.0
Radio repairman	267	115.3
Teacher	256	112.8
Toolmaker	60	112.5
Foreman	298	109.8
Electrician	289	109.0
Mechanic	421	106.3
Carpenter	451	102.1
Bartender	98	102.2
Welder	493	101.8
Chauffeur	194	100.8
Cook and baker	436	97.2
Truck driver	817	96.2
Barber	103	95.3

Source: T. W. Harrell and M. Harrell, "Army General Classification Test Scores for Civilian Occupations," *Educational & Psychological Measurement,* Vol. 5 (1945), pp. 231–232.

TABLE 2–3. Intelligence of Occupational Groups, Census Classification

Census classification number	Classification title	Number of cases	Mean score
0	Professional	68	14.56
1	Farmers	45	10.22
2	Managers	78	12.60
3	Clerical	102	12.40
4	Sales	48	11.52
5	Craftsmen	102	10.62
6	Operatives	154	10.02
7	Service	81	9.19
8 and 9	Laborers	67	9.63

Source: J. B. Miner, *Intelligence in the United States.* New York: Springer, 1957, p. 73.

question. Let us turn now to the data on occupational differences in personality.

DIFFERENCES IN PERSONALITY

The idea that there are basic differences in the personalities of members of different occupations has its roots in the writings of the Greek philosophers and continues to be of interest today. A considerable amount of research into the interests, attitudes, motives, and emotional adjustment of various occupational groups has been carried out by a number of investigators, and as a result a number of generalizations that are important for the personnel process can be made in this area.

Interests. Research dealing with interests has firmly established that the higher level occupational groups in our society can be clearly distinguished from one another on this basis. For example, the Strong Vocational Interest Blank can now be scored for forty-seven male occupations, such as Architect, Musician, and Certified Public Accountant (7). This means that members of at least forty-seven different occupations responded in a consistently different manner to the 400 questions on the test, thus establishing a pattern of responses that was typical and unique for their type of work. The test asks for a like-indifferent-dislike categorization of a variety of activities.

Some of these occupations, however, exhibit more differences vis-à-vis certain occupations than toward others, at least insofar as the Strong Vocational Interest Blank responses are concerned. Thus, the higher level occupations tend to cluster into a smaller number of groupings. Table 2–4

TABLE 2–4. Vocational Interest Groups As Measured by the Strong Vocational Interest Blank

Group	Group title	Occupations
1	Creative-scientific	Architect, dentist, psychologist
2	Technical	Mathematician, engineer, chemist
3	Production manager	Production manager
4	Subprofessional technical	Farmer, carpenter, aviator
5	Uplift	Personnel manager, social science teacher
6	Musician	Musician
7	Certified public accountant	Certified public accountant
8	Business detail	Accountant, banker
9	Business contract	Sales manager, life insurance salesman
10	Verbal	Lawyer, journalist
11	President of manufacturing firm	President of manufacturing firm

Source: L. J. Cronbach, *Essentials of Psychological Testing,* 2nd ed. New York: Harper & Row, 1960, p. 410.

lists the groups that had been clearly identified by the late 1950's and some of the occupations in each category.

It has also been shown that occupational groups at lower levels seem to have some significantly different interest patterns (6). There are indications that plasterers, bakers, truck drivers and so on, differ substantially from one another in the pattern of their interests. Also, it appears that there are significant differences in interests between the higher level occupations generally and those at lower levels. Business and professional men tend as a group to have very different types of preferences than unskilled workers.

The implication of these findings, of course, is that it may be very difficult to get an individual to perform in a job that deviates in many ways from his personal interest pattern. People are not in any sense perfectly interchangeable across jobs. A man may be shifted to a job in the same interest grouping without much difficulty insofar as his levels of satisfaction and performance are concerned. But transferring him directly into work that normally satisfies a very different set of interests may well be accomplished at considerable cost to organizational goal achievement.

Attitudes. There is little doubt on the basis of the research evidence that there is a strong relationship between occupational groupings and general socioeconomic attitudes. In a typical study, a nationwide sample of the adult white male population was subdivided into the following occupational groups: large business, professional, small business, white collar, skilled manual, semiskilled manual, and unskilled manual (4).

The greatest conservatism was found in the two business groups and among the professionals, the greatest radicalism among the manual workers, and the greatest variation among the white collar workers. Apparently, many white collar employees identify with the business management and professional groups, whereas others react in a manner commensurate with their income levels. Taken as a whole, of course, these results provide some indication of the amount of unconflicted support for organizational goals, especially the productivity or profit goal, that may be expected in different occupational groups.

Managerial Characteristics. Research indicates that managers as a group have a homogeneous set of values, which are highly pragmatic in nature (9). Furthermore, top level managers differ significantly from middle managers, in that they view themselves as being more dynamic, daring, and less cautious (44). And this trend extends on down in the organization. A direct positive relationship exists between both self-assurance and initiative and the level of job held in the hierarchy (14). The evidence on this latter point is contained in Table 2–5.

Other studies have indicated that there is a similar positive association between the motivation to assume managerial responsibilities and exercise power over others and actual managerial level. The extent of the relationship is indicated by the fact that the correlations obtained have consistently been in the low .40's (39). Furthermore, graduate business

TABLE 2–5. Mean Scores on Self-Assurance and Initiative for Various Occupational Levels

Occupational level	Number of cases	Self-assurance score	Initiative score
Higher management	110	28.56	32.46
Middle management	67	24.27	29.51
Lower management	87	24.14	29.07
Line workers	152	23.22	26.75

Source: E. E. Ghiselli, "The Validity of Management Traits in Relation to Occupational Level," *Personnel Psychology,* Vol. 16 (1963), p. 110.

students who aspire to managerial positions have more such motivation than those who do not (40).

There is also some research evidence available regarding power motivation in different types of managerial groups. The results of one such study are contained in Table 2–6. It is clear that whereas the sales man-

TABLE 2–6. Miner Sentence Completion Scale Scores in Various Corporate Manager Groups

Group	Mean score	Number of cases
Sales management	8.94	35
Engineering management	6.35	43
Research management	4.45	40

Source: J. B. Miner, *Studies in Management Education.* New York: Springer, 1965, p. 200.

agers are strongly motivated to exercise power, the research managers are much less so.

Results of the same kind have been obtained with business school students majoring in different job areas (27,39). It seems likely that differences between managers working in the various areas of specialization are not entirely a consequence of experiences occurring *after* managerial responsibilities have been assumed. Men who choose sales work, for instance, are not the same as those who prefer other fields.

A particularly extensive study of occupational personalities at the higher levels of management involved the administration of a number of personality tests to a large group of executives, followed by a comparison of the results obtained by those working in different specialities (22,45). Among the tests used were the Minnesota Multiphasic Personality Inventory, Bernreuter Personality Inventory, and Thematic Apperception Test. The results are summarized, in a general way, below:

- 1. Sales managers tend to be highly dominant, sociable, thick-skinned, people-oriented, and to some extent self-centered.
- 2. Production managers are somewhat defensive in nature and are marked by strong self-control; they shy away from self-analysis and tend to prefer the practical.
- 3. Administrative and accounting managers are not very creative or original and are given to moods of depression.

It is clear from the studies described that managerial positions do contain individuals with certain specific personality characteristics, and there is reason to believe that major differences exist among managers working in different areas. For this reason, a company that has always operated within the marketing segment of its industry might have considerable difficulty expanding into the production and research areas. Similarly, individual and group differences can constrain too rapid growth of any kind, since many of the characteristics noted appear to be required for all managerial work, and a small company simply is not likely to have these resources available in sufficient quantity to staff a greatly expanded management group.

An additional constraint on rapid expansion derives from what is known about emotional illness and the symptoms of emotional disorder. It is clear that emotional problems are most prevalent among people in lower level occupations, among those in unskilled and routine semiskilled jobs in particular (28). They develop much less frequently among the more highly skilled and management (38).

Other evidence indicates that symptoms of emotional illness do not tend to have negative consequences for performance when the work is of a routine, repetitive nature. But they do interfere drastically when frequent decision-making is required and when a variety of problems must be thought through. Thus, a company with a high proportion of minimally skilled employees will not need, and probably will not have, a work force that is extremely stable and well-adjusted emotionally. If, however, a sizable upgrading of skills should appear desirable, as with the introduction of automated equipment, the lower level of emotional stability could limit management's freedom of action.

REMOVING CONSTRAINTS

In one sense, the constraints described are of a kind that a company may well prefer not to remove. Many of the abilities and personality characteristics noted are not only prevalent in the occupational groups where they occur, but are also essential for effective performance there. Thus, in many instances it would be disastrous for a company to attempt to eliminate them. Too much homogeneity within a total work force can be a source of difficulty.

It is also true that if an organization is to promote from within, it must have in lower level positions individuals who possess the abilities and other characteristics required for performance at higher levels. This means in the case of the factors associated with managerial work that some over-staffing or stockpiling is usually necessary. A company needs more people with high intelligence, managerial interests, a desire to exercise power, and so on than it can use at a given point in time, because a continuous flow of replacements must be maintained.

Where provision is not made for an adequate internal supply of the resources needed to permit a smooth managerial replacement process, the resulting constraints can be overcome by hiring managers from outside the company. A number of firms do, in fact, follow this procedure as a matter of policy. There are some disadvantages, primarily the lack of incentive for those at lower levels, when promotion from within is not the policy, but this is certainly one way of overcoming the restrictions imposed by an inadequate supply of managerial talent.

An obvious alternative is to change existing employees who do not possess the managerial characteristics, so that they may be more fully qualified for this type of work. In the case of intellectual abilities, this appears impractical, if not impossible, so that stockpiling on intelligence would appear to be essential. But the personality factors discussed are in many cases subject to modification.

Interests are known to shift rather frequently early in life, although they do become stable in adult life. Thus, there is some reason to believe that changes can be produced purposefully if the right conditions are established. However, little actual research has been done on this specific problem. Socioeconomic attitudes clearly may be altered, although the ease with which this may be accomplished varies from individual to individual. There is reason to believe that considerable change occurs normally as a function of the first promotion into the ranks of management (30). Certain other personality characteristics discussed can apparently be changed as a result of management development programs (39). Specific details on this will be covered in Chapter 8. In the case of some traits, the evidence that change can be produced is extremely strong; in other instances we do not really know yet whether management development can be effective. Finally, emotional stability can be improved and symptoms reduced through individual and group psychotherapy. The process may not be short, and it may never succeed with certain people, but it is possible to bring about a considerable change in emotional adjustment given the appropriate circumstances.

Cultural Differences

Our discussion to this point has been concerned with the *internal* constraints imposed by individual differences within a work force. There are at the same time, however, a great variety of *external* constraints that impinge on personnel decisions and limit the action alternatives. Many of these have received little, if any, attention from psychologists. They are primarily of a legal and economic nature. The legal structure may prescribe in large degree what can and cannot be done in terms of labor relations, pay scales, hours of work, and in many other areas. Similarly, the competitive economic structure and technology of an industry, as well as the geographical locale of a company, impose restrictions.

In addition to these nonpsychological factors, there are other external constraints associated with the particular culture, and these have been of major concern to psychologists—particularly the various cultural mores and values. In fact, psychology has been the major contributor to our understanding of such cultural differences within the modern world. And knowledge of the influence differences in national culture may have on the personnel process is of considerable importance to American companies today. International trade has reached a record peak with the countries of Europe, Latin America, and the Far East and promises to attain even higher levels as the underdeveloped nations rush toward economic self-sufficiency and higher standards of living. Large numbers of American firms are faced with the problem of staffing overseas offices and, in many cases, manning major production and distribution facilities in foreign countries (41). If these international operations are to be managed so as to maximize organizational productivity and maintenance, a very high priority must be given to how the management process should be varied in the light of cultural considerations.

That cultural variations do exist, even at the managerial level, can no longer be doubted. In one study of managerial attitudes, sharp differences were found between Nordic-European countries (Norway, Denmark, Germany, and Sweden), Latin-European countries (France, Spain, Italy, and Belguim), the United States and Great Britain, a group of developing countries (Argentina, Chile, and India), and Japan, which stood alone. Managers in these countries did hold many attitudes in common, but there were also a number of characteristics peculiar to each cultural grouping. Thus, whereas attitudes in the three developing countries tended to be autocratic, Japanese managers gave evidence of a considerably greater democratic trend (18).

How, then, do these cultural factors impinge on personnel practices? What are the specific characteristics of a culture that can be expected to influence the utilization of human resources? A descriptive framework for answering these questions is provided in Table 2–7.

Table 2–7 was originally devised with reference to the production process (47). However, it is clear from the last column that many of the activities and areas described as being subject to influence by cultural factors fall within the domain of the personnel process. Among these are management development, safety programs, supervisory selection, layoff policies, incentive systems, labor relations, merit evaluations, policies on

TABLE 2–7. The Cultural System As It Affects Production Management

Differences in these cultural factors—	. . . affect a people's values and habits relating to—	For example, the local employee might feel that—	. . . and this would tend to affect approaches in these (and other) areas of manufacturing management—
I. Assumptions and attitudes	Time	Time is not measured in minutes, but in days and years.	Production control, scheduling, purchasing
	One's proper purpose in life	The only purpose which makes sense is to enjoy each day.	Management development
	The future	The future is not in man's hands.	Short- and long-range planning
	This life vs. the hereafter	Life and death are completely ordained and predetermined.	Safety programs
	Duty, responsibility	Your job is completed when you give an order to a subordinate.	Executive techniques of delegation and follow-up
II. Personal beliefs and aspirations	Right and wrong	I give the boss inventory counts that please him.	Inventory control system
	Sources of pride	A college degree places one higher in society for life.	Selection of supervisors
	Sources of fear and concern	Jobs are hard to get for a man laid off, regardless of the cause of layoff.	Layoff policy
	Extent of one's hopes	Without the right education and social class, advancement is limited.	Incentives, motivation

TABLE 2-7. The Cultural System As It Affects Production Management—Continued

Differences in these cultural factors—	. . . affect a people's values and habits relating to—	For example, the local employee might feel that—	. . . and this would tend to affect approaches in these (and other) areas of manufacturing management—
	The individual vs. society	The individual's wants and needs must be subordinated to the whole group.	Labor relations
III. Interpersonal relationships	The source of authority	My men don't like the new process. It won't work.	Quality control
	Care or empathy for others	I'd rather give my salary raise to my foreman than have to tell him he is not to receive one.	Merit reviews
	Importance of family obligations	I had to stay home because my father was sick.	Absenteeism
	Objects of loyalty	Friendship is more important than business.	Work-group relationships
	Tolerance for personal differences	If you don't agree with your boss, he will be insulted.	The decision-making process
IV. Social structure	Interclass nobility	I'd refuse to work for a man without a trade school certificate.	Promotion from within

TABLE 2–7. The Cultural System As It Affects Production Management—Continued

Differences in these cultural factors—	. . . affect a people's values and habits relating to—	For example, the local employee might feel that—	. . . and this would tend to affect approaches in these (and other) areas of manufacturing management—
	Class or caste systems	Men with my standing don't move heavy objects such as typewriters.	Job descriptions—flexibility of job assignments
	Urban-village-farm origins	The company must take the place of the village in caring for its people.	Fringe benefit programs
	Determinants of status	Elderly people have wisdom. They deserve the most important jobs on big machines.	Equipment selection

Source: C. W. Skinner, "Management of International Production," *Harvard Business Review*, Vol. 42, No. 5 (1964), p. 129.

absenteeism, promotion procedures, job description, and fringe benefits. It seems evident that people in other parts of the world view things very differently than we do in the United States, and they may have very different conceptions of what is right and wrong.

JAPANESE CULTURE

A good example of the way in which cultural considerations affect personnel decisions comes from Japan. In connection with a research study, some 2,000 production workers, divided equally between the United States and Japan, were surveyed (54). The firms studied in the two countries were essentially comparable. Some of the questions dealing with personnel practices and policies that were asked of the workers in both countries are noted in Table 2–8.

TABLE 2–8. **Differences Between Japanese and American Employees' Cultural Values**

Questionnaire items	United States, %	Japan, %
1. *I think of my company as:*		
The central concern in my life and of greater importance than my personal life	1	9
A part of my life at least equal to my personal life	23	57
A place for me to work with management during work hours to accomplish mutual goals	54	26
Strictly a place to work and entirely separate from my personal life	23	6
2. *When a worker wishes to marry, I think his (her) supervisor should:*		
Help select a mate and serve as a possible go-between	2	6
Offer personal advice to the worker if requested	29	70
Merely present a small gift from the company	9	19
Not be involved in such a personal matter	60	5
3. *In regard to housing for workers, management should:*		
Provide company housing at no charge	2	29
Provide company housing at special low rent	8	39
Provide low-interest loans to assist workers in owning their own homes	56	29

TABLE 2–8. Differences Between Japanese and American Employees' Cultural Values—Continued

Questionnaire items	United States, %	Japan, %
Avoid direct financial assistance in housing	34	3
4. *If a worker, although willing, proves to be unqualified on his job, management should feel a responsibility to:*		
Continue his employment until he retires or dies	23	55
Continue his employment for as long as one year so that he may look for another job	19	23
Continue his employment for three months so that he may look for another job	38	18
Terminate the employment of unqualified workers after giving about two weeks' notice	20	4

Source: A. M. Whitehill, "Cultural Values and Employee Attitudes: United States and Japan," *Journal of Applied Psychology*, Vol. 48 (1964), pp. 70–71.

An examination of the responses indicates that the perceived permanence of the employment relationship, which is so typical in Japan (5), has some very direct implications for personnel practice. Thus, question 1 indicates that an American firm doing business in Japan would have to give less consideration to matters of company loyalty than in the United States, because loyalty is a basic aspect of the Japanese culture. This loyalty comes at some cost, however, as questions 2 and 3 demonstrate, for the company is expected to assume roles not included in the value expectations of American employees. The Japanese production worker anticipates that the company will take a much more active interest in him and his problems.

In general, however, it would seem that organizational maintenance as a goal would be relatively easy to achieve in a Japanese plant. On the other hand, productivity might well present something of a problem. The responses to question 4 suggest that sanctions against ineffective performance, which if not widely accepted in the United States are not widely rejected either, may be almost entirely proscribed in Japan.

INDIAN CULTURE

Studies carried out in India provide a picture of a cultural climate that again differs from that found in the United States. In one such investigation, a group of 200 Indian factory workers were asked to rate the importance of various job factors (46). These factors were then ranked in terms of their average rated importance and the results were compared with findings from similar studies conducted in the United States. The most relevant of these comparisons, for our purposes, involves a survey carried out among workers at the General Motors Company (10). The results are presented in Table 2–9.

TABLE 2–9. Comparisons of Rankings of Job Factors by Indian and American Workers

Job factor	Ranking among Indian workers	Ranking among American workers
Job security	1	6
Adequate earnings	2	1
Personal benefits	3	2
Opportunity for advancement	4	8
Comfortable working conditions	5	9
Suitable type of work	6	7
Opportunity for increased income	7	
Hours of work	8	
Sympathetic supervision	9	5
Opportunity to learn the job	10	

Source: P. N. Singh and R. J. Wherry, "Ranking of Job Factors by Factory Workers in India," *Personnel Psychology*, Vol. 16 (1963), p. 31.

Although some factors included in the Indian survey were not studied among the General Motors workers, and some ranked at General Motors were not ranked in India, several very interesting differences are identified. The Indian workers show a much greater concern with job security, opportunity for advancement, and comfortable working conditions and emphasize sympathetic supervision much less. In part, these differentials can be accounted for by the very high unemployment rates that have plagued India; it is not surprising that job security is so important. But a very different attitude toward authority in the two cultures is also reflected. Increased consideration and kindness from supervisors would seem to be a much less effective way of building commitment to the company in India than it is in the United States. Sympathetic supervision is just not that important to Indian workers.

RUSSIAN CULTURE

Russia, with its Communist social system, provides an example of a cultural context for business that is almost the direct opposite of that existing in the United States. Although it is unlikely that many American firms will open plants in Russia in the near future, it is still of interest to contrast the two cultures, in view of the current status of world power relationships. Fortunately, information is available on the types of restrictions on personnel decisions existing within the Russian economy (12).

One very clear difference between the two countries is in relation to such factors as work motivation and employee morale. For many years, those responsible for the utilization of human resources in the Soviet Union were unconcerned with matters of this kind. The Communist ideology assumed that workers exert more effort merely because they want to in a noncapitalistic, socialist system. The incentive procedures used in the United States to increase individual productivity have rarely been employed in Russia, since such tools have characteristically been perceived as unnecessary. There has been a similar lack of interest in programs designed to increase worker morale, and thus contribute to organizational maintenance. Recently, some emphasis on the use of incentives has appeared under the sponsorship of high government officials, but change in this area has been extremely slow.

A similar pattern is present in the area of personnel selection. Traditional Communist ideology assumes that there are few important differences between people; consequently the view that some individuals may be more capable workers than others is not acceptable. Since the logic of personnel selection is that within a given framework and for certain purposes some people *are* more capable than others, specialized selection techniques have rarely been used as a management tool in the Soviet Union. In fact, it would be unwise for a manager to attempt to use them.

Instead of selection, the Russians have concentrated primarily on training and skill development, since it is part of the professed ideology that all individuals must be brought to a high level of performance. Thus, training has been the preferred route to the productivity goal. Organizational maintenance, however, has been sought in a different manner. Because all organizations are considered to be arms of the state, it is the state that has been employed as the central unifying point, and the usual approach has been to attempt to build loyalty and faithfulness to the state rather than to the particular business organization.

BRITISH CULTURE

One might expect that differences of this kind would not appear when American culture patterns are contrasted with those of another Western country such as England. Information is available, however, from a comparative study employing insurance clerks in Great Britain and the United States as subjects (11). Among the British, self-reliance, kindness, politeness, obedience, and not creating a nuisance were relatively more important, whereas the Americans placed greater emphasis on respect for parents and authority, sincerity, honesty, getting along with others, individuality, and being unselfish.

These differences suggest that rather different approaches should be taken to foster organizational maintenance in the two countries. For example, an organization placing considerable stress on rules of procedure and tending to minimize individual spontaneity would be expected to produce higher levels of satisfaction in Great Britain. Perhaps this is why a highly structured and planned incomes policy regulating prices and wages throughout the economy has emerged there since World War II (33). A smaller, more informal type of organizational unit should be preferable in the United States, and the general nature of the economy appears to reflect this.

THE UNDERDEVELOPED COUNTRIES

Although many other examples could be given indicating how cultural constraints can operate to restrict management's freedom of action and specify acceptable routes for the attainment of company goals within various foreign countries (19), it is probably more appropriate at this point to turn to the difficulties that may be encountered in underdeveloped countries. These appear to be of two general types—ideological and educational.

In one comparative study of thirty-four nations, an attempt was made to relate the level of economic development to the values and motivational patterns of the people (31). A major portion of these findings are of direct relevance here, since they indicate that there are certain countries where, because of the value systems, organizational productivity may be relatively easy to achieve and organizational maintenance difficult and others where the converse is true. In countries that had maintained high levels of economic growth, the people were marked by a strong emphasis on hard work and achievement and, perhaps even more important, by the view that social relationships should occur with some specific purpose in mind, such as a business deal, rather than for purely social reasons. Such a culture pattern should facilitate the productivity goal, but it would appear that special measures would have to be taken so that these individuals could work together cooperatively. It seems less likely that they would spontaneously create the feelings of camaraderie and friendship that are necessary to a stable organization.

On the other hand, in those countries where economic growth was slow, social relationships tended to be valued for their own sake and people did not have to have particular purposes or goals to engage in them. Here organizational maintenance might be expected to come more easily, but the lower level of achievement motivation would suggest that commitment to a company's productivity and profit objectives might be much more difficult to obtain. Countries where the desire to achieve was low and economic growth minimal were by no means all in the underdeveloped category, however. Many had experienced considerable growth in the past, but not in the past few decades. Thus, this low group included such diverse nations as Belgium, Algeria, Denmark, Chile, and Switzerland. In these and other countries, the values necessary to productivity and continued economic growth were lacking.

A deficiency in the required values is not the only factor that may serve to limit goal achievement in underdeveloped areas, however. An equally important factor, at least insofar as productivity is concerned, is education (20). In many countries, certain personnel programs are out of the question, because the labor market does not contain individuals with the necessary basic education, skills, or professional training. Countries such as Afghanistan, Ethiopia, and Haiti not only have a very limited economic capacity, but they lack the educated personnel needed for advancement.

REMOVING CONSTRAINTS

In general, the approach in this section has been to point out some of the constraints within which personnel decisions must be made in foreign countries. Little has been said about the possibility of circumventing these restrictions, largely because this is not easily done. An obvious procedure, of course, is to move the business operation to a cultural context where the limitations no longer exist. This may or may not be feasible on other grounds; personnel considerations are not always paramount. Or it may be possible to staff the organization in large part from outside the culture that imposes the restrictions, perhaps with United States citizens. This may or may not solve the problem.

Another alternative is to induce change in the culture itself. Because of the widespread support for cultural values within a society, however, these are not easily altered. This is not to suggest that societies and cultures do not change. They most certainly do, and the psychologist can play a role in this process. For example, there is good reason to believe that rather basic changes are taking place in Japanese society at the present time; the shift is toward a much more Westernized perception of the employment relationship (5,55). The group responsible seems to be the segment of Japanese management that has had the greatest contact with the West.

A personnel psychologist may do much to foster change through the development of appropriate training and communications programs within the company. Similarly, he may serve as a public relations agent within the external community by discussing the virtues of the desired change. Although these attempts to modify attitudes may meet with only limited success, they can contribute a great deal to an ongoing change process. Combined with other socioeconomic and political forces in the culture, they can make a very real difference.

In education, even more can be done. Although it may not be economically feasible to do so, companies can have a rather dramatic impact on the educational systems of foreign countries. The accomplishments of the oil companies in Venezuela provide a case in point (48). Although union and governmental pressures were without question an important factor, it remains true that through their direct investment in schools and hospitals, American oil companies have done a great deal to improve the educational level and the health of the Venezuelan populace.

REFERENCES

1. Allport, G. W., P. E. Vernon, and G. Lindzey, *Study of Values: Manual of Directions*, rev. ed. Boston: Houghton Mifflin, 1951.
2. Anastasi, A., *Differential Psychology*, 3rd ed. New York: Macmillan, 1958.
3. Bentz, V. J., "A Test-Retest Experiment on the Relationship Between Age and Mental Ability," *American Psychologist*, Vol. 8 (1953), 319–320.
4. Centers, R., *The Psychology of Social Classes*. Princeton, N.J.: Princeton Univ. Press, 1949.
5. Chandler, M., *Management Rights and Union Interests*. New York: McGraw-Hill, 1964.
6. Clark, K. C., *Vocational Interests of Non-professional Men*. Minneapolis, Minn.: Univ. of Minnesota Press, 1961.
7. Cronbach, L. J., *Essentials of Psychological Testing*, 2nd ed. New York: Harper & Row, 1960.
8. Dreger, R. M., and K. S. Miller, "Comparative Psychological Studies of Negroes and Whites in the United States," *Psychological Bulletin*, Vol. 57 (1960), 361–402.
9. England, G. W., "Personal Value Systems of American Managers," *Academy of Management Journal*, Vol. 10 (1967), 53–68.
10. Evans, C. F., and V. Laseau, *My Job Contest*. Washington, D.C.: Personnel Psychology, Inc., 1950.
11. Farber, M. L., "English and Americans: Values in the Socialization Process," *Journal of Psychology*, Vol. 36 (1953), 243–250.
12. Fleishman, E., "Some Observations of Industrial Psychology in the U.S.S.R.," *Personnel Psychology*, Vol. 16 (1963), 115–126.
13. Fuchs, E. F., and C. H. Hammer, "A Survey of Women's Aptitudes for Army Jobs," *Personnel Psychology*, Vol. 16 (1963), 151–156.
14. Ghiselli, E. E., "The Validity of Management Traits in Relation to Occupational Level," *Personnel Psychology*, Vol. 16 (1963), 109–114.
15. Gordon, L. V., *Gordon Personal Profile: Manual*. Yonkers-on-Hudson, N.Y.: Harcourt, Brace & World, 1953.
16. Guilford, J. P., and W. S. Zimmerman, *The Guilford-Zimmerman Temperament Survey: Manual*. Beverly Hills, Cal.: Sheridan Supply, 1949.
17. Gurin, G., J. Veroff, and S. Field, *Americans View Their Mental Health*. New York: Basic Books, 1960.
18. Haire, M., E. E. Ghiselli, and L. W. Porter, *Managerial Thinking: An International Study*. New York: Wiley, 1966.
19. Harbison, F., and C. A. Myers, *Management in the Industrial World*. New York: McGraw-Hill, 1959.
20. Harbison, F., and C. A. Myers, *Education, Manpower, and Economic Growth*. New York: McGraw-Hill, 1964.
21. Harrell, T. W., and M. S. Harrell, "Army General Classification Test Scores for Civilian Occupations," *Educational and Psychological Measurement*, Vol. 5 (1945), 229–239.
22. Huttner, L., S. Levy, E. Rosen, and M. Stopol, "Further Light on the Executive Personality," *Personnel*, Vol. 36 (1959), 42–50.

23. Jacobsen, E., D. Trumbo, G. Cheek, and J. Nangle, "Employee Attitudes Toward Technological Change in a Medium Sized Insurance Company," *Journal of Applied Psychology*, Vol. 43 (1959), 349–354.
24. Karon, B. P., *The Negro Personality*. New York: Springer, 1958.
25. Katzell, R. A., R. S. Barrett, and T. C. Parker, "Job Satisfaction, Job Performance, and Situational Characteristics," *Journal of Applied Psychology*, Vol. 45 (1961), 65–72.
26. Klineberg, O., "Negro-White Differences in Intelligence Test Performance: A New Look at an Old Problem," *American Psychologist*, Vol. 18 (1963), 198–203.
27. Korman, A. K., "Self-esteem Variable in Vocational Choice," *Journal of Applied Psychology*, Vol. 50 (1966), 479–486.
28. Kornhauser, A., *Mental Health of the Industrial Worker*. New York: Wiley, 1965.
29. Lee, E. S., "Negro Intelligence and Selective Migration: A Philadelphia Test of the Klineberg Hypothesis," *American Sociological Review*, Vol. 16 (1951), 227–333.
30. Lieberman, S., "The Effects of Changes in Roles on the Attitudes of Role Occupants," *Human Relations*, Vol. 9 (1956), 385–402.
31. McClelland, D. C., *The Achieving Society*. Princeton, N.J.: Van Nostrand, 1961.
32. McClelland, D. C., J. W. Atkinson, R. A. Clark, and E. L. Lowell, *The Achievement Motive*. New York: Appleton-Century-Crofts, 1953.
33. McKersie, R. B., "Incomes Policy in Great Britain," in G. G. Somers, *Proceedings of the Nineteenth Annual Winter Meeting*. Madison, Wis.: Industrial Relations Research Association, 1967, pp. 139–148.
34. McNemar, Q., *The Revision of the Stanford-Binet Scale*. Boston: Houghton Mifflin, 1942.
35. Miner, J. B., *Intelligence in the United States*. New York: Springer, 1957.
36. Miner, J. B., "The Concurrent Validity of the PAT in the Selection of Tabulating Machine Operators," *Journal of Projective Techniques*, Vol. 24 (1960), 409–418.
37. Miner, J. B., "The Validity of the PAT in the Selection of Tabulating Machine Operators: An Analysis of Predictive Power," *Journal of Projective Techniques*, Vol. 25 (1961), 330–333.
38. Miner, J. B., *The Management of Ineffective Performance*. New York: McGraw-Hill, 1963.
39. Miner, J. B., *Studies in Management Education*. New York: Springer, 1965.
40. Miner, J. B., "The Early Indentification of Managerial Talent," *Personnel and Guidance Journal*, Vol. 46 (1968), 586–591.
41. Myers, A. S., "Recruiting and Selecting Foreign National Personnel for Overseas Operations," *Personnel Administration*, Vol. 28 (1965), No. 4, 25–30.
42. Owens, W. A., Jr., "Age and Mental Abilities: A Longitudinal Study," *Genetic Psychology Monographs*, Vol. 48 (1953), 3–54.
43. Pettigrew, T. F., *A Profile of the Negro American*. Princeton, N.J.: Van Nostrand, 1964.
44. Porter, L. W., and E. E. Ghiselli, "The Self-Perceptions of Top and Middle Management Personnel," *Personnel Psychology*, Vol. 10 (1957), 397–406.
45. Rosen, E. H., "The Executive Personality," *Personnel*, Vol. 36 (1959), 8–20.
46. Singh, P. N., and R. J. Wherry, "Ranking of Job Factors by Factory Workers," *Personnel Psychology*, Vol. 16 (1963), 29–33.

47. Skinner, C. W., "Management of International Production," *Harvard Business Review*, Vol. 42 (1964), No. 5, 125–136.
48. Taylor, W. C., and J. Lindeman, *United States Business Performance Abroad—The Creole Petroleum Corporation in Venezuela.* Washington, D.C.: National Printing Association, 1955.
49. Toch, H., "Attitudes of the Fifty Plus Age Group: Preliminary Considerations Toward a Longitudinal Survey," *Public Opinion Quarterly*, Vol. 17 (1953), 391–394.
50. Tomkins, S. S., *Affect Imagery Consciousness, Vol. II: The Negative Affects.* New York: Springer, 1963.
51. Tyler, L., *The Psychology of Human Differences*, rev. ed. New York: Appleton-Century-Crofts, 1956.
52. Wechsler, D., *The Measurement and Appraisal of Adult Intelligence*, 4th ed. Baltimore, Md.: Williams & Wilkins, 1958.
53. Welford, A. T., *Aging and Human Skill.* London: Oxford Univ. Press, 1958.
54. Whitehill, A. M., "Cultural Values and Employee Attitudes: United States and Japan," *Journal of Applied Psychology*, Vol. 48 (1964), 69–72.
55. Whitehill, A. M., and S. Takezawa, *Cultural Values in Management-Worker Relations. Japan: Gimu in Transition.* Chapel Hill, N. C.: School of Business Administration, Univ. of North Carolina, 1961.

QUESTIONS

1. Discuss the relationship between age and the various abilities. What influence does the degree of education appear to have on this relationship?
2. What are some of the important sex differences? Which of these differences appear to be susceptible to change?
3. What are the general characteristics of different types of managers? What are the implications of these differences for personnel decisions?
4. What do we know about the prevalence and consequences of emotional disorder in the world of work? What is the significance of this problem for human resources utilization and planning?
5. Discuss the prevailing attitudes toward work motivation in the United States and the Soviet Union. Why do some people think these differences are narrowing?
6. What are some ways in which constraints owing to cultural differences may be overcome? What are some of the problems involved?

3

Establishing Role Prescriptions

It has become increasingly common, in recent years, to conceive of business organizations, and, in fact, all organizations, as behavioral systems that operate in accordance with the input-output model (22). Since this conception serves as a basis for the discussion in this chapter and will also be utilized in a variety of other connections through the remainder of the book, it is important to establish a clear understanding of what is meant at the outset.

On the input side, we will be primarily concerned with people, the human resources that become available to an organization as a result of employment. As indicated in Chapter 2, people enter the firm with various abilities, skills, personality characteristics, cultural values, and so on that may constrain personnel decisions. But these individual differences are also the raw material with which productivity and maintenance goals must be attained. Screening and selection, as they will be discussed in Chapters 6 and 7, are techniques for controlling this human input so that, insofar as possible, the people hired will be those most likely to contribute to organization objectives.

It should be emphasized that human resources are not the only inputs that are considered in a truly comprehensive analysis of organizational functioning. Financial resources, materials, facilities, technology, and so on are also important. Since, however, this is a book about personnel psychology, rather than finance, or production, or real estate, the discussion will be restricted to specifically human inputs. It is important to keep in mind, nevertheless, that management increasingly is faced with the alternative of having a variety of tasks performed *either* by a human being *or* by a machine. As new developments in technology and automation occur, decisions must constantly be made as to whether a specific type of work will be assigned to a man or to a machine. Decisions of this kind are strongly influenced by economic considerations: Labor costs are compared against anticipated capital expenditures (25). Thus, personnel people may have only a limited amount of influence on the outcome.

On the output side, in an ultimate sense, the major consideration is the degree to which the firm is able to utilize all of its resources to attain the goals of organizational productivity, or profitability, and organizational maintenance. Insofar as the personnel process is concerned, however, the primary consideration is the behavior of the individual as an organization member. Do the firm's employees do the things required to maximize their contribution to goal attainment?

This means that any discussion of organization outputs from the personnel viewpoint must be concerned with three factors:

1. The things that the people who work for the company say and do.
2. The things that the people who work for the company are *expected* to say and do.
3. The relationship between these expectations and what actually occurs.

ROLE PRESCRIPTIONS

In this chapter, primary attention will be given to the matter of establishing expected patterns of behavior. These expected patterns, which are more appropriately called *role prescriptions,* may be developed for managerial positions, in which case we are essentially concerned with organization planning. Or they may be established for positions where actually doing the work, rather than managing or supervising it, is paramount. In this latter case, it is more common to speak of job analysis. Nevertheless many companies do carry their job analysis procedures well up into the managerial ranks for purposes of salary administration. Thus, the distinction between organization planning and job analysis on the basis of level of position is not entirely clear-cut.

In Chapters 4 and 5, the focus will be on the techniques used to determine whether individuals actually do approximate the established role prescriptions for their positions. When a person acts in a way that is highly congruent with the expected pattern, he is normally defined as successful or effective. When he deviates too far from existing role prescriptions, he is likely to be considered unsuccessful or ineffective. Establishing role requirements and determining the degree of deviation from them in actual behavior is what is meant when we speak of the evaluation of individual outputs.

It may seem strange that a discussion of the output side has been placed ahead of any description of such input processes as recruitment, selection, and placement. There is, in fact, some logical inconsistency in this approach. Yet, to do otherwise would be even more confusing. The individuals selected for employment must most closely approximate in their work behavior the role prescriptions for the positions they will fill. Hiring should be oriented toward obtaining successful people who will contribute the most to the company's goals. But this cannot be done without a full understanding of what kinds of behavioral outputs are desired, of how success is defined in a given job and in a given company. Thus, the discussion of what we select *for* must precede any detailed treatment of *how* we select.

Although job analysis and organization planning are carried out in order to produce a company structure that will, hopefully, maximize goal attainment, an additional consequence should be noted. Role prescriptions, once established, can also operate as internal constraints on personnel decisions. Thus, individual differences are not the only source of restriction within the firm. The way in which an organization has been designed and job duties assigned can impose similar limitations. For instance, established patterns of communications, indicating which individuals should be contacted in what order about various types of problems, can severely restrict personnel actions. They not only tend to bind solutions to a limited set of alternatives because of veto power invested in certain positions, but they may also introduce sizable delays. Such constraints resulting from an existing set of role prescriptions, and the consequent organizational structure, can of course be overcome through the introduction of revised prescriptions, but that in itself is time-consuming and often may not be feasible. This topic of change will be considered in detail later in this chapter.

THE TERMINOLOGY OF OCCUPATIONAL STUDY

Before turning to a discussion of the methods and procedures employed in performing a job analysis, it is essential to understand some of the terms that will be used. The definitions that follow constitute what has come to be the generally accepted terminology among personnel specialists. They are in line with the terminology used by the Occupational Research Program of the United States Employment Service (20).

- A *task* is a distinct work activity carried out for a distinct purpose. An example would be a retail clerk in a department store dusting off merchandise. Another example would be the same clerk setting up the same merchandise in an attractive display. When there are enough such related activities, a position is created.

- A *position* is a specific set of tasks and duties performed by a given individual in a given firm at a given time. The number of positions in a company at one time is equal to the number of employees at the same time.
- A *job* is normally made up of a number of similar positions in a given company. However, a job may involve only one such position at a given time. For example, a store may have one retail hardware clerk, or many, depending on the size of the store and the scope of its business.
- An *occupation* is a number of similar jobs existing in different companies and at different times. Examples of occupations are carpenters, civil engineers, and so on.
- A *job description* is a written statement of the tasks, duties, and behaviors required in a given job, plus the personal qualifications that all candidates for the job must of necessity possess. (This latter aspect is often referred to separately as the *job specification*.)
- A *job family* is a collection of two or more jobs that either require similar worker characteristics or contain parallel tasks as determined by the job analysis.
- When a study is made of the tasks performed by a single person, the term *position analysis* is usually employed. When the scope is broadened to include two or more positions which are similar enough to be considered one job, it is more characteristic to speak of *job analysis*. Since in the business world, at least at lower levels, there are usually two or more similar positions within a firm, the designation job analysis is typically used (21). This analysis provides information about the job, the necessary activities and personal requirements involved, and its relationship to other jobs.

It is important to understand that although the job analysis frequently *utilizes* the actual behavior of incumbents, the job description, nevertheless, provides a statement of what *should* be; it is a set of role prescriptions or requirements. Job analysts develop their descriptions based on information that is usually derived from people actually doing the work, just as organization analysts do, but this does not mean that the final result is necessarily a specific statement of what any individual is actually doing. It is instead an idealized statement of what he and others holding the position are expected to do.

It is also true that on occasion job descriptions are written well before the company has actually employed anyone in positions of a particular type. In such instances, the role prescriptions cannot be based on the actual behavior of incumbents. Perhaps the most striking example of this derives from the field of space travel. Before each astronaut starts out on his flight, a detailed job description is developed specifying exactly what he is expected to do and when. Because of the physical and psychological stresses involved a great variety of factors have to be considered in constructing these role prescriptions. In many instances, simulated conditions are devised in order to determine which behaviors will contribute most effectively to goal attainment (8). Here, there can be no question but that an *ideal* behavior pattern is being developed.

THE USES OF JOB ANALYSIS

As noted earlier in this chapter, the data derived from job analysis are of considerable value in evaluating the behavior of individual organization members. Jobs are structured to contribute maximally to productivity and maintenance goals; then individual behaviors are compared against these expected patterns. In this way, an evaluation of the individual outputs of the organization is obtained.

This contribution to the appraisal and evaluation process is an important function of job analysis, but it is by no means the only use to which this information may be put. There are, in fact, many ways in which job descriptions may be utilized by a company (16). Some of these are noted below:

Job Evaluation. Perhaps the most widespread application to which the data of job analysis are put is in job evaluation. Job descriptions are used to evaluate jobs in terms of their worth to the company. Wage and salary differentials are then established to reflect the existing differences in job requirements. In this connection, it is important to make a clear distinction between job analysis, job evaluation, and individual evaluation. The first refers to the establishment of role prescriptions; the second to the rating of *jobs* for payment purposes; the third to the rating of *people* in relation to role prescriptions.

Selection and Placement. Job descriptions are of considerable value as guides to hiring and placement practices. People who will be most successful, who will most closely approximate role requirements, should be selected for employment and assigned to appropriate kinds of work. Thus, selection procedures must be based on a detailed knowledge of position requirements. This consideration led us to take up the evaluation of individual outputs prior to discussing the evaluation of inputs into the organization.

Training and Development. Job analysis indicates the needs that training and management development must fulfill. Training programs should be devised to provide skills, knowledge, and motives that are lacking, but that are required for effective or outstanding performance and adequate morale. Thus, training should generate a closer match between actual and expected behavior.

Safety. The safety specialist can utilize the data of job analysis to identify job hazards and dangerous working conditions. In fact, many job descriptions include this information as an integral aspect. With this information, steps can be taken to minimize the possibility of accidents.

Labor Relations. By providing a means to common understanding between management and the labor unions with regard to the duties of each position, job analysis eliminates, or at least reduces, one type of employee grievance. Suspicion of favoritism is considerably reduced to the extent that pay differentials are based on clear differences in job duties. Thus, a job analysis contributes to reduced internal conflict once the program is well established and widely accepted; the organizational maintenance goal is thereby fostered.

Methods Improvement. The data of job analysis provide an index of what are presumed to be the most appropriate work procedures, given the existing equipment. But once a job has been studied in this amount of detail, it may become apparent that certain changes in the man-machine balance are economically feasible, and desirable. Automatic equipment may be introduced, or on occasion human actions may be substituted for machinery. Thus, job analysis can provide a basis for re-engineering the positions involved.

Wage and Salary Surveys. Job descriptions from different companies provide a method of comparing pay rates within occupations. With such information it is possible to be reasonably certain that the jobs compared are in fact similar. Thus, a company may determine how its pay scales jibe with others for comparable work in the community and adjust its rates accordingly.

Counseling. This, of course, is primarily an application outside the company itself. Yet job descriptions such as those developed by the United States Employment Service, and occupational information based on extensive job analyses, can have considerable value in areas such as vocational guidance and rehabilitation counseling. With this type of data it is possible to guide the inexperienced and the disabled into occupations where they are most likely to succeed.

The Scope of the Job Analysis

What kinds of information must be obtained in connection with a job analysis? There is no simple answer to this question, since the specific job under consideration, the company, and the purpose to which the data are to be put all exert influences. Different jobs have quite different salient aspects, and companies develop varying procedures for a number of reasons. If the primary purpose is to prepare a set of training guidelines, the information sought may well differ considerably from that desired should the objective be to construct a wage system. Yet there are certain types of data that are included in most analyses, although by no means in all, and it is these that have been singled out for discussion here. Exactly where a particular type of information may appear within a given job description is, however, subject to considerable variation. A specific item may well initiate one job description and come at the end of another. There are, in fact, almost as many variants as there are companies with job analysis programs.

ELEMENTS OF THE JOB DESCRIPTION

Job Title. All job descriptions should contain a specific job title or name, since this is needed for bookkeeping purposes within the firm and to facilitate reporting of the firm's activities to the government and to other data-collection agencies. In many cases, alternate or sláng titles are also noted.

Work Activities and Procedures. One segment of the job description is devoted to describing, in whatever detail is necessary, the tasks and duties to be performed on the job, the materials used in carrying out these tasks, the machinery operated if any, the kinds of formal interactions with other workers required, and the nature and extent of the supervision given or received.

Physical Environment. Another aspect of job description is the complete description of the physical working conditions where the work is to be performed. Among the factors that should be noted are the normal heat, lighting, noise levels, and ventilation in the work situation. In addition, it is sometimes desirable to indicate the physical location of the work in terms of a rural-urban or some other geographic designation, since this may be of relevance in recruiting and for other purposes. Any particular accident hazards are also described.

Social Environment. An increasingly common part of the job description is a section devoted to specifying the social conditions under which the work will be carried out. This is a relatively new component, and as a result the types of information included tend to vary considerably from company to company. Often there is a statement regarding the number of individuals in the working environment of the particular job. In addition, there may be considerable information on the age, sex, and other characteristics of these work associates. Thus, some idea may be gained regarding the homogeneity or heterogeneity of the individuals who will be employed together.

Physical aspects of the job that bear on the social aspects may also be noted—time of work hours (night or day), work location (city, suburban, or rural), availability of noncompany facilities (stores, restaurants, and so on), and availability of recreation (company-sponsored or not). These and other features of the social environment are, of course, significant in relation to the organizational maintenance goal. Role prescriptions in the areas of conflict minimization, cooperation with superiors, maintaining continued employment uninterrupted by excessive absenteeism, and the like always exist, even though these requirements may not be explicitly stated in the job description. Knowledge of the social environment can be extremely helpful in minimizing disparities between prescriptions of this kind and actual behavior.

Conditions of Employment. This aspect of the job description is concerned with the place of the job in the formal organization in such terms as the wage structure, working hours, method of payment, permanency of the positions, seasonal or part-time nature of work, allowable fringe benefits, relation to other jobs, and opportunities for promotion or transfer. Although every effort should be made to have statements in a job description as clear and precise as possible, this is particularly important when the conditions of employment are being described, because of the possible legal implications of many of the items.

In Tables 3–1 and 3–2, two rather different types of job descriptions

TABLE 3–1. A Typical Generalized Job Description: Job Analyst °

A. TITLE: Occupational Analyst.

B. ALTERNATE TITLES: Job Analyst, Personnel Studies Assistant, Employment Service Analyst, Personnel Technician.

C. DUTIES: Analyzes jobs and prepares descriptions and specifications; prepares or revises trade tests; supervises subordinates in compiling material; performs other functions. (Occupational analysts sometimes specialize in job analysis or in aptitude or job performance testing work.)
Details of above:

   1. Analyzes jobs and prepares descriptions and specifications. Studies jobs in plants, describes work performed, analyzes abilities and training required and writes descriptions largely in form of specifications for the use of employment interviewers, counselors, and other personnel workers for use in employment, in-service training, transfer, and job evaluation.

   2. Prepares or revises trade tests. Prepares trade test questions and administers them to workers for standardization purposes. May analyze results and select questions which show highest validity.

   3. Supervises subordinates in compiling material. May direct others in making job analyses, developing trade questions, and in related work.

   4. Performs other functions. May be required to contact employers and workers to obtain their cooperation and to explain the value of the techniques developed. May assist in one or more phases in the development of aptitude test batteries or in the preparation of surveys of jobs in plants using the *Dictionary of Occupational Titles.* May assist or train other staff members in the use of the techniques developed.

D. QUALIFICATIONS:

   1. Educational—College graduation or substitution of experience year-for-year is generally required as a minimum. However, in specialized fields, such as test-development, an M.A. may be required. Courses in industrial psychology, tests and measurements, and statistics are most often required. Persons with a year or more of graduate training sometimes enter this work without previous experience.

TABLE 3–1. A Typical Generalized Job Description: Job Analyst—
Continued

---

2. Training—
    a. On-the-job: Knowledge of the industry if employed in private in-
        dustry or familiarity with the practices of public employment offices
        if so employed. This varies from two weeks to six months.
    b. Prior: Some experience in job analysis, employment interviewing,
        or use of testing techniques in industry is usually required. Amount
        necessary depends on amount of college training. Generally four or
        five years or its equivalent in college training is required.
3. Personal—Ability to meet and get along with others is essential. Must
    write clearly and concisely and have ability to supervise others.
E. PROMOTIONS: From Employment Interviewer to Senior Analyst or Sec-
    tion Chief in charge of test development.
F. RELATION TO OTHER POSITIONS: Related to positions of Employ-
    ment Counselor or Interviewer and Industrial Psychologist.

° Adapted from Carroll L. Shartle, "Occupational Description for Positions in Psychology." A Report submitted to Division of Anthropology and Psychology, National
Research Council, Columbus, Ohio.

Source: R. Bellows, *Psychology of Personnel in Business and Industry*, 3rd ed., p.
            198. Copyright 1961. Reprinted by permission of Prentice-Hall, Inc., Engle-
            wood Cliffs, New Jersey.

TABLE 3–2. A Typical Job Description for a Specific Position in a
Specific Firm: Dealer Sales Supervisor for a
Petroleum Company

TITLE: Dealer Sales Supervisor
SALARY GRADE: 12
DEPARTMENT: Domestic Marketing
TITLE OF IMMEDIATE SUPERVISOR: District Manager
DUTIES: Under direction, supervises 6–15 salesmen engaged in selling and
    stimulating resale of company products to and/or by assigned accounts,
    acquiring new business, and in developing stations. Plans and supervises
    direct marketing activities within district or assigned territory in order to
    acquire and maintain maximum amount of profitable business by securing
    and retaining superior operation of service stations, developing dealers,
    acquisition of new direct marketing accounts, etc.
    1. Performs supervisory duties; assigns work, answers questions, etc.; fol-
        lows current activities by review of reports, discussions with subordi-
        nates, etc. Interviews job applicants, and makes selection subject to
        District Manager's approval. Handles minor disciplinary matters. Is
        consulted relative to promotions, transfers, salary treatment, etc. En-
        dorses expense and mileage accounts.
    2. Plans and supervises direct marketing activities within the district or
        territory in order to acquire and maintain maximum amount of profit-

TABLE 3–2. A Typical Job Description for a Specific Position in a Specific Firm: Dealer Sales Supervisor for a Petroleum Company—Continued

able business by securing and retaining superior operation of service stations, developing dealers, acquisition of new direct marketing accounts, etc. Receives occasional special assignments from District Manager, consults him as necessary on policy problems, and keeps him advised as to direct marketing activities; otherwise, works independently in accordance with established policies. Keeps currently informed of current activities by field observations, advice of subordinates, etc.

a. Recruits new dealers through personal contacts, newspaper ads, etc.; interviews candidates in conjunction with salesmen and recommends selection to District Manager. Gathers necessary credit information and personal references. Schedules trainees in training school, and reviews periodic progress reports. Attempts to place graduate trainees awaiting station with established dealer for further training. Indoctrinates and motivates new dealers; makes in-station inspections to check on training, answer questions, etc. Upon request, arranges for dealer employee clinics to be held within the district and assigns service salesmen as instructors; acts as faculty member of Dealer Training Schools.

b. Reviews monthly profit and loss statement and housekeeping reports prepared by salesmen on each financed dealer; looks for possible trouble spots such as excessive personal accounts receivable, expenses, personal loans, unbalanced sales, etc.; discusses weak points with salesmen, recommends remedial measures, and follows for correction. Participates in annual district reviews of dealers for purpose of discussing past performance, planning future programs and goals, pointing out weak spots in operation and offering advice relative to elimination. Prepares dealer lease analysis forms recommending future rental treatment, and discusses with District Manager.

c. Trains, coaches and assists salesmen in selling and acquiring accounts, training their dealers, investigating and settling complaints, overcoming problems, negotiating contracts, planning and executing sales promotions, etc. by double teaming with them in the field. Requests assistance from regional staff personnel and supplier's representatives, and handles necessary liaison duties.

d. Inspects stations in conjunction with District Manager; checks on appearance, service rendered, personnel's working knowledge, customer contacts, etc.; prepares written report, and follows for correction of noted deficiencies. In daily travels around territory makes casual inspections of stations, and advises others of items needing correction. Follows closely, and handles non-routine matters in connection with dealer changeovers.

e. Performs sundry related duties; plans and may conduct periodic sales meetings. Attends districts staff meetings. Handles correspondence with regional and home office personnel, dealers, etc. relative

TABLE 3–2. A Typical Job Description for a Specific Position in a Specific Firm: Dealer Sales Supervisor for a Petroleum Company—Continued

---

to matters supervised. Contributes to district's monthly marketing letter. Assists District Manager in preparation of service station site justifications, budgets, quotas, performance reports, etc. Speaks at local service organizations, and may serve as member of various industry and trade associations and committees.

3. As individually assigned, substitutes partially for District Manager during vacations and other absences to the extent of signing forms, reports, etc. normally signed by District Manager, and handling familiar matters according to District Manager's known views or his handling of similar problems in past; refers questionable matters to Regional Office for advice or decisions; advises District Manager of matters handled.

EDUCATIONAL REQUIREMENTS: High school graduate.

SPECIFIC KNOWLEDGE TO START: General knowledge of dealer marketing; company products; district organization and facilities; company marketing policies and procedures; service station operation. Supervisory experience.

WHERE EXPERIENCE REQUIRED: 4–5 years' experience in dealer marketing with at least 1–2 years as Dealer Salesman.

KNOWLEDGE ACQUIRED ON JOB: Experience in motivating, training, and supervising salesmen; learn to develop and apply effective selling programs; familiarity with company and competitive direct marketing activities in district; learn responsibility limits of positions. (6–9 months to acquire.)

PHYSICAL EFFORT: Semi-active; drives car approximately 1,100 to 2,000 miles/month.

RESPONSIBILITY:

Men—Supervision of 6–15 salesmen.

Materials—Economical use of office supplies.

Equipment—Care and use of office machines; inspection of service stations.

Markets—Acquiring and efficient servicing of accounts; occasional public relations contacts.

Money—Economical use of company expense funds by self and subordinates.

Methods—Execution, selection and control of methods used in direct marketing.

Records—Preparation, analysis and endorsement of records, reports and forms relative to direct marketing activities.

WORKING CONDITIONS:

Regular working hours 8:30 to 5:00 five days a week.

Surroundings and hazards:

10–60% normal office conditions.

40–90% field and travel conditions, with related hazards.

are presented. The first is much more generalized and contains the type of information that might be used by a vocational guidance counselor in advising young men with regard to a career. The description has been written to cover role prescriptions that might be found in a variety of employing organizations. Constructing trade tests, which cover the specific knowledge required for job performance, for instance, may or may not be an aspect of such a position depending on whether such tests are actually used by a particular company.

By way of contrast, the dealer sales supervisor description is much more specific as to what is required in this particular company. Here the exact role prescriptions are spelled out in considerable detail. Note that considerable attention is given to differentiating between what the sales supervisor is expected to do and what is expected of his superior, the district manager. In this sense, the job description has clearly been co-ordinated with the organization planning function.

THE JOB SPECIFICATION

The job specification part of the job description may not be labeled separately or, if it is, may well appear under the heading of qualifications. It contains information on the personal characteristics that are believed necessary for job performance. Included are such factors as educational background, experience, and personal qualifications.

Although the job specification is not universally treated as a separate entity within the job description, there are strong arguments for doing so, for it performs an entirely different function from the other components. The job specification neither states role prescriptions nor describes the conditions of work. Instead, it attempts to indicate what kind of people can be expected to most closely approximate the role requirements. Thus, it is basically concerned with matters of selection, screening, and placement.

A detailed discussion of problems in the selection area will have to await Chapters 6 and 7. Nevertheless, it is important to note here that job specifications are often written with little knowledge as to their actual relationship to work performance. Thus, it has become common practice to require high school graduation for a great variety of positions. Yet this is often done without trying out individuals who have not graduated from high school to determine if they are capable of effective performance. In most jobs it seems likely that a reasonably intelligent and emotionally mature person who has not finished high school will do as well as the graduate who lacks one or both of these characteristics.

Numerous examples could be given of situations where job specifications artificially restrict the labor market, so that it is very difficult to find anyone who meets all the requirements. This sort of thing is fine, if the specifications must be met to assume satisfactory performance. But all too often the information that would indicate whether this is the case has not been obtained. Specifications are often written without the intensive study that should precede the introduction of any selection procedure.

The Methods of Job Analysis

The methods used to gather information about a job vary greatly in comprehensiveness and systematic rigor. In the discussions that follow an effort will be made to explain some of the more commonly used techniques. The advantages and disadvantages of each approach will be emphasized, and an attempt will be made to cite typical occupations for which the particular procedure is most useful.

OBSERVATION OF THE JOB OCCUPANT

Observation of the job occupant is a frequently used method of identifying the tasks and duties actually involved in fulfilling the demands of a particular job. It requires merely that the job analyst observe a number of job occupants as they perform the job in a normal, workaday manner and that he record these observations systematically. This may be done either by writing down what was done in narrative form or by using a check list. The check list approach, of course, requires some prior knowledge of the particular job and those closely related to it. The job description is then written to include any new role prescriptions that may be desired. It is important that more than one job occupant be watched at work, since to do otherwise might result in the highly idiosyncratic and unique behaviors of a specific individual being written into the description.

Unfortunately, the simplicity of this approach is somewhat misleading. There are, in fact, certain related problems that can be very significant in the business situation. First, this method assumes that the act of observing an individual at work does not have an impact on the work behavior itself. For the method to be of value, the worker must do the same things in the same way when he is being watched as when he is not. In many instances, this is clearly not the case.

Many people have a tendency to show off under circumstances such as this; others become anxious. Activities that are expected to yield approval are often exaggerated. If the worker feels he is being observed in order to set his wage rate (as may well be the case), it is very likely that he will pattern his activities so as to obtain as favorable a rate as possible. These difficulties can be avoided by setting up a procedure whereby the worker may be observed without his knowledge. This is not easily accomplished, however. If the subterfuge is found out, labor relations problems can be anticipated, and considerable damage to morale is almost inevitable. All in all, it would seem that some distortion of normal behavior as a function of observation is very likely in most instances.

A second difficulty with the direct observation method of job analysis is that it becomes almost meaningless in the case of work that is primarily mental in nature. Thus, there are many positions ranging from private secretary to chairman of the board that are not really subject to this type of study. Observation alone will not yield a clear and meaningful picture of what the individual is doing. It should be noted, also, that this particular objection will become increasingly significant as automation spreads into new areas, since the general trend with the introduction of new technology is for the amount of physical behavior to decrease while mental activities increase as a factor in job performance.

A final problem with observation is that it is not very practical when the *job cycle*—the time from the beginning to the end of a specific task—is rather long. For example, the individual who has only to punch holes in some material with the aid of a machine may have a cycle of only ten or twenty seconds. But the skilled machinist who is making up an extremely complex and sensitive die may have a cycle of three to six months. In any instance where a specific action occurs only infrequently, it is very uneconomical to attempt a complete job description based on observation alone.

For the reasons stated, then, it appears that the observation technique should be employed only when the work is largely automatically controlled (such as a conveyor belt system), is primarily physical, and when the job cycle is rather short (as with certain lower level clerical jobs and many unskilled and semiskilled factory jobs).

INTERVIEW OF THE JOB OCCUPANT

Many of the objections to observation as a method of establishing the tasks, duties, and responsibilities of a job can be overcome by utilizing the interview as a source of information. The job cycle problem is largely eliminated, since the worker can observe himself and briefly summarize in words behaviors that were spread over a long time span. Similarly, an individual can monitor his own mental processes even though an observer cannot. As a result, the difficulty with nonphysical tasks is minimized; mental and behavioral activities can both be described. Furthermore, the employee is made an active participant in the information-gathering process, with the result that negative attitudes and resistances are much less likely to develop. Finally, this procedure utilizes the often considerable information the worker has about his job, information that may not be available to the job analyst from any other source.

It is desirable, however, that this procedure be utilized only after considerable planning and forethought. The individual doing the interviewing, the job analyst, must be thoroughly trained in the techniques of interviewing. Questions should be worked out in advance, and there should be a clear concept of exactly what information is desired.

The job analyst needs to gain *rapport* with the worker whose job is being studied. Confidence must be elicited, and the worker must be induced to accept the usefulness of the job analysis procedure. This is not easily done. Sometimes it is impossible. But the difficulties are compounded when, for instance, a college-trained job analyst goes into a plant to interview a blue-collar worker, who has only a minimum of formal schooling, and uses a vocabulary well above the level that the worker can adequately comprehend. In such cases, misunderstanding is inevitable and resentment very likely. The information-gathering function will probably not be adequately served.

A second possible source of difficulty is that the person being interviewed may, consciously or unconsciously, present a distorted picture of his position. He may, for example, attempt to portray his work as more difficult and important than it really is, in the hope that his pay and status will be increased accordingly. Interview data derived from a number of individuals performing the same or very similar tasks can be used to correct this tendency in part, but it is sometimes difficult to fit several disparate interviews together to form a comprehensive picture. The important thing is that the job analyst retain a clear conception of his own role, that he keep constantly in mind that he is supposed to establish a set of role prescriptions. These will only rarely be identical with any one incumbent's statements regarding his work behavior. Thus, job descriptions must go beyond mere interview data to effectively structure the entire pattern of work within the organization.

JOB OCCUPANT DESCRIPTION

The method of job occupant description is similar in intent and procedure to the interview, except that the occupant either writes a narrative description or fills out a questionnaire, rather than giving the information orally. Usually he is expected to go into considerable detail regarding the tasks performed, the conditions of work, the materials and equipment employed, and so on.

As might be expected, this technique has many of the advantages and disadvantages of the interview. It is, however, somewhat more economical of time and effort, since the services of an interviewer are not required. On the other hand, there is a loss in flexibility, which means that mistaken impressions can go uncorrected, or require considerable time to correct. Also, the benefits of a face-to-face discussion, as they may contribute to rapport and, consequently, to the correctness of the information obtained, are lost.

Evidence from several studies indicates that job occupants are quite consistent in describing their work, even when the jobs are as complex as those of aircraft control and warning operator, aircraft control and warning radar repairman, and jet fighter crew chief (12). People holding these military jobs note much the same tasks at one time as they do at another. An equally high degree of consistency was obtained with the check list for various engineering occupations presented in Table 3–3 (5).

TABLE 3–3. Job Description Checklist for Research, Development, Production, and Sales Engineers (occupants are to rank the items in terms of importance)

A. Evaluating ideas.
B. Conducting negotiations.
C. Planning the best use of equipment and materials.
D. Investigating problems of a basic and fundamental nature which may not be undertaken for specific practical application.
E. Keeping informed about competitive products and activities.
F. Simplifying production methods.
G. Developing a working model of a new instrument or process.
H. Developing and testing useful hypotheses or generalizations.
I. Preparing initial specifications for equipment installation.
J. Completing experimental or pilot projects.
K. Performing liaison work with departments and personnel to maintain over-all efficiency of process or equipment production.
L. Applying theoretical and empirical principles to develop an economically feasible instrument or process.
M. Developing a fund of basic research knowledge.
N. Evaluating performance of present materials, designs, methods, processes, products, equipment.
O. Selling ideas to people.
P. Planning best use of personnel.
Q. Working with customers' representatives to suggest equipment and/or process modification.
R. Originating technical ideas.
S. Controlling expenses.
T. Preparing and making technical recommendations and proposals.
U. Attending seminars, symposia, and colloquia to keep abreast of current developments.
V. Trouble shooting and/or meeting emergencies.
W. Setting up pilot projects to develop and test new process and equipment designs.
X. Writing technical articles, correspondence, instructions, manuals, patent disclosures, reports, specifications.

Source: M. D. Dunnette and G. W. England, "A Checklist for Differentiating Engineering Jobs," *Personnel Psychology*, Vol. 10 (1957), pp. 194–195.

Both the interview and the written description suffer in that job occupants may report incorrectly regarding their work. Probably the most effective way to compensate for any such bias is to have the data obtained from the incumbent reviewed by his immediate superior. If the superior has actually performed the work in the past, he is likely to be particularly helpful. Even without such personal experience, however, he can be presumed to possess considerable knowledge, merely because of the nature of his relationship to the incumbent and to the job. Since the objectives of the worker himself and those of his superior are likely to be somewhat different, this review may well provide a valuable antidote to the worker's statements in certain areas.

In general, the methods that secure information directly from the job occupant have a considerable advantage when the job analyses cover positions at middle or relatively high levels, where the work is not very repetitive. Individuals in these types of jobs are also those with whom the typical job analyst is likely to be most capable of gaining rapport.

EXAMINATION OF PREVIOUS JOB DESCRIPTIONS

Another way of gathering information about a job is to determine what is already known about it. This cuts down on duplication of effort and can provide a substantial base for subsequent study. Thus, for those companies that have them, previous job descriptions can be of real benefit. Before utilizing such information or any job descriptions that may be available from other firms, it is important to look into the analysis procedures employed. A poorly prepared job description may well do more harm than good. Also, the possibility that technological and other changes may have altered the job should be considered. Many job descriptions become obsolete insofar as present-day activities are concerned, even though the job titles may have remained the same.

There are, in addition, several other sources of occupational information. Perhaps most important is the *Dictionary of Occupational Titles,* published by the U. S. Employment Service (24). This contains very brief job descriptions of over 20,000 jobs. Almost any job title in normal usage can usually be found there. The job descriptions are, however, quite short and are based on multicompany studies. Thus, they may well not be appropriate for establishing role prescriptions in connection with a specific job in a specific company.

Two other sources are the *Alphabetical Index of Occupations and Industries,* put out by the Bureau of the Census (23), and the *International Standard Classification of Occupations* (9). Both are intended primarily for use in connection with a census of population and thus provide only minimal information about each job in the job description sense. However, by providing classification information, they do indicate the general type of work to which each job title refers.

EXAMINATION OF WORK MATERIALS

In some cases, it is possible to gain important information concerning the tasks and duties of a particular job by examining the materials typically used during work performance. A good example would be the tools of a carpenter, or perhaps the typewriter used by a secretary. The usefulness of this method is quite limited, but it can be of considerable supplementary value in certain instances.

PERFORMANCE OF WORK ACTIVITIES

It has long been said that the best way to learn about something is to do it. More recently, this assumption has received considerable support from laboratory research in psychology. It is apparent that one of the best ways for a job analyst to obtain information about a job is to take on its duties himself.

In many cases, this is entirely feasible. Such jobs as retail clerk and truck driver can be learned rather rapidly, as can many others requiring relatively limited skills. However, it is obvious that this is a technique of rather restricted usefulness and generality, since many jobs take years of training. Probably as the complexity of our knowledge increases, there will be fewer and fewer jobs that can be studied by actually performing them. Nevertheless, the advantages of the approach where it can be used are considerable.

Developing Job Families

A primary goal of a job analysis program is to develop systematic knowledge of how the jobs in a given company are related to one another in terms of either the required tasks or the necessary personal characteristics, or both. Such information can be of considerable value in planning training programs, selection, transfer, promotion, and other personnel activities. If certain jobs can be shown to group together, the occupants of these similar positions can be treated as a unit for a number of purposes. Groupings of this kind are particularly valuable as a guide in the placement of employees.

A very useful way of constructing such job families has been based on the differing aptitudes presumed to be required by each job (15). This technique forms the basis of the ensuing discussion. It has considerable value and can be employed by any company, utilizing the total job pool identified within the firm as a starting point.

In the research under consideration, the jobs were drawn at random from the *Dictionary of Occupational Titles*. The analysis as a whole was based on more than 300 jobs. Each was rated from the brief job descriptions in the *Dictionary* by six specially trained raters, who indicated the degree of aptitude required for satisfactory, not maximum, performance. The aptitudes employed are described in Table 3–4. The scale values assigned by the raters were averaged, and an aptitude requirement was established in all nine areas. Profiles over the nine aptitude dimensions were developed for all of the jobs studied.

TABLE 3–4. Aptitudes Used in Rating Jobs

Code	Aptitude
G	*Intelligence:* General learning ability: the ability to "catch on" or understand instructions and underlying principles; ability to reason and make judgments.
V	*Verbal:* Ability to understand meanings of words and ideas associated with them, and to use them effectively; to comprehend language and understand relationships between words and to understand meanings of whole sentences and paragraphs.
N	*Numerical:* Ability to perform arithmetic operations quickly and accurately.
S	*Spatial:* Ability to comprehend forms in space and understand relationships of plane and solid objects: may be used in such tasks as blueprint reading and in solving geometry problems; frequently described as the ability to "visualize" objects of two or three dimensions.
P	*Form Perception:* Ability to perceive pertinent detail in objects or in pictorial or graphic material; to make visual comparisons and discriminations and see slight differences in shapes and lengths.
Q	*Clerical Perception:* Ability to perceive pertinent detail in verbal or tabular material; to observe differences in copy, to proofread words and numbers, and to avoid perceptual errors in arithmetic computation.
K	*Motor Coordination:* Ability to coordinate eyes and hands or fingers rapidly and accurately in making precise movements with speed; ability to make a movement response accurately and quickly.
F	*Finger Dexterity:* Ability to move the fingers, and manipulate small objects with the fingers, rapidly or accurately.
M	*Manual Dexterity:* Ability to move the hands easily and skillfully; ability to work with the hands in placing and turning motions.

Source: D. B. Orr, "A New Method of Clustering Jobs," *Journal of Applied Psychology*, Vol. 44 (1960), p. 45.

TABLE 3–5. Definitions of Rating Scale Values

Level 1—An amount possessed only by the top 10% of the working population.

Level 2—An amount possessed by the highest third, exclusive of the top 10%.

Level 3—An amount possessed by the middle third of the working population.

Level 4—An amount possessed by the lowest third, exclusive of the lowest 10%.

Level 5—An amount possessed by the lowest 10% of the working population.

Source: D. B. Orr, "A New Method of Clustering Jobs," *Journal of Applied Psychology*, Vol. 44 (1960), p. 45.

The total distance, or difference, between each job profile was then computed, ignoring the sign of the difference. As an example, three hypothetical jobs—A, B, and C might have shown the following aptitude profiles:

Aptitude Code	Job A	Job B	Job C
G	3	1	5
V	2	1	5
N	1	4	4
S	4	3	3
P	5	3	3
Q	5	2	1
K	1	1	1
F	3	5	4
M	2	1	1

The difference, or distance, between Job A and Job B is:

$$(3-1) + (2-1) + (4-1) + (4-3) + (5-3) + (5-2) + (1-1) + (5-3) + (2-1) = 15.$$

The difference, or distance, between Job A and Job C is:

$$(5-3) + (5-2) + (4-1) + (4-3) + (5-3) + (5-1) + (1-1) + (4-3) + (2-1) = 17.$$

The difference, or distance, between Job B and Job C is:

$$(5-1) + (5-1) + (4-4) + (3-3) + (3-3) + (2-1) + (1-1) + (5-4) + (1-1) = 10.$$

It is apparent that Jobs B and C are much more alike in their requirements than are A and B or A and C. Thus, Jobs B and C would probably be classified together in a single job family. Job A, on the other hand, would clearly be left out of this particular grouping, although it could be assigned to another family to which it showed greater similarity in an expanded analysis.

Thus, those jobs that demonstrate a small difference, or distance, from one another are clustered together. In the study using jobs from the *Dictionary of Occupational Titles*, six job families were found. These accounted for more than 300 jobs studied. The characteristics of these six families are presented in Table 3–6, together with a number of typical jobs. Within each grouping the aptitude patterns of the component jobs appear to be much more similar than when jobs from different families are compared. Thus, transferring individuals within job families should be more successful than transferring them across families.

TABLE 3–6. Job Families Based on Similarity of Aptitude Patterns

Job family characteristics	Typical jobs
I. High level technical, supervisory, and mechanical jobs. The aptitudes required are Intelligence, Verbal, Numerical, Spatial, and Form Perception. Clerical is rated low.	Meter Engineer X-Ray Technician Engineering Specification Writer Pattern and Foundry Inspector
II. Extremely low level jobs, primarily unskilled.	Cement Finisher Helper Hydraulic Riveter Helper Cameraman Assistant Cooky Mixer Helper
III. Fairly high level skilled jobs, mostly mechanical and artisan types. The emphasis is on Spatial, Form Perception, Manual Dexterity, and Finger Dexterity.	Transformer Tester Steam Fitter Tubular Furniture Maker Rock Cutter
IV. Jobs at a very high level with respect to their requirements of Intelligence and Verbal. Supervisory jobs are contained in this cluster, and there is some emphasis on clerical abilities.	Rate Analysis Clerk Public Accountant Law Examiner Actor
V. Clerical jobs and supervisory jobs at a lower level than those in I. The aptitudes required in the greatest amounts are Intelligence, Verbal, Numerical, and Clerical.	Coal Inspector Service Establishment Attendant Beef Weighing Clerk Depot Master
VI. Mechanical-manual jobs of a medium grade of skill. Intelligence, Finger Dexterity, and Form Perception are required, but no aptitude is needed in more than an average amount.	Machine Driller Steam Table Attendant Thermite Welder Cable Splicer

Source: D. B. Orr, "A New Method of Clustering Jobs," *Journal of Applied Psychology*, Vol. 44 (1960), pp. 46–48.

Criticisms of Job Analysis

The reader should be aware that this entire matter of job analysis is surrounded by some controversy. There are those who believe that such analyses are too restrictive in nature, that they are not desirable because the job is largely what an individual makes of it. According to this viewpoint, job descriptions, and the role prescriptions that they contain, impose undue limitations on the development of the individual in his job.

Although it is true that these criticisms have some validity, this does not mean that companies should dispense with job analysis. It is important that areas of work specialization and concentration be spelled out, both as an aid to the productivity objective and in order to minimize internal conflict and stress. To eliminate all types of job description would be tantamount to eliminating any attempt at planning the utilization of human resources.

A more appropriate answer would seem to be the development of better, more realistic job descriptions, perhaps utilizing several methods of getting information. In addition, it may well prove desirable to write job descriptions at a somewhat higher level of generality, especially in the more skilled, professional, and managerial occupations so that an individual would have more latitude to fulfill himself in his job and to utilize his own unique talents and skills.

The amount of research being done on problems in the area of job design is increasing steadily. Engineering psychology, in particular, has made important contributions aimed at a better fit between the requirements of the work and its technology, as they influence role prescriptions, and the characteristics or competencies of human beings (7,11). Job specifications are being established increasingly by investigating the factors that predetermine success in a given job. Finally, there has been a recent trend toward linking jobs vertically into career ladders, as well as horizontally into job families. Training requirements for movements up a ladder are specified, and different ladders are established for different entry occupations (6). These developments suggest that the job descriptions of the future will, in fact, be far superior to those that have been criticized.

Designing and Changing Organizations

Psychological research provides considerable evidence that certain role prescriptions operate with a rather high degree of consistency across a great variety of managerial positions in the business world (14). Because of their prevalence and their nature, these requirements are not likely to be specifically designated when organization plans are drawn up and managerial job descriptions devised. Yet, when people are selected for managerial work, there is a very high probability that an individual's ability and desire to behave in accord with these prescriptions will be an important consideration.

The evidence indicates that managers, as managers, are expected to have a relatively favorable attitude toward those above them in the hierarchy. In their relationships with other managers at comparable levels, the role prescriptions call for a generally competitive attitude. Finally, managers are expected to impose their own wishes on subordinates and to exercise power over them. It is the nature of the managerial role to get those who work for them to do what they want.

These general prescriptions are very likely to appear no matter what the particular position, as long as it is essentially managerial, and we will return to them again in connection with the discussion of management appraisal. But there are also specific role requirements that are unique to a given job or a group of jobs. These are the major concern of those involved in structuring and restructuring organizations. In what follows, we will discuss several role requirements related to organizational design that have been of particular interest to psychologists. A number of other requirements have to date been of concern only to management theorists.

VERTICAL AND HORIZONTAL DIFFERENCES IN DECISION-MAKING AUTHORITY

The line-staff concept has become rather confused over the years, but it is probably most appropriate to think of it in terms of an horizontal difference in decision-making authority that is comparable to the vertical differences that exist between upper, middle, and lower managements. Staff and lower managers' role prescriptions tend to limit severely the type of decisions they can make; in a relative sense, line and upper level managers' do not.

Line managers are in the direct chain of command and have role prescriptions that call for decisions concerning the main operations of the firm. Staff managers, although expected to make decisions regarding those subordinate to them in the staff unit, are primarily concerned with providing advice and assistance to the line. They function outside the direct chain of command.

The University of California Studies. Support for this view, that staff managers experience a deficiency in decision-making relative to line managers, which is in many ways comparable to the differential between the lower and top organizational levels, comes from research conducted at the University of California (17). Approximately 1900 managers from firms throughout the country completed a questionnaire that yielded an index of the extent to which various needs or motives are felt to be satisfied on the job. The results, presented in Figure 3–1, are broken down by position level within management and line or staff designation.

It is apparent that irrespective of the need area there is a rather marked tendency for dissatisfaction to be more pronounced in the lower level positions. This is true of both line and staff. If we add the 114 presidents and board chairmen to the table, this conclusion gains even more support. At the very top level, there is considerably more satisfaction in all areas than in any other group, with one exception. On social needs, the top executives have an average score of .34 (18). Apparently, these men experience some relative deprivation insofar as opportunities for social interaction are concerned.

With the exception of the social area, a tendency similar to that associated with hierarchic position is in evidence when line and staff are compared, although, in the case of the desire for security, only the lower

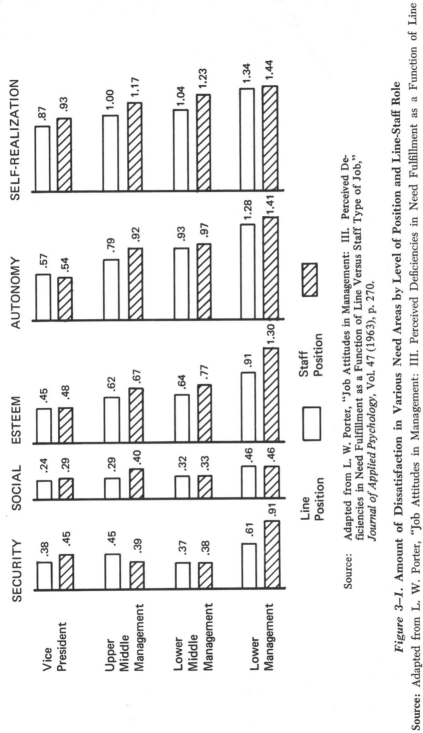

Figure 3–1. Amount of Dissatisfaction in Various Need Areas by Level of Position and Line-Staff Role

Source: Adapted from L. W. Porter, "Job Attitudes in Management: III. Perceived Deficiencies in Need Fulfillment as a Function of Line Versus Staff Type of Job," *Journal of Applied Psychology*, Vol. 47 (1963), p. 270.

management staff positions produce a real difference in the sense of deprivation. Apparently, satisfaction with the opportunities for social interaction is essentially comparable in staff and line and so is the feeling of security, except at the very lowest managerial levels. When we move to autonomy and self-realization, both clearly related to decision-making, however, there is no question but that the staff role yields a greater sense of deficiency, unless one is a vice president.

The evidence is clear that the staff-line differential is a real and meaningful aspect of most industrial organizations, although it may become blurred in certain research-based firms, such as those in the electronics industry (4). Role prescriptions for staff positions characteristically produce a sense of deficiency, insofar as freedom to make decisions is concerned, which is much more pronounced than in line work. Yet this line-staff differential is not as pronounced as that between upper and lower management. The vertical disparity in role prescriptions seems to be greater than the horizontal.

SPAN OF CONTROL AND GROUP SIZE

A second aspect of organizational structure that has been the subject of psychological research is the so-called span of control—the optimal size for the work group consisting of a manager and those who report directly to him.

Evidence from a sizable body of research indicates that, all other things being equal, there are distinct advantages associated with the relatively small work group (1). As we move up through the organization, a structure that minimizes the number of managers reporting to an individual at the next level would seem highly desirable. Small group size seems to produce greater output as well as better morale.

The ideal might be to keep this span of control consistently below eight throughout the organization. The number of people reporting to a manager must, however, reflect the nature of the work, the personality of the superior as it relates to the desire for social interaction, and the level of effectiveness of the subordinates. The importance of keeping the group small increases when the men are inexperienced, turnover is high, and conditions are such that a high incidence of performance failure requiring supervisory attention is likely to be present (13). This suggests that in the upper echelons of management, where highly selected and experienced men are characteristic, larger spans of control may be employed without negative effects.

It is apparent that keeping the size of groups small through the hierarchy produces a very tall organization with a large number of managerial levels. This has generally been assumed to be an undesirable state of affairs, partly because communication is inevitably more difficult and partly because the impersonality associated with such a structure might produce low morale and dissatisfaction.

At least on the latter count, it now seems clear that the negative consequences of the tall organization form are not so pronounced as often feared. In connection with the University of California studies, information was obtained on the number of managerial levels and company size for each firm employing the 1,900 managers, as well as on line-staff status. Over all, there was no evidence of any greater amount of dissatisfaction in the tall, as opposed to the flat, organizations (19). However, this statement needs some qualification. In companies with fewer than 5,000 employees, there was a tendency for managers to be somewhat less satisfied in the tall structure; in particular, they experienced some deprivation in self-realization. When there were more than 5,000 employees, the reverse was true, the tall structure producing somewhat greater satisfaction. In these larger companies, the tall organization form seemed to be particularly advantageous in yielding satisfaction with the degree of security a manager experienced.

Thus, it seems that, in the larger companies, a tall structure with relatively small groups is desirable, at least insofar as achieving organizational maintenance goals is concerned. In smaller firms, it would seem wise to keep the number of managerial levels to a minimum.

ORGANIZATIONAL CHANGE

As noted previously, changing organizational role prescriptions, such as level in the hierarchy, line-staff designation, or the managerial span of control, is not likely to be accomplished easily. Especially where the change is drastic, conflict may become rampant, and dissatisfaction can rise to high levels, resulting in considerable turnover among key people. What was intended as a move to achieve greater productivity and/or profits may result in a sizable loss in the organizational maintenance area. In view of this, it is important for a personnel psychologist to be thoroughly conversant with the phenomenon known as *resistance to change* and with the factors that may influence it (3,26).

For one thing, resistance is almost inevitable if those who will be affected are not advised of the exact nature of the anticipated shifts and the reasons behind them. Incomplete and ambiguous information is likely to be reinterpreted as a threat. People who might be affected can be expected to band together in a close-knit unit to fight the change. It is particularly undesirable to permit word to get around long before the change occurs that some type of major reorganization is in the offing. Such rumors, even though true, are very likely to be viewed with alarm, when the exact impact on each individual has not been spelled out.

Second, people will interpret an organizational change in different ways depending on their particular motives and other personality characteristics. Resistance may derive from a variety of causes. Yet, in management, especially at the highest levels, power considerations are very likely to be primary (14), and, accordingly, any resistance may well stem from a perceived threat to a manager's power position. One can assume that those who have no power will favor change, largely because they can only gain; they have nothing to lose. Similarly, those who have every reason to anticipate increased decision-making and thus greater power as a consequence of the organizational shift will also offer their support. Resistance will predominate among those who have some basis for believing their power within the company will be diminished, either through demotion, or movement to a staff role, or in some other manner. Reorganization almost always involves some alteration in the power balance.

Third, resistance is a common consequence when strong pressure for change, say from the organization planning group and perhaps higher management, is coupled with strong pressure against it, say from the group of managers at the same level. At such times, a manager may attempt to maintain the status quo, even after a new set of role prescriptions have been allocated. This may result in no real change in role *behavior*.

Fourth, to the extent a manager can participate in the decision to make a change and exert some influence in determining what the new allocation of role prescriptions will be, he is likely to support the change, and any potential resistance will in all probability be dissipated. When he is allowed to participate, a person will normally feel that he has had an opportunity to protect his power position and that any loss in this regard has occurred voluntarily. Under pressure, he can only assume, even if his decision-making authority is extended by the reorganization, that he is not very important to the firm, since he was not consulted on an action of direct significance to him.

Fifth, if an organizational change is promulgated as the personal action of some one individual or as an attempt to achieve the ends desired by a single manager, it is particularly likely to arouse resistance. If, on the other hand, the change is closely, and logically, tied to organizational goals, so that it can be viewed by many as a sensible means to achieve productivity and/or maintenance objectives, support can be expected to be maximum.

Sixth, resistance will be high when the mechanics of change ignore the established customs, values, and institutions. A shift in role prescriptions is ideally achieved by paying strict attention to other role prescriptions— by consulting those who can expect to be consulted, by having the change announced by the man who should announce it, by acting when such actions are supposed to be taken, and by relating the change to existing organizational values. The change must be viewed as legitimate.

Finally, organizational change will be easier when there is a readiness for change, when people are prepared and accept it as a fact of life, when the role prescriptions themselves emphasize a proclivity for change. Under these circumstances, resistance is difficult to justify, and a person who wants desperately to fight a change may not do so largely because he knows others will not go along with him. Here, organizational restructuring is viewed as inevitable and entirely legitimate. Managerial role prescriptions, in fact, include a proviso that all managers must expect major alterations in their roles at uncertain intervals. If this is the pattern of expectations, it is difficult for a particular manager to obtain much group support for any resistance when his role does change, and any opposition to reorganization will probably be short lived.

In view of these considerations, it should be apparent that carrying out a successful reorganization, even on a small scale, is no easy task. Gaining acceptance for the new structure and keeping repercussions in the organizational maintenance area to a minimum can be just as difficult and time-consuming a task as settling on the exact design that is to be instituted. Studies indicate that very sizable improvements in productivity and profits can be achieved without any major long-term loss insofar as other company goals are concerned (10). It is clear that a change in managerial role prescriptions need not create a greater disparity between expected and actual behavior, and thus less effective managers. An adequately planned and implemented reorganization will produce major shifts in *behavior*, in the direction of the new role requirements.

REFERENCES

1. Bass, B. M., *Organizational Psychology.* Boston, Mass.: Allyn & Bacon, 1965.
2. Bellows, R., *Psychology of Personnel in Business and Industry*, 3rd ed. Englewood Cliffs, N.J.: Prentice-Hall, 1961.
3. Coch, L., and J. R. P. French, "Overcoming Resistance to Change," *Human Relations*, Vol. 1 (1948), 512–532.
4. Dalton, M., "Changing Staff-Line Relationships," *Personnel Administration*, Vol. 29 (1966), No. 2, 3–5, 40–48.
5. Dunnette, M. D., and G. W. England, "A Checklist for Differentiating Engineering Jobs," *Personnel Psychology*, Vol. 10 (1957), 191–198.
6. Fine, S. A., *Guidelines for the Design of New Careers.* Kalamazoo, Mich.: W. E. Upjohn Institute for Employment Research, 1967.
7. Gagné, R. M., *Psychological Principles in System Development.* New York: Holt, Rinehart & Winston, 1962.
8. Grether, W. F., "Psychology and the Space Frontier," *American Psychologist*, Vol. 17 (1962), 92–101.
9. *International Standard Classification of Occupations.* Geneva, Switz.: International Labour Office, 1958.
10. Lawrence, P. R., *The Changing of Organizational Behavior Patterns.* Boston, Mass.: Graduate School of Business Administration, Harvard Univ., 1958.
11. McCormick, E. J., *Human Factors Engineering*, 2nd ed. New York: McGraw-Hill, 1964.
12. McCormick, E. J., and H. L. Ammerman, *Development of Worker Activity Check Lists for Use in Occupational Analysis*, Technical Report WADD–TR–60–67. Lackland Air Force Base, Texas: Personnel Laboratory, Wright Air Development Division, Air Research and Development Command, United States Air Force, 1960.

13. Miner, J. B., *The Management of Ineffective Performance*. New York: McGraw-Hill, 1963.
14. Miner, J. B., *Studies in Management Education*. New York: Springer, 1965.
15. Orr, D. B., "A New Method of Clustering Jobs," *Journal of Applied Psychology*, Vol. 44 (1960), 44–49.
16. Otis, J. L., and R. H. Leukart, *Job Evaluation*, 2nd ed. Englewood Cliffs, N.J.: Prentice-Hall, 1954.
17. Porter, L. W., "Job Attitudes in Management: III. Perceived Deficiencies in Need Fulfillment as a Function of Line versus Staff Types of Job," *Journal of Applied Psychology*. Vol. 47 (1963), 267–275.
18. Porter, L. W., *Organizational Patterns of Managerial Job Attitudes*. New York: American Foundation for Management Research, 1964.
19. Porter, L. W., and E. E. Lawler, "The Effects of Tall versus Flat Organization Structures on Managerial Job Satisfaction," *Personnel Psychology*, Vol. 17 (1964), 135–148.
20. Shartle, C. L., *Occupational Information*, 3rd ed. Englewood Cliffs, N.J.: Prentice-Hall, 1959.
21. Shartle, C. L., "Occupational Analysis, Worker Characteristics, and Occupational Classification Systems," in H. Borow, *Man in a World at Work*. Boston, Mass.: Houghton Mifflin, 1964, pp. 285–309.
22. Stogdill, R., *Individual Behavior and Group Achievement*. New York: Oxford Univ. Press, 1959.
23. United States Department of Commerce, Bureau of the Census, *Alphabetical Index of Occupations and Industries*, Washington, D.C.: Government Printing Office, 1960.
24. United States Department of Labor, *Dictionary of Occupational Titles*, 3rd ed. Washington, D.C.: Government Printing Office, 1965.
25. Wallis, W. A., "Some Economic Considerations," in J. T. Dunlop (ed.), *Automation and Technological Change*. Englewood Cliffs, N.J.: Prentice-Hall, 1962, pp. 103–113.
26. Zander, A., "Resistance to Change: Its Analysis and Prevention," *Advanced Management*, Vol. 15 (January 1950), 9–11.

QUESTIONS

1. In discussing occupations, it is important to be aware of the distinctions between terms that are part of the vocabulary. What major characteristics distinguish the following?
   a task and a position
   a job and an occupation
   the job description and the job specification
   position analysis and job analysis
   a job family and an occupation
   job analysis and job evaluation
2. What are the uses to which job analysis information may be put? Can you think of any uses not discussed in the text?
3. What are the disadvantages of observation of the job occupant as a method of obtaining job analysis information? To what extent do the interview procedure and job occupant description overcome these disadvantages?
4. Take four jobs with which you are reasonably familiar and assign aptitude ratings to them, using the aptitudes of Table 3–4 and the scale of Table 3–5. Determine the distance between each pair of jobs. Which would you group together in the same job family?

5. What research has been carried out by psychologists which is relevant to line-staff differentials? To span of control? Do such considerations appear to be a fruitful area for future psychological study?
6. What is resistance to change, and what considerations must be kept in mind in attempting to overcome it?

4

Management Appraisal

In Chapter 3, some of the methods used to establish and formalize role prescriptions have been discussed at length. Let us now turn to the various methods developed to evaluate individuals relative to these role prescriptions, more especially to the evaluation of managerial personnel.

It should be understood at the outset that evaluation in some form is inevitable. All organizations make some effort to determine whether individual members are contributing to the attainment of objectives. This may be done in an off-hand way by the top person or through the use of a complex, formal appraisal and evaluation system. The evaluations may be precise and accurate or vague and almost entirely in error. But we can almost certainly expect to be judged in some way when we join an organization, especially if it is an employing organization that rewards its members with money.

A great variety of techniques and procedures have been devised to aid in this process of evaluation and appraisal. All attempt to provide some indication of the extent to which an individual's behavior matches a conception of what he is expected to do. The basic consideration is whether behavior is so integrated with established role requirements as to be considered successful or so much at variance with them that it is considered ineffective.

Because any given position is likely to have a number of different role prescriptions, we can expect that job-related behavior will be evaluated in a number of ways. Particularly in the case of managers, it is not a matter

of doing one or even a few things correctly, but of doin
different things, all designed to meet one or another ro
Accordingly, an individual may be considered a great
regard, only to fail badly relative to some other requireme

It is characteristic, then, to evaluate people in terms or y.
of their behavior, or dimensions of performance. Generally, the ...
concern is with actual behavior, with the things a person does or says.
But on occasion, evaluation systems move one step back into the individual and attempt to deal with the abilities, motives, emotional patterns,
and so on that cause, or determine, the behavior. The most general pattern is to establish the extent of the match to a role prescription, or the
degree of success. Often, however, *standards* are introduced so that behavioral output is considered only as it relates to some minimal acceptable
level. Either the person is above or below standard in a particular regard.

Individual appraisal is carried out to determine what actions should
be taken with regard to a person, in the present instance a manager. The
result may be a decision to increase his pay, or decrease it, or leave it
the same. Or the evaluation may be used as a basis for a placement decision—promotion, demotion, transfer, retention, or even separation. Management appraisal data are also used to guide management development
activities, either directly, through a feedback of the conclusions to the
person evaluated, or indirectly, as an indicator of future educational
needs. Finally, the evaluations may be used to provide *criterion* data
when selection procedures are being developed. This topic will be a
primary concern in Chapters 6 and 7. It is sufficient to note here that a
company normally tries to select from among job applicants those who
have characteristics similar to the characteristics of its more successful
employees and to screen out applicants who appear to be like unsuccessful
workers.

The Behavior of Effective and Ineffective Managers

Before discussing the numerous techniques and procedures used in management appraisal, it is advisable to review what we know about the
behavior of managers who have consistently been judged successful in
their companies. In large part, managing is characterized by the attempt
to elicit high levels of productivity and a maximal contribution to organizational maintenance from others. The manager is assigned much
more work than he can do alone; therefore, he must get others to help
perform his role. Managerial behavior is consistently evaluated in terms
of its effects on others, that is, in terms of its supervisory aspects: Does the
manager facilitate the work efforts of his subordinates, or does he act in
such a way as to actually make them less effective than they might otherwise be?

RESEARCH ON EFFECTIVE SUPERVISION

The most extensive studies of supervisory behavior have been carried out by psychologists at the University of Michigan. This work has been done in a great many different types of firms, from insurance companies to manufacturing. As a result, a rather consistent picture of the typical, effective supervisor has been obtained (13).

For one thing, the ideal manager devotes his efforts primarily to supervisory and leadership tasks and does not become deeply involved in doing the work of his subordinates. The factory foreman who spends long periods operating a machine and the sales supervisor who is primarily engaged in direct selling are not likely to be effective. They do not have the time to plan the work of their groups, perform any required special technical tasks, provide materials as necessary, observe the group's performance, motivate their subordinates, and deal with less effective workers. The process of supervision is left largely undone.

Second, less successful managers maintain extremely close supervision. Some delegation, which permits subordinates a degree of freedom, is apparently essential. The manager who continually hovers over his men, giving them frequent and detailed instructions on all phases of their work, seems to have a primarily negative impact rather than the positive effect he presumably intends.

Third, more effective supervisors tend to be relatively employee-centered and to exhibit considerable concern for their subordinates as human beings. The less effective, on the other hand, maintain an unreasonable pressure for production with very little indication of human kindness. They take a punitive attitude whenever a mistake occurs, make no effort to develop their subordinates, rarely talk things over with their men, do not give praise, and usually neglect such special requests as their subordinates may make.

A fourth finding from the University of Michigan research indicates that the manager who exhibits none of the three negative behavior patterns just discussed may nevertheless remain relatively ineffective if he cannot influence his own superiors. He must succeed in getting support for his actions up the line. It is not enough to appear employee-centered; the results must be made to stick. A promised change in work schedules that is never put into effect or a salary increase that is turned down at higher levels indicates that the manager is not very important. Repeated occurrences of this type tend to produce a work group that largely ignores supervision.

Fifth, a successful manager assumes an active leadership role in his relations with his men. It is essential that the group be led and that the members be given some understanding of their role prescriptions. A laissez-faire approach is characteristically unsuccessful.

These findings, as well as others of more recent origin, have been interpreted as supporting a participative or democratic managerial style almost to the exclusion of other approaches (14,30). However, the evidence is not entirely consistent with this interpretation. There is good reason to believe that the permissive manager is more effective in certain structure toward their subordinates appear to be most successful (26, 29).

The Ohio State University Studies. A very similar series of investigations has been carried out by psychologists at Ohio State University. After conducting a number of detailed statistical analyses, these researchers conclude that behavior toward subordinates can be described adequately in terms of only two groupings, rather than five. In general, managers who exhibit both consideration and what was called initiating structure toward their subordinates appear to be most successful (26,29).

These studies indicate that a major factor contributing to failure is inconsiderate behavior toward subordinates. Being overdemanding and critical, "riding" one's workers, failing to consult the men on actions of concern to them, refusing to accept suggestions or to listen to problems, never doing a favor for a subordinate—these and similar behaviors were found to predominate among managers who were not meeting job requirements.

The second factor deals more directly with the work output of the group. Those managers who initiated structure for their men, who established standards and specified role prescriptions, were consistently found to be more successful. Managers who placed little emphasis on following rules, who gave the impression of being "one of the boys," who rarely assigned work duties or took a position on anything, and who neglected planning and organizing activities were identified as generally ineffective.

There is, of course, considerable similarity between the findings of the Ohio State studies and those of the Michigan studies. The first type of behavior noted by the Michigan psychologists, doing the work of subordinates, seems to be a failure to initiate structure. The second factor, too close supervision, and the third, a lack of employee-centeredness, are presumably comparable to the Ohio State conception of a deficiency in consideration and kindness. The fourth and fifth factors, which involve the exercise of influence both upward and downward in the organization, fall in the general category of initiating structure and exercising control. The successful manager is normally the one who acts to enforce role requirements and standards, but with a degree of consideration and human kindness toward his subordinates. This approach elicits the greatest contributions in both the maintenance and the productivity areas from a group. But, it must also be recognized that there are sizable variations from organization to organization in the types of individuals who will be viewed as successful in a leadership role (21).

ADDITIONAL ASPECTS OF
MANAGERIAL BEHAVIOR

Successful managing is not, of course, defined entirely in terms of behavior directed toward subordinates, although this may be extremely important. A manager, especially one at the upper levels or in some specialized aspect of the company's total operations, may also be called on to make decisions that have a direct impact on company profits and productivity. Decisions on new plant locations or converting to automated production processes or entering new markets are of this kind. If these decisions prove to be incorrect, the manager responsible for making them is likely to be considered unsuccessful, at least in this particular regard. Furthermore, any unwarranted wastage of company assets or deliberate reduction of company productivity and profits, through theft, for purposes of stock manipulation, or for any other reason can be assumed to produce a judgment of sizable departure from role requirements.

In addition, a manager may be evaluated in terms of his impact on internal stresses within the company. Does he act to reduce conflict and dissension, to negotiate peaceful solutions to conflicts with other managers? Does he attempt to head off labor difficulties? Or does he foment discord, antagonize others, and provoke union representatives? The answers to these questions can well exert considerable influence on judgments as to whether a manager is effective.

Decisions and actions of much the same kind are also required of many managers in relation to external threats to organizational maintenance. Thus, an acquisition involving the company in a costly antitrust suit, which is finally lost, may result in an extremely negative opinion of the managers involved. A highly articulate and successful lobbying effort that defeats a law unfavorable to the firm, on the other hand, can yield a very favorable evaluation.

These are the kinds of activities unique to managerial occupations and thus of particular concern in management appraisal. When added to the usual considerations of quantity and quality of work output, and the matter of being physically present on the job—absenteeism, tardiness, and so on—they largely cover the gamut of behaviors considered in connection with the management evaluation process. It should be recognized, however, that a number of psychologists employ methods of classifying managerial behaviors that differ in a number of respects from those used here.

Judgmental Appraisal

The most widespread method of evaluating managers is to obtain some type of judgment regarding their effectiveness. This may be done as required whenever a manager is being considered in connection with a personnel action, such as promotion or a proposed development activity. Or the appraisals may be conducted at regular intervals, so that all managers are considered within a specified time span. Ideally, this would be done once a year, or at most at two-year intervals. Any longer interval is likely to produce considerable error, since managers do change, and, consequently, badly outdated evaluations may be employed to guide personnel actions.

It is probably most common in the business world to have managers appraised by managers who are above them in the hierarchy. However, there are a number of other techniques that require discussion, some of which are gaining increasing acceptance. Among these are evaluations by peers, i.e., managers at the same level, or by subordinates; evaluations by, or with the assistance of, personnel specialists and psychologists; and self-appraisal.

In this chapter, little attention is given to specific rating procedures and the types of judgmental errors that may occur. It is sufficient here to cover the different sources of appraisal data and the relative merits of each. The details of rating scale construction and use will be taken up in Chapter 5. It is important to recognize, however, that what is said there regarding the techniques used with lower level employees is equally applicable to judgments regarding managers. Many management appraisal systems utilize rating systems identical in format to those discussed in Chapter 5, although the variables or dimensions measured may be different—because managerial work is different.

APPRAISAL BY SUPERIORS

One of the first questions that arises in constructing any management appraisal system is whether to use the judgments of a single superior or of several. On this point, the evidence is clear (3). The average of several evaluations made by equally competent raters is far superior to a single rating. If at all possible several levels of supervision should be tapped, provided, of course, that all the individuals involved are in a good position to observe the work behavior of the man being appraised. Sometimes it is possible to utilize managers at higher levels who are not in the direct chain of command above the man—an individual who works in close spatial proximity, a staff manager with whom he often deals, and so on. Even if the immediate superior is the only person who is really knowledgeable regarding the man, multiple ratings appear to be preferable. Thus, the average of successive evaluations made by the same superior over a period of perhaps six months is generally superior to a single report.

The difficulty with using managers at various higher levels to obtain multiple ratings is that the condition of equal competence is frequently not met. A manager several levels above the individual being appraised may well not have a really adequate opportunity to observe him. His conclusions may be based on a limited number of isolated incidents, plus hearsay.

This is clearly demonstrated in Table 4–1. In this particular study,

TABLE 4–1. Correlations Between Supervisory Ratings at Three Different Levels and an Independent Index of Job Proficiency ($N = 100$)

	Supervisory level		
Rating scale question	Commissioned officers	NCO flight chiefs	Immediate NCO superiors
How much does he know about his job?	.24	.19	.42
How well does he do his job?	.25	.18	.40

Source: D. K. Whitla and J. E. Tirrell, "The Validity of Ratings of Several Levels of Supervisors," *Personnel Psychology*, Vol. 6 (1953), p. 464.

100 lower level noncommissioned officers were rated first by their immediate superiors, then by the next higher level of NCO's, and finally by the commissioned officers responsible for their work (32). (Each man was rated three times.) These ratings were then correlated with scores obtained by the men being appraised on a special written test of job knowledge and proficiency. Ideally, of course, the correlations could go as high as 1.00, which would indicate a perfect relationship between the ratings and the test scores, the best ratings matching the highest scores and so on down the line.

Although this degree of precision was not obtained (it never is in studies of this kind), there was a tendency for the ratings and test scores to correlate (all values in Table 4–1 are well above .00). More important for our purposes, however, are the higher correlation coefficients of the immediate NCO superiors. These men apparently had picked up information that was also reflected in the test scores, but that was not available to those at higher levels. The immediate superiors, because of a greater amount of contact, were in a better position to evaluate the men than were those further up the hierarchy. In any averaging of the three ratings, one would want to give their opinions much greater weight.

This raises an additional problem with regard to multiple ratings by superiors. Many companies conduct what they call appraisal sessions, where several of the manager's superiors meet and discuss his work in detail. They then make what amounts to a group rating, which is the particular composite of their individual opinions that they can agree on or that the majority favors. This composite, however, is likely to be heavily weighted with the views of the highest level individual present, or the highest level person who clearly states his opinions. Yet, as we have seen, this person may not be in the best position to appraise the manager. As a result, the degree of error can be considerable.

In order to overcome this difficulty, it is generally considered desirable to have the evaluations made separately, and to record all of them in the personnel office before any group appraisal session is conducted. If a composite rating is then made by the group, it can be checked against the average of the independent ratings to see if it represents a shift in the direction of the highest level person.

The Appraisal Summary. In companies that maintain an ongoing appraisal system with periodic evaluations, the typical procedure is for a member of the personnel department to write an appraisal summary. This summary may be merely a brief synopsis, but more frequently it is an extensive and detailed description of the individual. An outline for an appraisal summary of this latter type is presented in Table 4–2.

TABLE 4–2. Outline Covering Items Included in a Typical Appraisal Summary

---

1. Personal Background
   Age
   Family background
      Marital status
      Children
   Education
      Types of specialization and degrees
      Extracurricular activities and offices
   Military experience
      Period of service
      Rank at start and end
      Nature of chief assignments
      Campaigns and decorations
   Work history
      Employers
      Position titles and duties
   Special accomplishments
      Honors and awards
      Professional or trade organization memberships and offices
      Community and church activities and offices
      Publications
   Special limitations
      Health
      Family problems
   Hobbies and recreational activities
2. Nature of Work
   Generalized statement based on organization planning and job analysis
      data

TABLE 4–2. Outline Covering Items Included in a
Typical Appraisal Summary—Continued

Committee assignments
Number and titles of people supervised
3. Job Performance and Personal Qualifications
General statement of value to company and probable future contribution
Technical performance
    Evaluation against expectations in each of the key areas noted in job
        description
    Specific achievements in each of key duties
Motivation in current position
    Attitude toward superiors, company, and job
    Acceptance of and desire for responsibility
    Personal desire for accomplishment and drive
    Self-reliance in making decisions
    Degree and fairness of competition
    Loyalty to company and general managerial orientation
Intelligence as manifested on the job
    Selection of realistic goals and methods of goal attainment
    Ability to learn new techniques
    Resourcefulness in new and trying situations
    Quality and speed of thinking
    Organizational and planning ability
    Judgment
    Thoroughness and accuracy
    Ability to sell ideas
    Flexibility in dealing with ideas of others
    Creativity
Emotional stability
    Adjustment to frustrations and constraints
    Capacity to take calculated risks
    Ability to get along with others
    Reaction to criticism and pressure
    Objectivity and freedom from prejudice
    Excessive emotionality
    Impairments caused by off the job problems
Leadership skills
    Ability to elicit cooperation from subordinates
    Ability to criticize and give orders if necessary
    Skill as a team worker with other organizational units
    Development of subordinates
    Delegation and use of controls
    Capacity to establish and publicize performance standards
    Type of subordinates sought and ability to appraise
Three accomplishments in present job that indicate what he is capable of
Summarizing snapshot covering major strengths and weaknesses

TABLE 4–2. Outline Covering Items Included in a
Typical Appraisal Summary—Continued

---

4. Overall Performance Rating
   Individual rating relative to what is expected
   Ranking among others at same level doing similar work
5. Potentiality
   Promotability and expected rate (or timetable) of progress
   Actual jobs or job types (job families) qualified for
   Long-range potential
6. Recommended Actions
   Changes in placement
   Ideal duration of current placement
   Development needs and plans based on comparison against following list
      of management knowledges and skills
      Knowledge of: Technical information bearing on job
                    Related specialties and jobs
                    Labor relations and labor law
                    Business economics
                    Company and departmental objectives
                    Job evaluation and payment policies
                    Safety
                    Employee benefits and privileges
                    Company organizational structure
                    Legal constraints
                    Industry practices and competitive picture
         Skill in: Delegation to subordinates
                    Coaching subordinates
                    Setting performance standards
                    Establishing controls and follow-up
                    Long-range planning
                    Decision making
                    Selling ideas
                    Negotiation
                    Evaluation of individuals and groups
                    Taking disciplinary action
                    Maintaining morale
                    Communications
                    Analyzing accounting reports and other data
                    Cost control
                    Discussion leadership
                    Report and letter writing
                    Public speaking
                    Interviewing and meeting people
                    Developing budgets
                    Reading (speed and comprehension)

The data used to write the appraisal summary on a specific individual are derived in large part from his superiors. But, in addition, the typical program utilizes psychological tests, a personal history form filled out by the manager himself, and in many cases a personal interview with the manager conducted by a personnel representative. The summary is characteristically considered confidential and is made available only to the manager's direct-line superiors and to appropriate personnel managers and psychologists.

When all these appraisal summaries have been completed for a given company unit, it is common practice to prepare a management personnel inventory. This indicates future replacement needs and lists the candidates for anticipated vacancies, who may qualify immediately or after further development. Anticipated needs for at least five years are usually considered, based on performance, expected promotions, retirement schedules, health, projected organizational changes, and so on.

Replacement candidates are obtained not only from the specific unit, but from other segments of the company as well. It is entirely possible for an individual to appear as a candidate on inventory lists for several units, depending on the breadth of his training and experience. The lists are maintained on a continuing basis, and thus are reviewed and updated frequently. On occasion the management inventory is developed in chart form along the lines of Figure 4–1.

APPRAISAL BY PEERS OR SUBORDINATES

During World War II, a technique known as *buddy rating* was developed by Navy psychologists. This procedure requires each member of a group to rate all other members on certain aspects of their work performance. The ratings on each individual are then averaged to provide an index of the man's competence.

In the years since these initial applications, much has been written about the advantages of this technique, especially as an aid in evaluating managers. Either all managers at a comparable level in a given unit, perhaps all first-line foremen in a small manufacturing plant, rate each other or as a variant each manager is rated by his subordinates. In this way, it is possible to obtain evaluations from those who are likely to be well acquainted with the man being appraised, to have observed his work closely over a long period, and thus to be capable of making extremely accurate ratings.

Despite these apparent advantages, buddy rating procedures have not achieved widespread acceptance in the business world for a number of reasons. For one thing, men at the same level in the managerial hierarchy are apt to be either friends or rivals. In the former instance, the ratings may be elevated inappropriately; in the latter, they may be depressed. Also, where there is mutual rating, there is always the possibility that both parties have agreed to do well by each other.

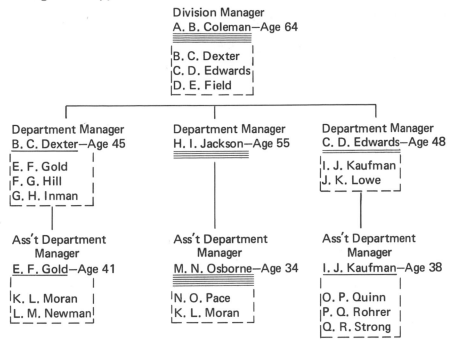

Code for Underlining of Incumbents

———————— Outstanding potential. Ready for job above. High promise for unit head.

════════ Good potential. Fair promise for unit head.

▬▬▬▬▬▬▬▬ Potential for some growth. Not likely to make unit head.

▬▬▬▬▬▬▬▬ Not likely to advance beyond present position.

▬▬▬▬▬▬▬▬ Age or health make replacement necessary within 5 years.

▬▬▬▬▬▬▬▬ Unsatisfactory performance. Replacement needed.

Figure 4–1. **Management Inventory Chart**

Where subordinates are asked to evaluate their superiors other problems arise. The anticipation of reprisal, whether justified or not, means that only the reckless or those who are on the verge of quitting may be willing to express a negative opinion. Furthermore, subordinates are likely to have personal objectives that differ from corporate objectives and that may exert an undue influence on the ratings. This is a problem in any rating system, but its impact tends to be increased when evaluations are made by people far removed from the policy-making level. Subordinates may well view a superior in terms of the degree to which he has served to satisfy or frustrate their own personal motives, rather than in terms of his contribution to company goals.

Certainly, as Table 4–3 indicates, the ratings made by peers or subordinates do tend to differ considerably from those made by superiors. In this study, 100 candidates for promotion at North American Aviation were evaluated by their coworkers and also by both their foreman and assistant

TABLE 4–3. Correlations Obtained when Candidates for Promotion are Rated by Coworkers and Superiors ($N = 100$)

	Ratings compared	
Item rated	Co-workers and superiors	Pairs of superiors
Job knowledge	.15	.63
Cooperation	.29	.67
Job performance—quality	.25	.61
Job performance—quantity	.33	.66
General fitness for promotion	.39	.71

Source: D. Springer, "Ratings of Candidates for Promotion by Coworkers and Supervisors," *Journal of Applied Psychology*, Vol. 37 (1953), pp. 348–349.

foreman (27). Although the two levels of supervision agreed reasonably well, as indicated by correlations in the .60's, the coworkers apparently were taking somewhat different factors into account: The correlations between coworker and superior ratings on the same men are considerably lower. In addition, the coworkers gave more favorable ratings. These findings are consistent with the view that coworkers may be influenced to some degree by personal considerations, whereas superiors tend to hold to a managerial orientation.

APPRAISAL SYSTEMS INVOLVING PERSONNEL
MANAGERS AND PSYCHOLOGISTS

One variant on the standard methods of evaluation by superiors involves much more active participation on the part of the personnel department. In this approach, the appraisal data are collected orally rather than through the use of written forms (9). Normally, a personnel representative will go to the office of the man's superior with a specific list of questions. Answers to these questions are obtained in conversation and recorded in note form. The notes are then converted to a written description once the personnel man returns to his own office. A draft of this written description is reviewed by the superior and then it is put in final form.

The advantages of this approach are that an oral procedure is more likely to elicit specific information regarding the man being appraised. Superiors will say things about a person in a free discussion that they will not put in writing. In addition, that a personnel representative will spend an hour or more conducting the interview conveys the impression that the appraisal process is considered quite important, thus eliminating the superficial, hurried responses that written rating forms sometimes produce.

Finally, this technique has the advantage that the personnel representative can maintain similar standards of evaluation across a large number of interviews. This control over the general level of ratings and the factors to be considered is much more difficult to exercise when written forms are used or when appraisal sessions are conducted by differing groups of managers each constituted to judge a particular individual. In this latter instance, it has become common practice to have a management appraisal specialist, often a psychologist, sit in on the group meetings for just this reason. Usually this person writes the appraisal summary also. Such an individual can establish common standards for the ratings within a department or division, or across the company as a whole. If he feels a particular group of superiors is being excessively lenient, or harsh, as compared with other such groups, he can take steps to correct this variation in standards, either by inducing the group to change its views or by introducing compensating statements into the final appraisal summary.

Psychological Appraisal. A markedly different type of appraisal is typically carried out by industrial psychologists who have had some training in the techniques of personality assessment. These appraisals usually involve extensive interviewing coupled with individual psychological testing (2,8,17). They are often employed in conjunction with other evaluation procedures. But even if this is not the case, efforts are made to integrate the test and interview data with information available from personnel files and other sources. The psychologist attempts to get as clear an understanding as he can of the underlying intellectual, emotional, and motivational characteristics of the man and then converts this into a picture of how such a person might be expected to behave. The resulting psychological description, as Table 4–4 indicates, is not so much a summary of actual behavior as a prediction of anticipated behavior under certain specified circumstances.

TABLE 4–4. Example of a Psychological Description on a Candidate for Promotion

---

Albert W. Woodworth, sales training representative

Mr. Woodworth appears to be the outstanding man among the four candidates for District Marketing Manager evaluated. The evidence suggests that Mr. Woodworth would not only make a major contribution in the position for which he is currently being considered, but that he also has the potential to perform very effectively at higher levels in the company. The following strengths are apparent:

TABLE 4–4. Example of a Psychological Description
on a Candidate for Promotion—Continued

1. Mr. Woodworth's general verbal intelligence level is very high. He has a Wechsler Verbal IQ of 136. This is the top score obtained among the 31 members of marketing management who have been evaluated to date. This showing is particularly surprising in view of the fact that Mr. Woodworth has no formal college education. Reasoning and problem-solving ability are also at a high level, as indicated by the results of the Terman Concept Mastery Test. Apparently Mr. Wood-worth has not only accumulated a great deal of knowledge: He is capable of bringing his intellectual abilities to bear in the solution of complex problems.

2. Mr. Woodworth is very strong on problem solving in the numerical area, being particularly adept in quickly grasping a problem and coming up with a solution. He should be outstanding in drawing inferences from an analysis of sales figures and in the accounting aspects of his work.

3. Mr. Woodworth's mechanical ability is at a very high level. In fact, his ability in this area is actually quite outstanding.

4. Mr. Woodworth has very wide interests and keeps himself informed in a great variety of fields. This breadth of interest plus his capacity for very rapid learning should permit Mr. Woodworth to adapt readily to new situations. It is unlikely that he will require a very long training period if promoted.

5. From the Picture Arrangement Test it is apparent that Mr. Woodworth has very strong work motivation. He can be counted on to push himself hard. He has the capacity to get things done and will keep at a problem until he has it licked. He appears to be happiest when he is working hard and effectively.

6. Mr. Woodworth is a rather independent person. He is unlikely to lean on others and is quite capable of reaching his own decisions. He would much prefer to figure out problems himself and do things his own way. Although he will on occasion follow the advice of others, he tends to distrust it. However, he can be counted on to follow directions and company policy meticulously when this is necessary. There is little question but that Mr. Woodworth will do his best work when given a free hand.

7. It is evident from the Thematic Apperception Test stories that Mr. Woodworth is an extremely competent planner and organizer. He will take risks but prefers to do so only after he has made a careful analysis of the alternatives. He has his own ideas about how things should be done and these ideas are likely to be both original and practical.

Although these strengths taken as a whole seem to argue very strongly for Mr. Woodworth's selection as District Marketing Manager, there are two problems which should be mentioned:

1. At the present time Mr. Woodworth is somewhat uncertain about his

TABLE 4–4. Example of a Psychological Description
on a Candidate for Promotion—Continued

own ability. Although he seems to enjoy management responsibilities and likes to participate in the solution of complex marketing problems, he has no clear conception of his own capacities and tends to underestimate them. He realizes that he has never held a job that has really challenged him, but, on the other hand, perhaps because of this lack of challenge, he has no idea of the level at which he might be able to function. It seems probable that Mr. Woodworth is the type of person who will perform more effectively the higher he rises in the organization. He needs to find out how good he really is, and only by facing greater challenges is he likely to gain confidence in his own ability. He needs to prove himself to himself and only after he has done this is he likely to realize his full potential. This entire problem came out quite clearly during the course of the interview.

2. Mr. Woodworth tends to be rather impatient with mediocrity. He holds himself to very high standards and expects others to perform at the same high level. He may find it hard to delegate to people whom he feels are not as competent as he would wish. As a result he may try to do too much himself and thereby fail to develop his subordinates to the full. He is also unlikely to establish warm relationships with his men, tending to remain somewhat at a distance from people. Mr. Woodworth is well aware of these problems but appears to be incapable of solving them at the present time. As Mr. Woodworth becomes more confident of his own abilities, he may well feel freer to let subordinates learn through an occasional failure and become capable of greater freedom in his own emotional relationships. This problem, like the other, should largely solve itself if Mr. Woodworth rises to higher levels of management responsibility. Nevertheless, it should be recognized that Mr. Woodworth will probably never be as effective in his handling of people as he is in problem-solving and organizing efforts.

Evaluations of this kind are particularly helpful when decisions must be made regarding promotion or transfer, since they provide information on how the man might be expected to act in the new position relative to revised role prescriptions. However, psychological procedures are also used by many companies in connection with a regular, periodic appraisal program. Although some companies do maintain an internal staff of industrial psychologists to conduct assessments of this type, a large proportion of the work is done by outside consultants. Because the actual techniques and procedures used are in many respects comparable to those of performance control, any further discussion will be delayed until we take up this latter approach in Chapter 11.

SELF-APPRAISAL

In some companies, it has become standard practice for the superior to conduct an appraisal interview with his subordinate manager after the appraisal summary has been prepared in an attempt to induce the man to overcome his deficiencies and improve his performance. The feedback of appraisal results in this manner has as its primary objective the *development* of a more effective manager. Unfortunately, the accumulated evidence indicates increasingly that these interviews are not very effective as developmental tools. Furthermore, the introduction of a feedback requirement tends to have unanticipated effects on the ratings that may vitiate them for other purposes.

Intensive studies of appraisal interviews conducted at General Electric indicate that any criticism by a superior is usually rejected as incorrect (12,20). Defensiveness was the characteristic attitude among the subordinates, and indications of a desire to improve performance occurred fewer than one time per interview. Yet, without the development of carefully stated goals for improvement, criticism was unlikely to produce an increase in effectiveness. Clearly, feedback procedures may well yield a considerable loss insofar as the organizational maintenance goal is concerned and very little, if any, improvement in productivity.

The experience of many companies has been that it is very difficult to get managers to actually conduct appraisal interviews with their subordinates. Because the situation is perceived as unpleasant, managers avoid it, and the interviews are actually held only after considerable pressure, and dissension. Many are never held in any real sense at all.

Another response to the anticipated unpleasantness of feeding back negative evaluations is an actual distortion of the ratings. In one study, the average rating on 485 supervisors moved from a score of 60, under normal nonfeedback conditions, to 84, when a rerating to be combined with appraisal interviews was obtained two weeks later (28). One way of making the ratings easier to report to others is to make them more favorable. Obviously, therefore, evaluations that are to be used for development purposes in an appraisal interview should not be used for other purposes, such as pay and promotion.

As a result of the deficiencies in the feedback approach, several writers have suggested that the development goal can be better served if managers appraise themselves (15,16). Although the various advocates differ somewhat on the specifics, the usual approach is for the man to sit down with his immediate superior and establish a series of targets or objectives for the next six months or for some other appropriate time period. Then, at the end of the specified interval, the two have a second discussion during which the man evaluates his performance relative to his objectives, attempts to solve any newly recognized problems, and sets new objectives for the next period. Throughout this process, the superior assumes the role of a listener and, on occasion, a guide, never that of a critic. Since there is no external criticism, there is no defensiveness. To the extent that the man criticizes himself, the basis for a change in his behavior has presumably been established. Unfortunately, however, research to date provides little support for the view that goal setting of this kind contributes either to increased job understanding or increased managerial effectiveness (18).

It should be emphasized that self-appraisal cannot be a substitute for other approaches, except possibly insofar as the self-development goal is concerned. If appraisal data are desired for other purposes, they should not be obtained from the man himself. The evidence on this is quite strong.

For one thing, self-appraisals tend to be considerably more favorable than ratings by superiors, as Table 4–5 indicates. In this particular study,

TABLE 4–5. Mean Ratings Given by Immediate Superiors and by Self (N = 117)

Scale	Superior rating	Self-rating
Ability to work with others	8.9	10.7
Amount of work done	9.4	10.5
Quality of work done	9.5	10.4
Leadership potential	5.9	8.9
Ability to do complicated jobs	8.5	10.4
Ability to work with minimum supervision	9.2	11.6
Conscientiousness	8.9	10.4
Overall performance	9.8	10.5
Average of 8 scales	8.8	10.4

Source: J. W. Parker, E. K. Taylor, R. S. Barrett, and L. Martens, "Rating Scale Content: III. Relationships Between Supervisory and Self-Ratings," *Personnel Psychology*, Vol. 12 (1959), p. 51.

the men rated themselves on the various characteristics, and, at the same time, similar ratings were obtained from their superiors (22). In no instance were the superiors' ratings lower; on leadership potential and the ability to work with minimum supervision the differences were sizable. Other studies in which self-ratings and supervisory ratings were correlated indicate that the two measure quite different things. In one instance, ratings by the two levels of supervision immediately above the men correlated .60 on ninety-six individuals. The self-ratings yielded values of only .25 and .13 when correlated with the two superior ratings (23). Clearly these individuals were not evaluating themselves in terms of the same type of standards their superiors employed with considerable consistency.

Objective Measures of Productivity and Profit

Although subjective rating procedures are probably the most widely used in evaluating managers, at least in connection with formal appraisal programs, a variety of hard or objective indexes may also be employed. These characteristically are based on the behavior of the manager's unit. If the productivity and contribution to profit of a unit is high, the manager is considered effective. If the average level of stress originating within a unit is low and the capacity to reduce external stresses high, the manager also is evaluated favorably.

At the present time, it is probably safe to say that the various productivity and profit indexes are more frequently obtained than are measures of organizational maintenance. This is particularly true at the higher levels of management. There is a tendency to assume that maintenance considerations are primarily a matter of concern for lower level supervisors and that profitability should weigh more heavily in the role prescriptions of managers toward the top of the hierarchy. This situation may well change in the future, but currently it does appear to be a fact of business life.

PRODUCTIVITY MEASURES

Largely because of the central interests of the industrial engineers who have made major contributions in this area, objective indexes of manufacturing output are available in the greatest number. Some of these measures of group productivity which can be used to evaluate the effectiveness of a manager are the following:

- Units produced.
- Number of rejects.
- Training time to reach standard production.
- Meeting of production schedules.
- Machine down time.
- Scrappage.

Many of these indexes, when computed on an individual basis and attributed to a single worker, are more relevant to employee evaluation (see Chapter 5) than to management appraisal. Only when such individual measures are combined to provide a group statistic can they be used to evaluate the competence of supervision.

The same holds for the evaluation of managers in areas of work other than direct production. Thus, the total sales figures or gains and losses over a prior period for a group of salesmen can be used to evaluate sales managers; so, too, can the number of customer complaints. Research and development managers may be appraised using variables such as the number of patents resulting from the efforts of their subordinates or the number of assigned projects that are completed. Office managers may be considered in terms of subordinate activities such as words typed, filing errors, and IBM cards punched.

The important thing is that these indexes must be relevant to the role prescriptions for the specific position and that measures of some kind be developed for all important role prescriptions. Unfortunately it is easier to establish objective, numerical measures in some areas than others. The result is that these areas may receive undue emphasis, purely because of their measurability, whereas other factors in the job description are entirely neglected in the appraisal. If this happens, a manager can easily learn to direct his efforts toward those job requirements that form a basis for evaluation. The consequence may be a major imbalance in the distribution of work, especially if a number of managerial jobs have similar role prescriptions and are evaluated in the same manner. This is why it is crucial that appraisal systems be developed by working back from a knowledge of the total job and its requirements, rather than by utilizing a few easily obtained measures that appear to be relevant. It is also absolutely essential that the factors selected be subject to the influence and control of the manager.

Some companies have gone to considerable lengths to establish comprehensive evaluation systems of this kind for managerial jobs, introducing very specific criteria to indicate acceptable levels of performance. Thus, one may find such standards as the following:

- Warehouse turnover is greater than 200 per cent per year.
- Frequency of vehicle accidents is less than .35 per hundred thousand miles.
- Operating overtime hours are less than 2.5 per cent of scheduled hours worked.
- Training sessions are held once each month.

ACCOUNTING MEASURES

In recent years, some major developments in the field of accounting, especially cost accounting, have made it increasingly feasible to evaluate managers in terms of their contributions to profits. It has long been common practice to establish budgets for various groups and to consider managers who unnecessarily exceed their budget as unsatisfactory in this particular regard. Similarly, many companies have evaluated wastage, equipment maintenance, labor, and so on in terms of the costs involved.

Now, however, much more sophisticated procedures are being introduced to deal with the entire gamut of factors influencing profitability in a single comprehensive analysis. For instance, cost centers may be established to coincide with the divisional boundaries of a company that has decentralized along product lines (6). The division is then treated as a separate firm, and the manager is evaluated in terms of share of the market, net sales, profit as per cent of sales or invested capital, and the like. If, in such cases, the divisional unit utilizes services, materials, or components from segments of the company outside the manager's jurisdiction, transfer prices are negotiated in terms of market value.

Increasingly, these procedures are being moved down through the managerial hierarchy so that the contributions to profit achieved by lower level managers, especially those within the line organization, can be determined. Standard costs are established for labor, materials, and overhead on the basis of prior experience and judgment. Cost variances are then computed by comparing actual figures with these standards (1,4), and managers are evaluated in accordance with the direction and amount of these variances. The technique requires a detailed organization plan with clear-cut designation of areas of responsibility. Also, there is considerable subjectivity inherent in setting the standard costs. But variance analysis of this kind does appear to provide an extremely valuable tool in appraising managers.

Objective Indexes in the Maintenance Area

As with productivity, organizational maintenance measures taken within the group, or unit, that is a manager's responsibility may also be used for purposes of appraisal. This assumes that a major factor contributing to any lack of job satisfaction, or sense of attachment to the work organization, can be the behavior of the manager in charge. Thus, if the various indexes suggest that a certain manager has a highly dissatisfied group, the undesirable situation can be attributed to him.

Unfortunately, using this type of information to evaluate individual managers has not been developed to the level of sophistication achieved in the productivity and profit areas. Although such studies as those conducted by the University of Michigan and the Ohio State University researchers do emphasize the importance of supervisory consideration and kindness, other evidence is consistent in indicating that a number of additional factors may also influence the level of satisfaction (31). Thus, immediate supervision is not the only factor that must be considered.

Clearly, policies and decisions made at a variety of managerial levels can have an impact. Yet, very few companies have worked out their role prescriptions and allocations of responsibility among the various levels of management with the same precision in the organizational maintenance area that they have achieved when dealing with productivity and profits. There appears to be a tendency at the present time to exaggerate the role of immediate supervision, when higher level management may actually be exerting greater influence. The various maintenance indexes should be used with caution when appraising individual managers. It is important to know who or what actually is responsible for the existing state of affairs. Yet, because of their relationship to an important company goal, some measures of this kind are essential.

MEASURES OF WITHDRAWAL FROM THE JOB

A number of indexes seem to reflect the tendency of people to avoid or escape from what they experience as unpleasant. Thus, in units where dissatisfaction is marked and there is little sense of group cohesion, employees may seek ways of leaving the specific work situation, either temporarily or permanently.

Separations and Turnover. Research indicates that employees who experience a sense of deprivation on the job insofar as important motives are concerned are particularly likely to leave the firm (24). Thus, turnover has been demonstrated to be closely related to the level of satisfaction at work and to the degree to which work interferes with other satisfactions. Whether or not the sources of frustration involved are under the control of any particular manager must be ascertained for each case.

A variety of different procedures are used to compute turnover. For purposes of evaluating managers, it is generally desirable to eliminate involuntary separations such as those caused by death, illness, and mandatory retirement from the statistics, because these causes are not normally subject to managerial influence. Often a ratio of some kind such as the following is computed for each unit:

$$\text{Turnover} = \frac{\text{Number of separations}}{\text{Midmonth employment}} \times 100$$

It is important in using statistics of this kind to include data collected over a period of time in order to eliminate the effects of seasonal and other temporary fluctuations. Only when a manager has consistently high turnover figures should the possibility that he is less effective be actively considered. Also, it is important to hold the general type of occupation and certain employee characteristics relatively constant in evaluating these figures. Turnover among young female clerical employees, for instance, is invariably high owing to marriage, family moves, returning to school, pregnancy, and other factors that are less likely to operate in other groups.

Absenteeism. Although it is by no means universal practice to keep absence statistics for individual work units, these data can be of considerable value in appraising managers. One way of avoiding an unpleasant work environment is to stay away from the job as much as possible. There are, of course, a variety of types of excused absences—sick leaves, military leaves, and so on—that normally do not reflect a desire to withdraw from a disturbing situation. Nevertheless, much that passes for sickness is probably not, and many illnesses are emotionally caused.

Thus, it does seem appropriate to consider a manager unsatisfactory in the maintenance area if his group has a continuing, disproportionately high absenteeism rate.

As with turnover, a variety of formulas are used to indicate absence rates. A common approach is the following:

$$\text{Absenteeism} = \frac{\text{Number of man-days lost through job absence during period}}{\text{Average number of employees} \times \text{number of work days}} \times 100$$

Some firms keep records covering not only the number of days lost, but also the number of times. Usually older work groups will have a higher number of days lost from work than those with more younger employees, but the actual frequency of separate incidents of absenteeism may not be so great.

Closely related is the use of tardiness statistics, which may well reflect a similar withdrawal tendency and which are easily obtained for any group that punches time cards. Probably, however, measures of lateness are much less frequently maintained on a regular basis than absenteeism data. Certainly they are less commonly used to evaluate managers.

Injuries and Dispensary Visits. The use of accident statistics as indexes of managerial competence is probably more appropriately explained in terms of the direct relationship to profits, nevertheless, it is true that people who are more upset and disturbed at work are particularly susceptible to injury. Thus, maintenance considerations can be involved. In the case of dispensary visits, the relationship is still clearer. A common method of escaping an unpleasant work environment is to seek medical attention. At the most, one might be sent home; at the least, one will be away from the work place for a period.

In many cases, injuries that involve lost time are recorded separately from those that do not require that the man be sent home. Both lost time and minor injuries are expressed as a frequency per man-hours worked in the unit. Statistics on dispensary visits are only rarely maintained as a basis for evaluating managers, but there is reason to believe that a count of the number of initial visits for a new complaint within some specified time span can be an effective method of identifying a widespread desire to avoid a particular work situation (19).

MEASURES OF RESISTANCE
AGAINST MANAGEMENT

Another way in which internal stress may manifest itself within a work unit is through direct resistance and conflict. Dissatisfied group members may not avoid the situation that disturbs them; they may attack the management that they see as causing their difficulties. Such resistance may be covert or overt. In any event, the manager who heads a unit where signs of resistance are numerous can find himself judged less competent, although whether this is justified or not must depend on the degree of influence he has over the situation.

Disciplinary Actions. One way that dissatisfaction may appear is through overt flouting of work rules and intentional deviation from role prescriptions. Such behavior characteristically results in a warning, suspension, or discharge, after a formal disciplinary hearing. When such formal disciplinary actions occur frequently within a given unit, it may well be that the manager has provoked considerable resentment by his actions. Among the behaviors that may elicit formal action of this kind by the company are:

- Unauthorized absence.
- Insubordination or impertinence.
- Loafing or sleeping.
- Misrepresentation such as tampering with time cards or records.
- Smoking when forbidden.
- Drinking or carrying liquor.
- Dishonesty or stealing.
- Fighting on the job.
- Gambling.
- Willful breach of safety rules.
- Repeated lateness.
- Leaving the job without permission.
- Immoral conduct.

Grievances. Another commonly used index is the number of grievances filed by employees within a given time period. Although complaints of any kind theoretically can be used, the usual procedure is to count the number of separate, formal grievances filed in writing under the terms of the union contract.

By filing a grievance, an employee is acting in a way that he is well aware management does not wish him to. Furthermore, in most cases, the grievance statement is directly critical of some managerial behavior. The union may make this particular outlet for dissatisfaction readily available and may even ask the employee to act. It is doubtful, however, that many grievances occur in the complete absence of some measure of discontent. Therefore, a manager with a high grievance rate can be presumed to have a group that represents some threat to the integrity of the firm.

Other Indications of Resistance. There are several other possible measures that may be appropriate depending on the company and situation. Among these are the number of man-hours lost from work owing to work stoppages, strikes, slowdowns, and the like—or the total number of separate incidents of this kind. The manager who experiences a high incidence of such occurrences is not likely to be fulfilling the requirements of his job, whether or not the resistance behavior is union inspired (provided, of course, that he is in a position to exert some influence over such events).

Actually, any failure to behave in ways that management is widely known to desire, if it is prevalent enough in a group, may yield evidence regarding the extent of dissatisfaction. A consistent refusal to join the company retirement system or to participate in group insurance plans might be used as an index in evaluating managers. The extent of participation in suggestion systems and in company-sponsored recreational programs might also be used. Obviously, the more relatively independent indexes developed, the more certain one can be in describing a particular manager as successful or unsuccessful in his efforts to foster organizational maintenance.

ATTITUDE OR MORALE SURVEYS

A final procedure for evaluating managers is the attitude survey. In general, the results of these surveys tend to be closely related to other measures, such as turnover and absenteeism, discussed previously in this section, although they do not necessarily yield a high correlation with measures of productivity and profits (5).

When used to evaluate managers or to predict labor relations problems, attitude surveys are normally handled on a group basis. That is to say, it is not so much the feelings of a particular individual that are of concern, but the over-all level of morale in a given unit. For this reason, the surveys are usually conducted on an anonymous basis, and on occasion, only a sample of the employees in a group is measured. In this latter instance, it is important that the sample be truly representative. The usual procedure is to select a random sample, so that each individual has the same chance of showing up in the survey group.

Although a detailed discussion of attitude measurement techniques is contained in Chapter 5, several points should be made here. First, surveys of this kind normally contain questions dealing with working conditions, supervisory behavior, attitude toward the job, loyalty to the company as a whole, company policies, and other considerations. If the questionnaire is this broad in scope, it is inappropriate to use the total result to evaluate immediate supervision. The various sections of the survey form must be sorted out in terms of the particular level of management with the appropriate responsibility. One cannot expect a manager whose role prescriptions do not call for action in a given area to exert influence over attitudes in that area.

Second, a decision as to whether a particular unit is satisfied or dissatisfied should be based on information that can be presumed to be valid and that is characteristic of the group as a whole. To do otherwise can only produce a biased evalution of the unit's management. There must be reason to believe that the people surveyed have given evidence of their true feelings. The survey should include all, or nearly all, members of the unit. If a sample is used, the respondents should not be permitted to select themselves. Replies obtained from the 30 or 40 per cent who may take the trouble to return a mailed questionnaire may reflect only the attitudes of those who are relatively satisfied. It is essential to obtain evidence regarding the attitudes of those who did not reply and correct the results accordingly. This is a difficult and time-consuming process, but only after it has been done can a manager be appraised correctly.

Career Appraisal

Management appraisal is normally concerned with determining how well a man is doing on his present job relative to a given set of role prescriptions, but there are instances where a measure of over-all career success to date is desired. This is a particularly important consideration when evaluation data are being used as a criterion for selection procedures. Usually, it is more desirable to select management trainees who will achieve continuing success in a variety of positions, rather than those who will do an outstanding job as trainees or perhaps in their first subsequent assignment.

Perhaps the most frequently used career index is the managerial level attained. Most firms maintain a system of salary grades, with each job from assistant foreman to president assigned to some point on the scale. The particular grade for the position held by an individual then becomes a measure of his success. Because these grade levels may be closely related to age or seniority and because they are strongly influenced by the level at which a man started with the company, it is probably more desirable to employ some index of grade progression than the absolute level. Thus, one can use a promotion rate measure such as the following:

$$\text{Success} = \frac{\text{Present grade} - \text{starting grade}}{\text{Total years of employment}}$$

In recent years, there has been considerable interest in the use of salary data as a basis for evaluation (10,11). Certainly such a measure is consistent with popular sentiment. When employed within a company that awards salary increases on grounds of merit and that maintains a stable salary scale utilizing comparable standards for all managers, it appears to offer a number of advantages. Usually when salary is employed as a success index, some correction for age or tenure is introduced to produce a change rate rather than an absolute amount. On occasion more complex statistical procedures are developed so as to provide data on the degree to which each man's salary deviates from the figure to be expected for people of his age and experience.

Rating procedures may also be used to evaluate career success as well as success on the current job. Probably the most commonly used technique is a promotability index of the type noted in Figure 4–1. When a man is said to have outstanding potential for advancement, a major determinant of this evaluation is likely to be a pattern of consistent accomplishment in prior positions. Predictions of future progress are in large part predicated on past successes. Of course, potential ratings are conditioned to some degree by age, and thus probably should not be used to evaluate career success among individuals over fifty. A man of, say, fifty-five may have little prospect of progressing further in his remaining ten years with the company and yet have had a very outstanding career.

REFERENCES

1. Axelson, K. S., *Responsibility Reporting*. New York: Peat, Marwick, Mitchell, 1961.
2. Balinsky, B., "Some Experiences and Problems in Appraising Executive Personnel," *Personnel Psychology*, Vol. 17 (1964), 107–114.
3. Bayroff, A. G., H. R. Haggerty, and E. A. Rundguist, "Validity of Ratings as Related to Rating Techniques and Conditions," *Personnel Psychology*, Vol. 7 (1954), 93–113.
4. Bierman, H., *Financial and Managerial Accounting*. New York: Macmillan, 1963.
5. Brayfield, A. H., and W. H. Crockett, "Employee Attitudes and Employee Performance," *Psychological Bulletin*, Vol. 52 (1955), 396–424.
6. Dean, J., "Profit Performance Measurement of Division Managers," *The Controller*, Vol. 25 (1957), 423–426, 449.
7. Fiedler, F. E., *A Theory of Leadership Effectiveness*. New York: McGraw-Hill, 1967.
8. Glaser, E. M., "Psychological Consultation with Executives: A Clinical Approach," *American Psychologist*, Vol. 13 (1958), 486–489.
9. Habbe, S., "Merit Rating—Plus," *Management Record*, Vol. 15 (1953), 323–324.
10. Hilton, T. L., and W. R. Dill, "Salary Growth as a Criterion of Career Progress," *Journal of Applied Psychology*, Vol. 46 (1962), 153–158.
11. Hulin, C. L., "The Measurement of Executive Success," *Journal of Applied Psychology*, Vol. 46 (1962), 303–306.
12. Kay, E., H. Meyer, and J. R. P. French, "The Effects of Appraisal Interviews upon Attitudes and Performance: An Experimental Study in General Electric," in A. F. Zander (ed.), *Performance Appraisals—Effects on Employees and Their Performance*. Ann Arbor, Mich.: The Foundation for Research on Human Behavior, 1963.
13. Likert, R., *New Patterns of Management*. New York: McGraw-Hill, 1961.
14. Likert, R., *The Human Organization: Its Management and Value*. New York: McGraw-Hill, 1967.
15. Maier, N. R. F., *The Appraisal Interview*. New York: Wiley, 1958.
16. McGregor, D., "An Uneasy Look at Performance Appraisal," *Harvard Business Review*, Vol. 35 (1957), No. 3, 89–94.
17. Megargee, E. I., *Research in Clinical Assessment*. New York: Harper & Row, 1966.
18. Mendleson, J. L., *Manager Goal Setting· An Exploration into Its Meaning*

and Measurement, DBA Thesis. East Lansing, Mich.: Michigan State University, 1967.

19. Merrihue, W. V., and R. A. Katzell, "ERI-Yardstick of Employee Relations," *Harvard Business Review,* Vol. 33 (1955), No. 6, 91–99.

20. Meyer, H. H., E. Kay, and J. R. P. French, "Split Roles in Performance Appraisal," *Harvard Business Review,* Vol. 43 (1965), No. 1, 123–129.

21. Miner, J. B., *The School Administrator and Organizational Character.* Eugene, Ore.: Univ. of Oregon Press, 1967.

22. Parker, J. W., E. K. Taylor, R. S. Barrett, and L. Martens, "Rating Scale Content: III. Relationships Between Supervisory- and Self-Ratings," *Personnel Psychology,* Vol. 12 (1959), 49–63.

23. Prien, E. P., and R. E. Liske, "Assessments of Higher-Level Personnel: III. Rating Criteria: A Comparative Analysis of Supervisor Ratings and Incumbent Self-Ratings of Job Performance," *Personnel Psychology,* Vol. 15 (1962), 187–194.

24. Ross, I. C., and A. F. Zander, "Need Satisfactions and Employee Turnover," *Personnel Psychology,* Vol. 10 (1957), 327–338.

25. Seashore, S. E., B. P. Indik, and B. S. Georgopoulous, "Relationships among Criteria of Job Performance," *Journal of Applied Psychology,* Vol. 44 (1960), 195–202.

26. Shartle, C. L., *Executive Performance and Leadership.* Englewood Cliffs, N.J.: Prentice-Hall, 1956.

27. Springer, D., "Ratings of Candidates for Promotion by Coworkers and Supervisors," *Journal of Applied Psychology,* Vol. 37 (1953), 347–351.

28. Stockford, L., and H. W. Bissell, "Factors Involved in Establishing a Merit-Rating Scale," *Personnel,* Vol. 26 (1949), 94–116.

29. Stogdill, R. M., and A. E. Coons, *Leader Behavior: Its Description and Measurement.* Columbus, Ohio: Bureau of Business Research, Ohio State Univ., 1957.

30. Tannenbaum, A. S., *Social Psychology of the Work Organization.* Belmont, Calif.: Wadsworth, 1966.

31. Vroom, V. H., *Work and Motivation.* New York: Wiley, 1964.

32. Whitla, D. K., and J. E. Tirrell, "The Validity of Ratings of Several Levels of Supervisors," *Personnel Psychology,* Vol. 6 (1953), 461–466.

QUESTIONS

1. What are the findings of the Michigan and Ohio State studies regarding effective managerial behavior? How do the two sets of findings relate to each other and to our conception of organizational goals?

2. Suppose that you were asked to design a management appraisal system based primarily on judgmental procedures. What would your recommendations be? Cover the various aspects in detail. Why do you prefer these specific approaches over other available alternatives?

3. In what ways does psychological appraisal differ from the other techniques? What are some of the problems that may arise if this type of approach to management appraisal is introduced in a company? When would it seem particularly desirable to use an outside consultant for this purpose?

4. Formulas have been presented to measure turnover and absenteeism in a group. Can you think of any variants of these formulas, perhaps including additional variables, that might prove useful.

5. What kinds of behaviors among work-group members are likely to reflect problems in the organizational maintenance area? Note as many as you can think of.

5

Employee Evaluation: Rating Systems and Attitude Surveys

Inasmuch as Chapter 4 devoted considerable space to the so-called hard, or objective, measures of productivity and maintenance, there is little need to recapitulate here. It is important to remember, however, that in evaluating managers, at least insofar as their supervisory skills are concerned, we were interested primarily in average or total measures for the subordinate group as a whole. Now, as we move on to nonmanagerial employees, we are concerned with the number of units produced, or the number of absences, or the number of disciplinary actions for each individual.

Although the preceding discussion covered the hard measures in some detail, it did not deal with the specifics of rating scale construction and the techniques of judgmental evaluation. These will be of primary concern in this chapter. One task that nearly every personnel psychologist must perform at one time or another is to construct a new rating form, or to revise an old one that is not working properly. At first glance, this may seem to be a relatively simple task, but there are a number of pitfalls. It is extremely helpful to have some familiarity with the relevant research and the experience of others.

A second emphasis of this chapter will be in the area of attitude measurement. One method of evaluating the attitudes of employees, usually relative to the organizational maintenance goal, is to obtain ratings from superiors and others who are in a good position to observe job behavior. Another approach involves the actual measurement of employee attitudes on the assumption that these attitudes currently, or will shortly, serve to determine employee behavior. The techniques of conducting surveys of this kind were touched on briefly in Chapter 4; they will be considered in much greater detail here.

Finally, a section will be devoted to the various obstacles and resistances that may obstruct the effective utilization of these techniques. For various reasons, the systematic evaluation of employee behavior relative to role prescriptions may face a number of difficulties and, in fact, become a source of considerable internal conflict. It is important for a psychologist to be sensitive to these problems, especially as they relate to seniority provisions in union contracts.

Rating Systems

There are, unfortunately, a number of presumed biases or errors that may creep into any rating process. Most newer developments in the field of rating scale construction attempt to reduce one or another of these, and it seems desirable to become conversant with the problems that may arise at the outset (1).

Halo. There is a tendency for people to judge others almost entirely with reference to some one factor that they consider important. Thus, a man who is easy to get along with may be evaluated favorably in all other areas quite independent of his actual behavior. When a halo of this kind is operative, and it nearly always is to some degree, rather sizable correlations between the different scales of a measuring instrument—quantity, quality, cooperativeness, and so on—will emerge. Those who are high on one scale tend to be high on others, and those who are low tend to be low consistently. As a consequence, the value of ratings in different areas, relative to different role requirements, can be dissipated.

Constant Error. The tendency of superiors to use somewhat different sets of standards in judging subordinates has already been noted. The situation is essentially the same as that existing in colleges and universities, where every student is familiar with the existence of difficult and easy graders. When evaluations made by different managers are compared, as they must be, considerable error may result. All men rated by one manager may score below those rated by another, even though the two groups are in actual fact very similar. The differences obtained are due to a difference in managerial standards, not in performance.

Recency Error. Most ratings cover the preceding six months or a year. Ideally, they should represent the average, or typical, behavior for this period. There is a tendency, however, to base ratings on what is most easily remembered, i.e., the most recent behavior. This may well not be characteristic of the total period, especially if the man is aware of the approximate date when he will be evaluated.

Error of Central Tendency. Whatever the level of the standards employed by a given superior, there is a good possibility that he will rate all of his subordinates within a narrow range. For one reason or another, the difference between the best and the worst employee on a particular scale often turns out to be minimal, even though much larger differences do exist. In small units, it is not unheard of to find the whole group clustered at one point on the scale. Errors of this kind tend to obviate the value of the evaluations.

Personal Bias. Perhaps the most important error of all arises because no one is capable of judging entirely independent of his values, prejudices, and stereotypes. All kinds of inappropriate criteria and standards may be introduced into the evaluation process with the result that, on occasion, ratings relate not so much to company goals as to the personal goals of a particular manager (18). Thus, evaluations can be influenced by such factors as an employee's racial or ethnic background, physical attractiveness, religion, manner of dress, alcoholic consumption, social standing, treatment of wife and children, and ancestry that are normally of little significance in meeting occupational role requirements.

RATING SCALES

One method of classifying judgmental procedures utilizes the categories of rating scales, employee comparison systems, check lists, and critical incident techniques (23). The free-written or essay approach should probably be added to this list. Let us take these up in order.

Rating scales may take various forms, but the primary characteristic is the requirement that a check be placed at some point along a scale of value. There may be a line along which a manager is to place a mark (the graphic scale) or numbers may be used, one of which is to be circled, or the approach may be that of Figure 5–1. The high and low ends are identified as such, and intermediate points may be defined through the use of appropriate adjectives.

Scales of this kind are widely used, primarily because they are simple to construct. Yet, in contrast to other techniques, they make no provision for reducing halo, constant error, and errors of central tendency, all of which can have a considerable impact.

Studies indicate, however, that the central tendency problem can be overcome through training and discussion with the raters (13). Probably other sources of error can be similarly reduced. Thus, with an adequate awareness of the factors that introduce bias, and a desire to overcome them, rating scales apparently can be employed effectively by managers in evaluating their subordinates. In actual practice, this degree of freedom from error may not be too common. This is particularly true if the rater is asked to mark a great variety of scales, which appear frequently to be overlapping, on each man. When the number of dimensions exceeds ten,

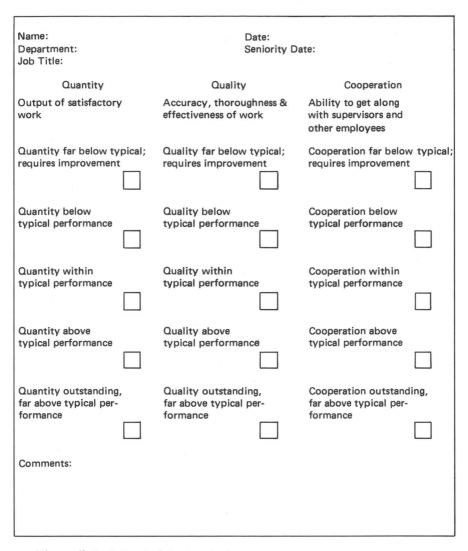

Name: Date:
Department: Seniority Date:
Job Title:

Quantity	Quality	Cooperation
Output of satisfactory work	Accuracy, thoroughness & effectiveness of work	Ability to get along with supervisors and other employees
Quantity far below typical; requires improvement ☐	Quality far below typical; requires improvement ☐	Cooperation far below typical; requires improvement ☐
Quantity below typical performance ☐	Quality below typical performance ☐	Cooperation below typical performance ☐
Quantity within typical performance ☐	Quality within typical performance ☐	Cooperation within typical performance ☐
Quantity above typical performance ☐	Quality above typical performance ☐	Cooperation above typical performance ☐
Quantity outstanding, far above typical performance ☐	Quality outstanding, far above typical performance ☐	Cooperation outstanding, far above typical performance ☐

Comments:

Figure 5–1. **A Typical Rating Scale**

the prospect of appropriate motivation in the rater becomes rather low.

Figure 5–2 presents a rating scale that has been constructed for a slightly different purpose than the scale of Figure 5–1. This particular measure is designed to obtain information as to whether an employee should be retained at the end of the initial probationary period, which may be from two to six months. It has a strong negative orientation, because the major concern is to identify those incapable of effective

Name: Current Date:

Department: Date Probationary Period Ends:

Job Title:

Please check the appropriate statement or statements in each area to indicate extent of employee's progress.

Quantity of Work

Slow to learn _____

Has to be pushed on occasion _____

Consistently meets requirements _____

Does more than required _____

Quality of Work

Not really very good _____

Sometimes drops below acceptable level _____

Acceptable _____

An accurate worker _____

Personal Characteristics

Does not cooperate with other workers _____ Cooperates _____

Is absent frequently _____ Rarely absent _____

Wastes time _____ Does not waste time _____

Is not a safe worker _____ A safe worker _____

Demands frequent supervision _____ Can work alone _____

A troublemaker _____ Does not stir up trouble _____

Are you satisfied to have the employee remain working for you? _____

If not suitable for retention in present job, would you recommend another job? _____

Comments:

Figure 5–2. **Typical Probationary Employee Evaluation**

performance. Perhaps, the greatest value of scales of this kind is to remind a manager of the great variety of behaviors that must be compared against role requirements in reaching a decision on retention. Note that this decision actually is not requested until the end of the scale, after all the aspects of the employee's behavior have been considered.

EMPLOYEE COMPARISON SYSTEMS

Employee comparison systems, unlike the rating scales, do not require the use of an absolute standard. Instead of comparing each man to some generalized concept of acceptable behavior, the rater compares the various individuals being evaluated. Thus, other workers provide reference points for the ratings, and the result is a relative evaluation.

Ranking. With this method, the manager merely ranks his subordinates on as many dimensions, or characteristics, as are required. Each dimension is treated separately. Because ranking may not be an easy task when a relatively large number of employees are involved, various aids have been developed for this purpose.

One of these, the alternation-ranking method, attempts to get the easier discriminations, those involving the poorer and better individuals, out of the way first, so that the rater can concentrate on the middle range where decisions are more difficult (7). The best person is selected first, then the worst, then the next best, the next worst, and so on, working inward, until the last person noted is the one in the median position.

An alternative approach has the manager assume a hypothetical role as the head of a newly formed firm. He is then asked to select the one individual from among his present subordinates who, on the basis of performance and potential, he would like to have as his vice president. This name is recorded. The manager then is asked to assume that this particular individual has refused the appointment and to select a second person from among his current group. This procedure is repeated until all members have been ranked. Although this technique provides only a single measure, on an over-all effectiveness scale, the approach does appear to meet most criteria for a satisfactory rating system (24).

The major advantage of any type of ranking is that it spreads individuals out over the entire range of performance. The error of central tendency is eliminated, and constant errors as such cannot occur. In addition, halo appears to be minimized, because the dimensions are ranked separately and person-to-person comparisons must be made on each. The biggest problems arise when there is a need to combine ratings made by different supervisors on different groups. It is always possible, although not probable, that the best man in one group is actually below the poorest in another. This difficulty will be discussed in more detail shortly.

Paired Comparisons. A second method of employee comparison produces a ranking as a final result, but requires only that the superiority of one individual over another be established by judgment. From a series of such comparisons of pairs, a rank ordering may be constructed. The nature of the technique should be apparent from Figures 5–3 and 5–4. These latter are derived from a study in which ratings of office tabulating machine operators were used to establish criteria for a selection testing program (16,17).

In Figure 5–4, a group of five operators are rated on one dimension by their superior. If the number of "better" evaluations is totaled for each man, the results are:

- Cooper   4
- Adams   3
- Dalton   2
- Baker   1
- Emory   0

These data provide a ranking within this particular group with Cooper the most effective man and Emory the least. The actual study combined similar information on four different tabulating units, most of them considerably larger than this one.

Table 5–1 provides information on the similarity between the paired

TABLE 5–1. Correlations Between Paired Comparison Ratings Made by Two Superiors and Between Ratings Made at a One-Year Interval (tabulating machine operators)

Aspects rated	Average correlations between ratings of two superiors (average N = 16)	Correlations between ratings separated by one-year interval (N = 35)
Application	.85	.75
Accuracy	.79	.72
Speed	.81	.78
Cooperation	.67	.64
Overall effectiveness	.79	.75

comparison ranking of the same individuals by pairs of superiors and on the similarity between ratings made by the same superior at an interval of one year. The results suggest that the procedure is generally effective, but that the cooperation ratings are, at least relatively, defective. This may be the result of certain inadequacies of the instructions to raters (Figure 5–3) in this particular area. Placing cooperation with fellow workers and with superiors together in one dimension may produce some ambiguity, with the raters emphasizing one aspect at one time, another

The purpose of these rating forms is to see how the various members of the group you supervise compare with each other in important aspects of tabulating machine operation.

In making the ratings, compare the employees under you on the following aspects of tabulating machine operation:

1. *Application*—Which employee is stronger in his application to the job? Which shows more interest in the work and strives to do well in it?
2. *Accuracy*—Which employee produces more consistently accurate work? Which do you feel you do not have to check on as much?
3. *Speed*—Which employee gets his assigned jobs done faster? Which one can produce more in a given time?
4. *Cooperation*—Which employee demonstrates a greater spirit of cooperation with his fellow workers and his supervisor? Which gets along better with people on the job?
5. *Overall effectiveness*—Considering the four factors above, and others not mentioned, which are important in tabulating work, which employee would you say is a more effective tabulating machine operator?

A separate form for each of these aspects on which you will rate your employees is attached. In completing these forms, you are to compare each employee with every other employee once on each of the five aspects.

1. In the column running down the left side of each form are the names of employees in your group who do the tabulating work. The same names in the same order appear in the row running across the top of the form.
2. No ratings are required in the blanks below the diagonal line running from the top left to the bottom right corner of the sheet. Obviously you cannot compare any man with himself.
3. Beginning with the name of the first employee in the left column, you are to compare him with each of the other employees whose names appear in the upper row. If, in your opinion the employee whose name is to the left is better in the aspect of the job which is being judged, place a "1" in the square made by the intersection of the column and the row. If you feel the employee whose name is in the upper row is better, place a "0" in the square.
4. Repeat the process for the succeeding names in the left column until the form is finished.
5. Even though two employees may be nearly equal on any characteristic, you must decide who is better and assign a "1" or "0".
6. Leave no blank spaces and use only "1's" or "0's."

Figure 5–3. Instructions to Raters Used in the Tabulating Machine Operator Study

aspect at another time. If fellow workers and superiors are separated by setting up two different dimensions, this would probably produce more satisfactory results.

Aspect: *Overall effectiveness*—Considering application, accuracy, speed, cooperation, and any other aspects which are important in tabulating work, which employee would you say is a more effective tabulating machine operator?

Mark "0" if the man is better

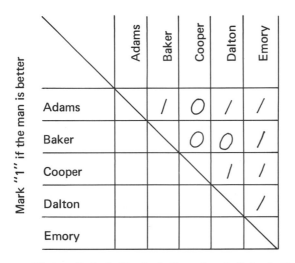

Figure 5–4. **A Typical Completed Paired Comparison Rating Form from the Tabulating Machine Operator Study**

Forced Distribution. One difficulty with ranking, and particularly paired comparisons, is that when the unit to be evaluated is large, say over twenty-five, it is often necessary to break down the total group into subgroups for purposes of rating. An alternative to this is a forced distribution.

In a sense, this is a variant of the rating scale procedure, with a provision eliminating constant errors and errors of central tendency. Managers place their men in categories on each dimension according to certain predesignated proportions. The common distribution is:

     Low 10%   Next 20%   Middle 40%   Next 20%   High 10%

Thus, for a unit of forty-six men the foreman would be asked to sort his men as follows:

     Low 5   Next 9   Middle 18   Next 9   High 5

Note that no assumption is made regarding the absolute level of performance. The lowest five are not necessarily unsatisfactory, only relatively less effective.

Combining Employee Comparison Data. The major difficulty with all the techniques discussed in this section is that although the relative position of each *man* within a group is established, there is no provision for determining the relative status of various *groups.* Two rankings on separate work units by their separate supervisors do not reflect any existing differences between the groups. One unit may have many more outstanding performers than the other, yet the ranking data will not indicate this fact.

The most common approach has been to assume that the groups to be compared or combined do not differ appreciably. If the groups are of different sizes, the ranks obtained from ranking or paired comparisons are translated into *standard scores,* through the use of appropriate conversion tables (9), and then combined into a single list. Sometimes rating scale data are obtained along with the employee comparisons as a check on the assumption of equality of groups. If an average on a rating scale for one group should closely approximate that for another group, it is considered appropriate to combine the two.

Where, however, there is good reason to believe that real group differences exist, the employee comparison approaches have only limited application. The major exception is where a few individuals can be included in the evaluations of more than one rater. These key individuals provide reference points around which the data for the various groups in which they have been included may be combined (10). It is important, however, that all who rate these key men be well acquainted with their work.

CHECK LISTS

The major characteristic of the check list procedures is that they deal with specific, on-the-job behaviors rather than the more abstract generalities of the rating scales. The manager actually reports on, or describes, the behavior of his subordinates rather than evaluating it. This means, of course, that separate check lists must be developed for each position that differs to any sizable degree in role prescriptions from the other positions. Although job descriptions can be of considerable assistance in constructing these check lists, it is time consuming and expensive to apply these techniques on a widespread basis within a company. On the positive side, however, is the fact that all types of error, including personal bias, tend to be reduced when the rating process moves to the level of differences in specific behaviors.

Because the manager provides only a number of checked behaviors that describe a particular man, the actual evaluation process must be carried out elsewhere. The behavior descriptions included in the check list must be categorized in terms of the degree to which they match role prescriptions. This is normally done by people who are familiar with the specific type of work—various levels of supervision, job analysts, and personnel specialists, perhaps industrial engineers or psychologists who serve in a staff capacity relative to the positions under consideration.

These evaluations of check list items may be carried out in a rough manner or by using the more precise techniques of attitude scaling that are described later in this chapter. In any event, the result is a designation of certain behaviors as good or desirable, and others as less so. Then, if the good behaviors are consistently checked by a particular employee's superior and the less desirable behaviors are not, he is considered to have been given an outstanding rating. The weights or evaluations attached to items are not normally known to the supervisors doing the rating.

Forced-Choice Procedures. A variant of the check list technique has been developed that appears almost completely to eliminate the personal bias problem. Unfortunately, however, it accomplishes this result while concurrently introducing a situation where those doing the rating have no idea whether they are evaluating a man favorably or not. Consequently, many managers have developed considerable resistance to this approach, so much so that very few firms are now using it. Yet, it is desirable to have some familiarity with the forced-choice procedure, if only because of the extensive discussions it has provoked within personnel management.

The basic elements of the measure are a series of blocks of two or more behavior descriptions. The descriptions within each block are selected so as to be approximately equal in their degree of favorableness or unfavorableness, but markedly different in the degree to which they have been found in prior studies to be associated with effective or ineffective performance, as defined by some other, external criterion. Thus, a block of items used for rating training skills and containing favorable descriptions is:

1. Patient with slow learners.
2. Lectures with confidence.
3. Keeps interest and attention of class.
4. Acquaints classes with objective for each lesson in advance.

A block of unfavorable items is:

1. Does not answer all questions to the satisfaction of students.
2. Does not use proper voice volume.
3. Supporting details are not relevant.

Within each block certain items have been found to discriminate between poor and good teachers, whereas others have little relation to success (3).

CRITICAL INCIDENT TECHNIQUE

This approach is best described by reference to a specific system developed for evaluating salesmen at the Minnesota Mining and Manufacturing Company (12). Initially, sales managers in the various divisions were asked to submit short stories or anecdotes, *critical incidents*, that illustrated what they considered particularly effective or ineffective salesman behavior. The result was sixty-one instances of effective, and thirty-five instances of ineffective performance. Analysis of these data revealed that fifteen basic types of behavior were involved such as following up, carrying out promises, and communicating all necessary information to sales managers.

A rating sheet was then constructed covering these fifteen areas, based on items as closely allied to the original critical incidents as possible. The rater was asked to indicate the degree of his agreement or disagreement should he hear a particular statement used to describe the salesman being evaluated. Examples of these statements based on critical selling incidents are:

- Follows up quickly on requests from customers.
- Promises too much to customers.
- Writes poor sales reports.

The major advantages of this technique are in establishing comprehensive definitions of role requirements, if these are not available from other sources, and in providing items that, because they are close to on-the-job behavior, can reduce personal bias. Other sources of error may well remain, however, and the basic procedures have been criticized as fostering excessively close supervision and blame finding (21).

ESSAY EVALUATIONS

In making essay evaluations, the superior merely writes out what he thinks of the subordinate, usually with very little by way of guidelines as to what points he should cover. An example is presented in Figure 5–5.

This approach does little to reduce the various types of error that may influence the evaluation process. Personal bias in particular may be marked, since the manager selects his own grounds for judging his subordinate. In addition, comparisons between individuals become difficult, because one man may be evaluated in one regard and another man on a completely different basis.

Specific role prescriptions may be introduced and free-written statements requested in each area. If this is done, however, a rating scale is normally much easier to use.

Name: Date:

Department: Seniority Date:

Job Title:

Type of Review

New Employee _____   Annual _____

Special   _____   Separation _____

Transfer _____   Promotion _____

Employee's Strong Points:

Employee's Weak Points—Areas Where Improvement Is Needed:

Comments with Regard to Any Contemplated Separation, Transfer, or Promotion:

Figure 5–5. A Typical Essay Evaluation

Attitude Measurement

When we move to the matter of attitude measurement, the primary focus is on factors related to a company's organizational maintenance objective. The major techniques are management estimation, interviews, questionnaires, attitude scales, and indirect measures (2). The techniques of sociometry should probably be added to this list, although they are based on somewhat different considerations.

MANAGEMENT ESTIMATION

As previously noted, rating procedures can be employed to obtain information regarding a man's attitudes and the behavior that is a consequence of these attitudes. Under most work arrangements, immediate superiors are in a good position to observe their subordinates. There is no reason why they cannot do as well in judging people relative to maintenance considerations as they do in the productivity area. Actually, almost all rating forms contain some items having to do with cooperation. Such questions deal directly with behavior that is a consequence of job attitudes and job satisfaction.

On the other hand, many supervisors may not wish to inform higher management regarding any widespread dissatisfaction within their groups for fear this condition will reflect on their own competence, or they may actually not be aware of the degree of discontent. Yet, such trouble spots are exactly what higher management wants and needs to know about, primarily because of their implications for labor relations trouble. As a consequence various techniques have been developed that involve obtaining information directly from the employees themselves.

INTERVIEWS

One obvious approach is to ask employees how they feel. The difficulty is that many will not feel free to express negative attitudes for fear of retaliation. Various techniques have been devised to deal with this problem, but it still remains the major barrier to effective attitude measurement.

Many companies have found it desirable to have interviews conducted either by a consulting firm or representatives of a university. In this way, they hope to reassure the employees that responses will not serve as a basis for retaliation against individuals.

In addition, efforts are usually made to ensure anonymity insofar as management is concerned. Thus, only the outside organization receives information on the names of those interviewed. The company's management is given a report in terms of group frequencies, rather than individuals' attitudes. This represents a major loss insofar as the process of comparing employees against role prescriptions is concerned. Certainly any management would much prefer to know the feelings of individual employees and thus the type of behavior it can expect. However, it is widely believed, probably correctly in many cases, that to attempt this would invalidate the survey entirely. Thus, companies tend to accept what from their viewpoint is the less desirable practice of comparing groups against role prescriptions in the maintenance area, in order to improve their chances of obtaining information that can be trusted as being predictive of behavior (19).

Interviews may be *guided* or *unguided*. In the latter instance, the interviewer encourages the employee to express himself in various areas, but does not follow a definite format. Questions may be worded quite differently when asked of different men. Attitudes are assessed by the interviewer based on what happens in the interview as a whole.

The problems here are maintaining comparability across interviews and minimizing the effects of interviewer bias. A talkative worker provides information differing in many ways from that derived from a reticent man. Questions will inevitably be worded differently, and the interviewer may well react much more favorably toward an employee who is willing to talk, thus making the interview easier to conduct.

Furthermore, because unguided interviews are difficult to quantify, the tendency has been to resort primarily to the guided approach. This approach tends to approximate the questionnaire procedure to be discussed in the next section, but the questions are asked orally. Administering such a standard questionnaire in an interview situation is costly, but it has the advantage of ensuring a high response rate within a group. Employees are much more likely to answer an interviewer than to return a mailed questionnaire. Thus, the bias that results when a nonrepresentative set of responses is obtained from a particular work unit tends to be reduced.

Exit Interviews. Some firms make it a regular practice to conduct exit interviews with employees who are leaving the company voluntarily, in order to assess attitudes in the groups where they worked. The assumption is that these people will talk freely because they have nothing to lose and that, therefore, the information obtained from them is more valid.

Although this assumption may be correct in some instances, it must be accepted with caution. Many employees will want references later, and in order to ensure a good report will avoid any criticism of the company. Others may feel rather guilty about leaving their jobs and to justify doing so will tend to exaggerate negative factors in the work situation. Thus, the blame for the separation is shifted from the individual to the company. Both these considerations make the exit interview a somewhat questionable source of attitude data.

QUESTIONNAIRES

In the past it has been a common practice to enclose attitude questionnaires with paychecks, to mail them to the employee's home, or even to hand them out at quitting time. These procedures rarely elicit a response from more than 50 per cent of a group, usually considerably less, and it is hard to know what the results mean. Since anonymity is usually protected in order to foster valid answers, it is not possible to follow up on those who do not return completed forms. A more desirable procedure, now widely adopted, is to assemble the employees in groups and have them complete the forms on company time. In this way, response rates comparable to those obtained with personal interviews can be obtained.

The topics covered in an attitude questionnaire vary with the particular needs of a company at a given time. Thus, firms carry out surveys because they are concerned about labor relations problems, attitudes toward fringe benefits, and so on. In these cases, the questionnaire should be constructed locally to fit the specific problem.

In other instances, where more general coverage is desired, some of the standardized forms that are available commercially may be preferable. These have the advantage that information on response frequencies in other companies are available for comparison purposes. Among these standardized measures is the Triple Audit Employee Attitude questionnaire that contains fifty-four items dealing with the following topics (6):

- Working conditions.
- Company.
- Pay.
- Hours.
- Coworkers.
- Type of work.
- Supervision.
- Promotions.
- Communications.
- Recognition.
- Security.

Another widely used measure is the SRA Employee Inventory (11), which covers:

- Job demands.
- Working conditions.
- Pay.
- Employee benefits.
- Friendliness, cooperation of employees.
- Supervisory-employee relations.
- Confidence in management.
- Technical competence of supervision.
- Effectiveness of administration.
- Adequacy of communication.
- Status and recognition.
- Security of job and work relations.
- Identification with the company.
- Chances for growth and advancement.

Attitude questionnaire items are of two basic types—fixed alternative and open ended. In the former category are questions with simple "yes" or "no" alternatives as well as those of a multiple-choice nature. Open-ended questions either ask for a free-written answer or require that blanks be filled in. In either case, the responses must be categorized after the answers have been obtained.

Open-ended questions can be expensive to use because of the need to construct categories (similar to multiple-choice alternatives) afterward, and to code responses into these categories. On the other hand, if one is not sure what alternatives should be included in a fixed-alternative measure, the open-ended approach may be preferable. Often it takes as much time and money to conduct preliminary studies aimed at setting up appropriate multiple-choice alternatives as it does to categorize free responses.

ATTITUDE SCALES

In instances where a more precise and reliable measure than can be obtained from a few questionnaire items is desired, attitude scales are frequently utilized. Measures of this kind have been developed for a great variety of purposes (20). There are several procedures, but in all various scores or weights are attached to different alternatives to indicate the degree of feeling characterizing a person who responds in a particular manner.

Perhaps the most frequently used approach is that developed by Thurstone (22), or some variant of it. The first step is to write out a great many statements bearing on the attitude to be measured, let us say satisfaction with one's present job. A number of people are then asked to classify these statements in terms of their favorableness. Traditionally, eleven categories are used ranging from 1, the least favorable viewpoint, to 11, the most favorable.

The *scale value* of each statement is the average of the category numbers assigned by the various judges. Not all the statements are normally used in the final attitude scale, however. It is important to select items indicating all variants of opinion. Thus, those finally used should be spread evenly throughout the range, from a scale value close to 1 to a scale value close to 11. Also, statements on which the judges cannot agree must be discarded. If several indicate that a statement should be in category 2 and the others have it in various categories up to 9, then agreement is clearly minimal, and the item should not be used. The scale of Figure 5–6 represents what remains from an original 246 statements (5).

If the Brayfield-Rothe scale were administered without the five multiple-choice alternatives for each item and employees were asked merely to check those of the eighteen items that applied to them, we would have a typical Thurstone scale. The score for an individual would be the sum of the scale values for the statements he checked. Such items as numbers

Some jobs are more interesting and satisfying than others. We want to know how people feel about different jobs. You are to cross out the phrase below each statement which best describes how you feel about your present job. There are no right or wrong answers. We should like your honest opinion on each one of the statements. Work out the sample item numbered (0).

0. There are some conditions concerning my job that could be improved.
   Strongly Agree   Agree   Undecided   Disagree   Strongly Disagree
1. My job is like a hobby to me.
   Strongly Agree   Agree   Undecided   Disagree   Strongly Disagree
2. My job is usually interesting enough to keep me from getting bored.
   Strongly Agree   Agree   Undecided   Disagree   Strongly Disagree
3. It seems that my friends are more interested in their jobs.
   Strongly Agree   Agree   Undecided   Disagree   Strongly Disagree
4. I consider my job rather unpleasant.
   Strongly Agree   Agree   Undecided   Disagree   Strongly Disagree
5. I enjoy my work more than my leisure time.
   Strongly Agree   Agree   Undecided   Disagree   Strongly Disagree
6. I am often bored with my job.
   Strongly Agree   Agree   Undecided   Disagree   Strongly Disagree
7. I feel fairly well satisfied with my present job.
   Strongly Agree   Agree   Undecided   Disagree   Strongly Disagree
8. Most of the time I have to force myself to go to work.
   Strongly Agree   Agree   Undecided   Disagree   Strongly Disagree
9. I am satisfied with my job for the time being.
   Strongly Agree   Agree   Undecided   Disagree   Strongly Disagree
10. I feel that my job is no more interesting than any other I could get.
    Strongly Agree   Agree   Undecided   Disagree   Strongly Disagree
11. I definitely dislike my work.
    Strongly Agree   Agree   Undecided   Disagree   Strongly Disagree
12. I feel that I am happier in my work than most other people.
    Strongly Agree   Agree   Undecided   Disagree   Strongly Disagree
13. Most days I am enthusiastic about my work.
    Strongly Agree   Agree   Undecided   Disagree   Strongly Disagree
14. Each day of work seems like it will never end.
    Strongly Agree   Agree   Undecided   Disagree   Strongly Disagree
15. I like my job better than the average worker does.
    Strongly Agree   Agree   Undecided   Disagree   Strongly Disagree
16. My job is pretty uninteresting.
    Strongly Agree   Agree   Undecided   Disagree   Strongly Disagree
17. I find real enjoyment in my work.
    Strongly Agree   Agree   Undecided   Disagree   Strongly Disagree
18. I am disappointed that I ever took this job.
    Strongly Agree   Agree   Undecided   Disagree   Strongly Disagree

Source: A. H. Brayfield and H. F. Rothe, "An Index of Job Satisfaction," *Journal of Applied Psychology,* Vol. 35 (1951), p. 309.

Figure 5–6. **Brayfield-Rothe Job Satisfaction Questionnaire.**

5 and 12 carry high scale values, whereas such items as numbers 4 and 18 carry low values.

In this particular instance, a modification of the standard Thurstone procedure has been introduced that allows employees to express the degree of agreement (14). Statements with scale values above 6 (positive statements) were scored 5 for a "strongly agree" response, 4 for "agree," and so on down to 1 for "strongly disagree." Statements with scale values below 6 (negative) are scored in the reverse direction with a 5 given for "strongly disagree." Thus, total scores range from 18 to 90.

As indicated previously, these approaches may also be used to scale items descriptive of some dimension of job performance, and thus to develop a weighted check list of job behaviors for rating purposes.

INDIRECT MEASURES

Most approaches to attitude measurement discussed to this point deal with the tendency of employees to suppress unfavorable feelings by protecting the anonymity of respondents. Thus, groups rather than individuals must be compared against existing role prescriptions.

The indirect measures attempt to solve the problem of suppressed attitudes in a different manner, one that does permit individual evaluation. The approach is comparable in certain respects to that employed in forced-choice rating. The employee does not know what he is revealing about his attitudes. As a consequence, he cannot withhold that which he might not wish to say.

Projective Methods. Here the essential element is that the employee "projects" himself into a situation portrayed by a picture or by a written statement, and then in responding to this situation reveals his attitudes. He may be required to describe a picture or to tell a story or complete a statement of some kind. In any event, he tends to ascribe to the situation and the people in it characteristics that belong to himself.

In general, these techniques are administered in an interview situation, but measures can be devised to fit the questionnaire format. The major problem is to be absolutely certain that the attitude measured is what one wants to measure. Devising a good projective attitude index requires considerable training and experience, and unfortunately little by way of standardized measures related to job problems is available commercially.

Structured Disguised Measures. A second approach requires the employee to respond to a series of questions that appear to constitute a test of general information or intelligence. However, the questions are so constructed that there either are no correct answers or the employee could not possibly be aware of the answers. Thus, any choice between alternatives must be based on attitudes. Employees are, of course, encouraged to guess.

One such measure of general morale makes extensive reference to the results of scientific research and pronouncements by unidentified well-known people (4). For instance, one question asks about the proportion of the workers in a group such as the respondent's who have been found in prior research to be particularly susceptible to discouragement when things go badly. Another question refers to statements by a social scientist and then asks what proportion of workers this man believes consider their jobs boring.

The major difficulty with these techniques in industrial situations is that, unlike the other approaches discussed, they are often deliberately misleading. Should employees become aware that management is not being entirely honest, considerable resentment may result. Especially in unionized firms, the losses can be greater than the gains. For this reason, a personnel psychologist should give considerable thought to the pro's and con's before undertaking an attitude survey with a structured disguised measure.

SOCIOMETRY

Although sociometric procedures have not been widely utilized in the business world, they appear to have considerable potential, especially as an aid in establishing the degree of attachment to a work group or organization, what has been called the cohesiveness of the group. They should provide particularly valuable information regarding a tendency to resort to escape behavior as a solution to discontent.

The sociometric questionnaire, in its most common form, merely asks each member of a group to indicate which among the other members he would like to have as companions in some activity, such as teaming up on a job or eating lunch. Usually, negative choices are also requested. Thus, each employee also indicates those he would not want as a companion. These choices provide valuable information regarding an individual's ties to his group, whether he is accepted by others and whether he feels close to certain group members. If the questionnaire is designed so as to permit choices both within and outside the specific work unit, an index of the pull of the group vis-à-vis external social forces may be obtained.

Resistance to Evaluation

In spite of the obvious significance of employee evaluation for the attainment of company goals, there are a number of sources of resistance that make it extremely difficult to install and maintain systems of this kind. As a result, there has been a clear-cut trend away from formal evaluation systems for blue-collar workers, at the same time that management appraisal has been on the increase (25). Although rating systems are still widely used, a number of firms have phased out their programs in the face of individual and union resistance.

One major difficulty is that employees who do not anticipate a favorable rating are likely to be opposed to the entire evaluation process, which is perceived as a personal threat. Because only a very limited number can have a feeling of certainty that theirs will be a favorable appraisal, the great majority of employees are likely to exhibit resistance in one form or another. Managers and supervisors may well experience considerable group pressure in this regard with the result that many of them, especially those who are particularly sensitive about such matters, may find it very difficult actually to do the ratings. Thus, there may be delays and other difficulties that, although probably not intentional, do reflect the conflicting pressures to which lower level managers are exposed. Finally, the whole system may well collapse as these individual considerations are added to the long-standing union position on such matters.

There is reason to believe that problems of this kind are not unique to rating programs. A number of companies have also found it difficult to maintain a system of periodic attitude measurement (8). A great many firms have at one time or another instituted continuing procedures aimed at obtaining data relative to the organizational maintenance goal. For various reasons, however, a number of companies have discontinued the procedures after a relatively brief trial.

Part of the difficulty seems to be that, historically, organizational maintenance has never attained quite the same stature as productivity. Thus, a number of managers have considered attitude survey results relatively unimportant. Although appreciation of the significance of this goal is now on the upswing, attitude measurement in the past has not had the support that other evaluation techniques have enjoyed.

Perhaps related to this consideration is the fact that if attitude surveys are to be of real value, they must be tied to action. When a number of employees in a unit are discontented, and a survey identifies the source of the difficulty, an effort should be made to improve the situation and thus to improve attitudes. Unfortunately, this has not always been done. Accordingly, periodic surveys have often yielded almost identical results, time after time, to the point where measurement was finally discontinued, because no new information was obtained.

Finally, and perhaps this is the underlying difficulty, what management typically wants from attitude measurement is individual employee evaluation, of the kind produced by rating procedures. Yet, many of the commonly used procedures yield only group results. Although these group data do have considerable value in appraising managers and in pinpointing labor problems, the return on the investment may be insufficient to convince some managers that continuing measurement is warranted.

All this does not mean that employee evaluation should be eliminated. Rating procedures and attitude measurement, as well as the various objective indexes discussed in Chapter 4, are an important aspect of the personnel process. But it would be misleading to suggest that these techniques can be utilized without provoking some resistance.

SENIORITY AND UNION RESISTANCE

Perhaps the greatest present source of difficulty in employee evaluation stems from the unions. Attitude surveys are frequently opposed because they are viewed as an attempt to undermine the union. Rating procedures are almost universally condemned as being inconsistent with a long-standing labor union commitment to the seniority principle.

When seniority holds for purposes of lay-off, promotion, shift-selection, eligibility for overtime, work assignment, and the like, it is the senior employee in terms of service with the company, or in the seniority unit, who gets the preferred treatment. This, of course, tends to eliminate most, if not all, need for a merit rating system.

Union contracts contain a variety of provisions insofar as seniority is concerned. In the most extreme case, only seniority is mentioned. Other contracts say that seniority governs provided the senior employee is minimally capable of doing the work. Still others indicate that seniority is the deciding factor where ability is equal. This, of course, places the burden of proof on management. Evidence must be presented that a person with less seniority is the more capable if, for instance, he is to be promoted. Even in this latter case, however, close inspection of actual practices often reveals that merit characteristically takes a position secondary to seniority. This may be because of expediency, the belief that adherence to seniority will foster labor peace, a lack of adequate criteria of ability, or the feeling that the existing evidence of merit differences would not convince an arbitrator should the union file a grievance (15). In any event, there is a strong tendency where seniority is mentioned at all in the labor agreement for it to govern.

Various union contracts contain widely varying provisions regarding the date that seniority starts to accumulate, loss of seniority, individuals who are exempted from the standard seniority provisions, and so on. It is almost impossible to generalize on these matters. There are also wide differences in how the seniority unit is defined. Seniority may be computed in terms of the company or the plant. It may hold only within certain occupations, occupational groups, departments, or even pay ranges.

In general, management prefers to keep the seniority unit as small as possible. The reason for this is that when lay-offs occur and higher level positions are eliminated, it is common practice to permit *bumping* within the unit, i.e., an employee with seniority may demand the job of another employee with less seniority. This can extend down through the unit until the person with the least seniority, in the lowest level job is the one laid off. Where seniority is company-wide and a highly skilled position is eliminated, the amount of dislocation occasioned by successive bumping can be considerable. Where the seniority unit is small, changes in the job structure are much more easily accomplished.

One final point should be made regarding the union and rating procedures. Even where seniority provisions have not obviated the need for employee evaluation, the unions may exercise a certain degree of control over an existing rating system. Thus, some contracts call for a review procedure under which a combined union-management committee reconsiders certain supervisory evaluations and may change them. Normally, such reviews are restricted to a certain percentage of the bargaining unit, perhap 1 per cent.

It is apparent, therefore. that when employee evaluation systems are installed, it is necessary to be sensitive not only to possible sources of individual resistance, but to union attitudes as well.

REFERENCES

1. Barrett, R. S., *Performance Rating*. Chicago: Science Research Associates, 1966.
2. Bass, B. M., *Organizational Psychology*. Boston: Allyn & Bacon, 1965.
3. Berkshire, J. R., and R. W. Highland, "Forced-Choice Performance Rating: A Methodological Study," *Personnel Psychology*, Vol. 6 (1953), 355–378.
4. Bernberg, R. E., "The Direction of Perception Technique of Attitude Measurement," *International Journal of Opinion and Attitude Research*, Vol. 5 (1951), 397–406.
5. Brayfield, A. H., and H. F. Rothe, "An Index of Job Satisfaction," *Journal of Applied Psychology*, Vol. 35 (1951), 307–311.
6. England, G. W., and C. I. Stein, "The Occupational Reference Group— A Neglected Concept in Employee Attitude Studies," *Personnel Psychology*, Vol. 14 (1961), 299–304.
7. Foundation for Research on Human Behavior, *Assessing Managerial Potential*. Ann Arbor, Mich.: The Foundation, 1958.
8. Foundation for Research on Human Behavior, *Assessing Organization Performance with Behavioral Measurements*. Ann Arbor, Mich.: The Foundation, 1964.
9. Guilford, J. P., *Psychometric Methods*, 2nd ed. New York: McGraw-Hill, 1954.
10. Guion, R. M., *Personnel Testing*. New York: McGraw-Hill, 1965.
11. Industrial Relations Center, University of Chicago, *SRA Employee Inventory*. Chicago: Science Research Associates, 1951.
12. Kirchner, W. K., and M. D. Dunnette, "Identifying the Critical Factors in Successful Salesmanship," *Personnel*, Vol. 34 (1957), No. 2, 54–59.
13. Levine, J., and J. Butler, "Lecture vs. Group Decision in Changing Behavior," *Journal of Applied Psychology*, Vol. 36 (1952), 29–33.
14. Likert, R., S. Roslow, and G. Murphy, "A Simple and Reliable Method of Scoring the Thurstone Scales," *Journal of Social Psychology*, Vol. 5 (1934), No. 3, 51–57.
15. McConkey, D. D., "Ability vs. Seniority in Promotion and Layoff," *Personnel*, Vol. 37 (1960), No. 3, 51–57.
16. Miner, J. B., "The Concurrent Validity of the Picture Arrangement Test in the Selection of Tabulating Machine Operators," *Journal of Projective Techniques*, Vol. 24 (1960), 409–418.

17. Miner, J. B., "The Validity of the Picture Arrangement Test in the Selection of Tabulating Machine Operators: An Analysis of Predictive Power," *Journal of Projective Techniques,* Vol. 25 (1961), 330–333.
18. Miner, J. B., *The Management of Ineffective Performance.* New York: McGraw-Hill, 1963.
19. Selltiz, C., M. Jahoda, M. Deutsch, and S. W. Cook, *Research Methods in Social Relations,* rev. ed. New York: Henry Holt, 1960.
20. Shaw, M. E., and J. M. Wright, *Scales for the Measurement of Attitudes.* New York: McGraw-Hill, 1967.
21. Strauss, G., and L. R. Sayles, *Personnel: The Human Problems of Management,* 2nd ed. Englewood Cliffs, N.J.: Prentice-Hall, 1967.
22. Thurstone, L. L., and E. J. Chave, *The Measurement of Attitude.* Chicago: Univ. of Chicago Press, 1929.
23. Tiffin, J., and E. J. McCormick, *Industrial Psychology,* 5th ed. Englewood Cliffs, N.J.: Prentice-Hall, 1965.
24. Ward, W. H., "The 'It's Your Business' Approach to Ratings," *Personnel Psychology,* Vol. 14 (1961), 183–191.
25. Whisler, T. L., and S. F. Harper, *Performance Appraisal—Research and Practice.* New York: Holt, Rinehart & Winston, 1962.

QUESTIONS

1. Describe the different types of error or bias that may appear when rating procedures are used. What effect does each have on the ratings?
2. What particular difficulties must be considered when the following techniques are used?

   - Paired comparison rating
   - Exit interviews
   - Essay evaluation
   - Structured disguised measures

3. Describe how a Thurstone scale might be constructed to provide a check list type of rating system.
4. What are the various techniques or procedures that may be used to ensure that valid information is obtained from an employee attitude survey?
5. What are the various ways in which the seniority-merit problem may be handled in the union contract? Why do you suppose the unions have tended to place so much emphasis on the seniority principle?

6

Selection: Validation Models and Nontest Techniques

Dealing with the individual human inputs to a company is basically a personnel function. First a pool of applicants or potential employees (perhaps candidates is the best word) must be recruited. Information must then be collected on these individuals in terms of which some will be selected for employment and others screened out. The primary consideration in reaching such a decision on employment is whether the individual is likely to be successful, that is, whether he will contribute to the attainment of organizational objectives.

Chapters 3, 4, and 5 discussed at some length the various ways in which the behavioral outputs of managers and other employees can be measured and evaluated. Thus, a man could be rated high or low on the quality of his work, he could have a good absenteeism record or a poor one, and so on. This chapter and the next discuss the techniques—interviews, psychological tests, reference checks, physical examinations, application blanks, and so on—that are used to select people who will obtain favorable evaluations on these various success indexes.

The first part of this chapter is a general treatment of the logic of selection. Much of our knowledge in this area was originally developed with reference to psychological testing. However, these approaches have much wider applicability, and the considerations involved are just as relevant for interviews, application blanks, and other selection procedures as they are for psychological tests. Basically, we will be concerned with the various methods used to relate the preemployment, or preplacement, data on an individual to indexes of the degree of matching between role behaviors and role prescriptions. These latter measures are usually referred to as *criteria* in the selection context.

The second part of the chapter deals with selection techniques other than psychological tests. Among these are the employment interview, application blanks, biographical inventories, references checks, and background investigations. All these procedures tend to focus on the collection of information regarding past behavior. The assumption is that the individual remains relatively constant and that, accordingly, the past may be used to predict the future.

The Longitudinal Prediction Model

The logic of the selection process has been most completely developed in the longitudinal prediction model. When a selection measure meets the requirements of this model, it is said to possess *predictive validity*. There are two major variants or cases involved.

CASE 1—SINGLE PREDICTOR

Step 1. Study the job, or group of related jobs, for which selection is to occur in order to identify characteristics that might be related to success. These may be intellectual abilities, personality factors, prior experience, physical attributes, or anything else that can be measured prior to actual job placement.

Step 2. Decide on the specific measures of these characteristics to be used. If verbal ability is a potential predictor, is it to be estimated from an interview or measured by a test? If a test, which one?

Step 3. Obtain these predictor measures on a relatively large group of job applicants or candidates. Then hire from this group without reference to the predictor data. That is, select the individuals to be employed without looking at the measures obtained and without taking this information into account in any way. This normally means that employment decisions should be made by a person other than the one conducting the study. If, on the other hand, the measures are used to select those who will be hired at this initial stage, and these predictors do have some validity, only relatively good performers will be found on the job and the possibility of identifying predictors that differentiate between good and poor performers will be to that degree lost. The sample may be accumulated over time as hirings occur, but there should be a bare minimum of thirty individuals in the hired group.

Step 4. Gather criterion data on the individuals hired after such information becomes available. The measure used may be any of those discussed in Chapters 4 and 5. Usually these data are not suitable for use as criteria until after the man has been on the job long enough for his performance level to stabilize.

Step 5. Determine the degree of relationship between the predictor values and the criterion values. Usually a correlation coefficient is used to indicate the degree of this relationship. The specific statistical index may vary depending on the distribution of predictor and criterion values in the group, but the result will be a coefficient ranging from -1.00 through 0 to $+1.00$ with the larger values, both negative and positive, indicating a closer relationship between predictor and criterion. The larger the coefficient, the greater the predictive validity of the measure taken before hiring.

If a summary statement of the kind a correlation coefficient provides is not needed, a simple chart of the relationship may be established. At each level on the predictor index the number of people falling at each point on the criterion might be indicated as follows, assuming a sample of fifty:

Predictor Values	Criterion Values				
	1	2	3	4	5
5			1	2	2
4		2	1	4	3
3	2	2	12	4	
2	1	5	4		
1	2	1	2		

It is not necessary to compute a correlation coefficient from this chart to ascertain that the predictor is rather closely and positively related to the criterion.

Step 6. If the results of step 5 indicate a relatively good predictive validity, under most circumstances a second study should be carried out on the same job using the same predictor and criterion measures. This *cross-validation* is undertaken because any relationship established in the first group might have resulted from a mere chance fluctuation. A second study is done to be sure the relationship is there and that it can be relied on when people who obtain high values on the predictor are actually selected for employment.

Obtaining a cross-validation sample is not always easy, especially if there is some urgency about getting the selection procedure into use. Under these circumstances it is relatively common to collect data on both groups at once, If, say, 100 men are hired for a job, the total group may be split in half with the initial validation done on one subsample and the cross-validation on the other. In any event, step 6 should be carried out. It is particularly crucial when a number of different predictor measures have been tested for a relation to the criterion and only one or two have produced significant results. Under these circumstances, chance may well be operative, and the one or two predictors that seemed to work in the first group may not work in the second (6).

CASE 2—MULTIPLE PREDICTORS

Most jobs are not so simple that a single measure of a single predictor is sufficient to yield maximum results. Normally, the best predictions are obtained when a number of predictors measuring a variety of characteristics are combined in some manner.

Steps 1 through 4 are essentially the same under multiple prediction as they are when predictors are validated separately. The major difference emerges in step 5. Some way of combining the various factors in such a way as to maximally predict job success must be developed. There are four basic approaches to this problem.

Multiple Correlation. In the multiple correlation approach, the correlations between the predictors are computed, as well as the correlations between various predictors and the criterion. A multiple correlation coefficient is then derived that represents a maximal index of the relationship, one that automatically weighs the separate predictors so as to yield the best criterion prediction. So-called *regression weights* may then be developed. The values obtained by an individual on the various measures may be multiplied by these weights and then combined to produce a maximum estimate of the chances for job success. Because this procedure is particularly sensitive to chance fluctuations, it is essential that step 6, cross-validation, be carried out.

Additive Correlation. Additive correlation is essentially an approximation procedure for the multiple correlation coefficient. It involves adding the values obtained by an individual on all of the predictors together and then computing the correlation between this composite index and the criterion. Rather surprisingly, this technique does yield a close approximation to the results obtained from the multiple correlation approach.

Multiple Stage Prediction. In multiple stage prediction, the predictors are utilized one at a time rather than in combination. Correlations are computed as in case 1 for each of the predictors with, of course, the cross-validation step included. The predictor that consistently produces the highest relationship with the criterion is identified, and some value is established as minimally satisfactory for employment. All candidates who fall below this value are screened out. The remaining individuals must meet a similar test based on the predictor having the second highest correlation with the criterion. The process of successive screening out is continued until all predictors exhibiting a consistent relationship to the criterion are exhausted. Those who at least equal the minimum satisfactory value on all predictors are hired. Normally, three or four such hurdles are all that are required. Beyond that very little predictive power is added.

Clinical Prediction. In clinical prediction, the combining of predictors is accomplished by the personnel manager or psychologist based on his own experience and without resort to statistical aids. His decision takes into account all the information available, but weighs the different measures and factors on a largely intuitive basis. Selection decisions of this kind have been successfully simulated on a computer (30).

The Concurrent Model

The concurrent approach is identical to that of longitudinal prediction with one very important exception—the predictor and criterion measures are obtained at roughly the same point in time, usually on individuals who have been employed in the job to be studied for a considerable period. Thus, there is no long wait after the predictor data have been obtained to collect the criterion information. Either case 1 or case 2 may be applied, and the cross-validation is done on a second sample of employees selected from the current group.

This procedure is admittedly a short cut, and as such has certain rather marked deficiencies. For one thing, the motivation of present employees in taking a test or filling out a questionnaire or even in an interview situation may be quite different from that of job applicants—they may not try as hard. Yet, the results are to be applied to an applicant group. This can introduce considerable error into the selection process, especially when measures of interests and certain kinds of personality tests are used. With physical examinations, intelligence tests, application blank data, and the like, it probably matters very little.

Second, the results obtained from certain measures may be largely a function of job tenure. Indexes of job knowledge may yield higher scores the longer the person has been on the job. This can produce rather misleading results when the job knowledge measure is used as a predictor for applicants, none of whom have had prior experience in the particular type of work. If, however, one is aware of this problem, appropriate statistical procedures can be used to remove the effects of job tenure from the results, and this potential source of error can be eliminated.

Finally, it is possible with some predictors that success or failure on the job may serve to determine the values obtained, rather than the reverse. For instance, in one study, decreases in self-confidence as measured by a psychological test were found repeatedly over eight years of employment among less successful managers, but this same trend did not appear among the more successful (16). Clearly, any predictor-criterion relationship involving self-confidence established from a concurrent study would not necessarily appear under the more exacting conditions of a longitudinal prediction study. This problem of "what causes what" is particularly common when measures of certain attitudes, interests, and personality characteristics are used as predictors. Often a review of the relevant research literature will reveal whether a particular predictor should be trusted, based on evidence of concurrent validity.

AN EXAMPLE OF THE CONCURRENT MODEL WITH MULTIPLE PREDICTORS

A good example of the concurrent method as applied to the selection of lower level factory managers is a study carried out at IBM (32). The first task of the personnel researchers was to study thoroughly the managerial role requirements of the particular jobs through interviews with a number of incumbents. The interviews suggested that knowledge of the work done was not so important as such factors as supervisory interest, decision-making skill, and employee orientation. Accordingly, a number of predictors in these areas were selected for trial and administered to the managers.

The predictors that gave any hint of possessing value are described in generalized terms in Table 6–1. Several other measures were used, but

TABLE 6–1. Correlation Coefficients Showing Relationships Between Predictors and Criteria. First Sample ($N = 42$)

	Criteria		
Predictors	Peer rating	Corrected salary	Superior rating
Intelligence test	.26	.40	.13
Personality test			
Ascendancy	.29	.28	.22
Responsibility	.02	.25	.09
Emotional stability	−.03	.08	−.07
Sociability	.08	.07	.07
Total score	.19	.39	.22
Supervisory test	.11	.04	.12
Biographical questionnaire	.03	.23	.19
Age	−.16	−.47	−.16

Source: Adapted from M. E. Spitzer and W. J. McNamara, "A Managerial Selection Study," *Personnel Psychology*, Vol. 17 (1964), p. 32.

have not been noted because of the consistently negative results. The criteria were, first, the average of the performance ratings made by a number of fellow managers. This index proved to be of only limited value, because the peer ratings on the same manager were not generally in very close agreement. Second was a corrected salary figure that was constructed to eliminate the influence of seniority with the company and as a manager. Finally, there were ratings by superiors, which, like the peer ratings, suffered from considerable unreliability.

In the first sample of forty-two managers, as Table 6–1 indicates, a number of predictors yielded some evidence of concurrent validity. Six measures produced coefficients above .20. The corrected salary criterion proved the most predictable, as might be expected in view of the deficiencies in the other indexes.

As often happens, however, cross-validation washed out a number of these initial findings—the relationships were not consistently present in these managerial positions, and thus the predictors could not be relied on in a selection system. (See Table 6–2.) As a consequence, the measures

TABLE 6–2. Correlation Coefficients Showing Relationships Between Predictors and Criteria. Cross-Validation Sample ($N = 42$)

Predictors	Criteria		
	Peer rating	Corrected salary	Superior rating
Intelligence test	.14	.36	.11
Personality test			
Ascendancy	−.02	.16	.11
Responsibility	−.17	.09	.07
Emotional stability	−.06	.23	.17
Sociability	−.06	−.14	−.12
Total score	−.09	.12	.04
Supervisory test	.13	.17	.33
Biographical questionnaire	.34	.35	.24
Age	.13	−.03	.25

Source: Adapted from M. E. Spitzer and W. J. McNamara, "A Managerial Selection Study," *Personnel Psychology*, Vol. 17 (1964), p. 32.

of ascendancy, responsibility, personality test total score, and age had to be abandoned. Emotional stability and the supervisory test showed some new strength as predictors, but because both were totally ineffective in the first sample these later findings had to be discounted. Only the intelligence measure and the biographical questionnaire, which resembled an application blank and contained questions on personal experiences and interests, held up in cross-validation; primarily in relation to the salary criterion.

When these two predictors were combined to yield a multiple correlation coefficient, the value obtained in the first managerial sample was .43. In the cross-validation group it was .41. If the top 25 per cent of the managers, based on the weighted combination of intelligence and biographical measures, had been selected for these positions, 68 per cent of them would have proved to be above average performers. Thus, the new selection system yields an improvement of 36 per cent over existing procedures. In view of the nature of the predictors identified, there is little reason to believe a longitudinal study would have produced different results.

Newer Approaches to Selection

The methods described earlier are the most widely used in personnel selection, but there are other approaches to validation, not currently in widespread use, that offer potential solutions to important problems. There is reason to believe that these may be more widely used in the future. It is important, therefore, to be at least generally familiar with them.

SYNTHETIC VALIDITY

One major disadvantage of the longitudinal and predictive models is that both require a relatively large number of employees doing similar work. They are, thus, of limited value in small companies and in larger firms wherever the number of people employed in a given type of activity is small. The synthetic validity model was developed for application in such situations (17,18). Its approach is analogous to that of the methods engineer who, when developing a standard time for a specific job, combines the various estimated times for separate elements of the operation.

First, various work elements or job requirements must be identified using job analysis procedures. Then, the predictor measures must be validated on a number of jobs having a particular work element or job requirement in common. If a sizable relationship between the values on a given predictor and those on some criterion index can be established for these jobs having a common characteristic, the predictor can be used in selecting individuals for other jobs with the same work element or requirements. The essence of the approach is that a high level of accomplishment on a predictor is almost invariably associated with a high level of a certain type of job behavior. If this can be established, the predictor can be used for any job where the behavior is required and important.

THE DECISION MODEL IN SELECTION

A second approach that has fostered considerable discussion, though, because of certain practical difficulties, it has not been widely applied, derives from mathematical decision theory (4,9). Its premise is that the ultimate purpose of any predictor is to assist in making a *decision* as to what should be done with a given applicant or candidate, and therefore the soundest approach to evaluating a measure is by determining the benefits that accrue to the total organization as a result of a particular decision. The utility concept is used to provide an index of value. Utility is defined by the benefits that accrue from a given set of decisions less the total costs incurred in the decision-making process.

Although a detailed mathematical treatment is not contemplated here, it is possible to describe the basic elements of this approach. There is, first, certain information regarding the individual—interview data, a completed application blank, test scores, and so on. Second, various treatments may be utilized depending on the decision made—hire the man, reject him, collect further information, and so on. Third, the outcomes of decisions are expressed in terms of various criterion values, which may be based on ratings, objective indexes, and so on. Finally, there are the utilities attached to the various outcomes: the benefits less the costs, derived from having an individual perform effectively in a given type of work or the net benefit derived from rejecting an individual with somewhat different characteristics.

Probabilities are attached to these factors and a matrix constructed so that it is possible to evaluate each applicant in terms of his expected value to the firm in a particular position. The difficulty with this approach, and the reason for its limited use, is that good measures of the utilities associated with various decision outcomes have not been available. Recently, however, some solutions to this problem, based on psychological scaling methods analogous to the Thurstone procedure, have been developed (5). It may well be, therefore, that the future will see a much wider application of the decision model in personnel selection.

The Limitations of Selection

It should be apparent from the correlations between predictors and criteria noted previously, such as those in Tables 6–1 and 6–2, that available selection techniques are not a panacea for all ills. Effectively utilized, they can increase the level of goal attainment in a company, but instances of performance failure and individual discontent will inevitably remain. Certain inherent limitations in selection models and technology may never be completely overcome.

One major problem, and this will become increasingly apparent after the discussions in this and the next chapters, is that the available predictors are far from perfect. They do not always reveal a characteristic that is important in determining job behavior, nor do they consistently specify correctly the degree to which it may be present. Interviews, psychological tests, physical examinations and all the other techniques may not yield the information they should, and on occasion they may produce erroneous information.

Another difficulty is associated not so much with the techniques themselves as with the people who use them. Human error is almost inevitable, even though it can be reduced through effective selection and training of personnel managers and workers. In one instance, the writer had a sample of several hundred answer sheets for the psychological tests used in a company's selection battery rescored at a later date. Although, in most cases, the divergence was not large, some tests clearly had been scored with considerable error, error sufficient to produce an inappropriate selection decision. Similar errors, owing to the misunderstanding of an interview statement or the misreading of some physical measure, occur more often than is generally recognized.

Considerations of economy are also relevant. The physical exam probably provides the best example. Increasingly, medical science is developing complex procedures for the detection of various diseases. Many of these diagnostic aids are extremely costly and require highly trained personnel; some necessitate hospitalization during the period tests are carried out. There can be no question that these techniques have considerable value in predicting subsequent events. Yet, companies rarely use them in connection with the pre-employment physical examination. They are too costly in time and money, and the disorders they identify are frequently rather rare. As a result, a decision has been made in many instances to risk future absenteeism and perhaps ineffective job behavior rather than to invest in the available selection techniques.

The investment decision here is analogous to that in a deferred maintenance policy for equipment and machinery. Instead of attempting to spot potential breakdowns before they occur, and correcting the situation, one allows the breakdown to develop. This procedure is based on the assumption that the resulting costs will be less than those of preventive maintenance. Many companies have not adopted psychological testing programs and other selection procedures for much the same reason. They assume that a sizable investment in selection procedures is not warranted, because any difficulties that develop can be handled later. Emphasis is placed on the output processes rather than on organizational inputs. As firing becomes more difficult, owing to union pressures and other factors, however, a number of these firms may recalculate the relative costs and come to a somewhat different conclusion regarding investment in the selection process (22).

In addition to these limitations associated with the selection procedures themselves, there are other problems. One major reason for the failure of selection predictions is that people change in unexpected ways. A physical disorder may develop, personality changes may occur, and so on. Marital difficulties may produce discontent that subsequently is transferred to the job. Or financial problems may arise, which could not have been anticipated, but which leave the employee preoccupied and upset. The list of possibilities is endless. The point is that things happen to people over the years of employment that change them. When these changes are added to the normal alterations associated with aging (see Chapter 2), it is obvious that selection procedures have a somewhat limited potential.

Certainly, prediction, in the short run, is much better than it is over a long period.

The problem of change is not restricted to the individual himself, however. Jobs also change. A man who was quite effective on an assembly line may not do so well when his job is automated more fully. A salesman who can sell one type of product in one market may run into difficulty when competitive pressures force the company to shift to a somewhat different consumer market or product. It is difficult, if not impossible, to select for the jobs of the future, especially when, at the same time, one must select for the extant jobs of the present.

Change may also occur across jobs rather than within them. That is to say, a man may shift from job to job within the company rather than be faced with a change in the role prescriptions of a given position. Some amount of career change is the general rule rather than the exception. Certainly this is the case among college-educated employees, and within the ranks of management. This matter of career prediction is one of the most difficult in the entire field of personnel selection. It requires that predictors be validated against career criteria and that longitudinal studies extend over long time periods. It is not too difficult to successfully predict whether a man will do well during his training period or in his initial placement with the company. It is quite another matter to predict that he will perform effectively twenty years hence in a position whose level and nature are something of a mystery. Yet, there is no question that career selection of this kind is what most companies need, at least for a sizable proportion of the people they hire.

A final source of error has been mentioned already in a different context. Two managers may not evaluate their subordinates in exactly the same way using the same criteria and standards. This is particularly true when organization planning and job analysis have had only minimal application, with the result that role prescriptions are ambiguous and uncertain. A man who is considered satisfactory by one superior may be rated considerably lower by another, even though his behavior has not changed. Two workers whose role behavior is almost identical can be evaluated quite differently. Obviously, when criteria are unstable and unreliable in this manner, selection techniques will not come out looking very effective.

All of these limitations are, of course, superimposed on the constraints imposed by the available manpower pool and the restrictions created by the nature and extent of the recruiting process. No selection procedure can yield an effective work force, if the recruitment procedures cannot, or do not, provide an adequate group of candidates from which selection can occur. Recruitment, then, becomes the *sine qua non* for selection. If the number of possible hires equals the number of jobs to be filled there is no selection. It is crucial, therefore, to develop recruiting procedures that will provide a sufficiently large and varied candidate manpower pool so that the selection techniques can at least achieve their maximum potential. Actually, any valid selection technique will perform quite effectively if it can be used to skim the cream off a very large candidate group.

The Selection Interview

Two approaches characteristically provide a basis for selection decisions. One relies heavily on the assumption that a candidate's behavior in the past can serve as a guide for predicting his future. Accordingly, extensive information is collected regarding the person's previous behavior in various educational, occupational, and perhaps other situations. This information is evaluated relative to the role requirements of the position to be filled, or of several positions, if career considerations are involved. The individual is expected to remain much the same person in the future that he was in the past; he is expected to retain the same or similar characteristics and behave in accordance with the previous pattern.

This rationale underlies many of the procedures regularly employed in the selection interview. It also underlies most biographical inventories, application blanks, medical history forms, and reference checking techniques. In all these instances, the primary, although not exclusive, emphasis is on accumulating valid information about the past to provide a basis for selecting the particular human inputs to the organization that will maximize future effectiveness.

A very different rationale underlies most psychological testing, the physical examination, and certain adaptations of the interview and the application blank. As we shall see, these latter adaptations make the particular interviews and application blanks very similar to psychological tests. This second approach relies heavily on the sampling of present behavior as a basis for prediction. Relatively standardized situations, which presumably have some relation to the job or jobs, are established, and candidates are asked to behave within these contexts. It is assumed that their behavior in these limited situations is typical of their total present behavior and that they will remain sufficiently unchanged in the future to permit effective prediction.

Although it should be evident that interview procedures are widely used for a variety of purposes, the primary concern here is with specific applications in the evaluation of human inputs to a business organization. Thus, applications in such areas as marketing research, employee counseling, management appraisal, attitude surveys, and so on will receive very little attention.

Even within the input context, the interview serves a number of purposes. It is much more than a selection device. Probably this is why it has survived and even thrived in the face of extended attacks by industrial psychologists and others and of considerable evidence that as commonly used it is often not a very effective selection technique.

There are, in fact, a number of requirements connected with the input process that at present cannot be accomplished in any other way, although telephone and written communication might be substituted in certain instances. Interviews are used as often to sell the company and thus recruit candidates for employment as to select. A single interview frequently involves both selection and recruiting aspects. Furthermore, terms of employment characteristically are negotiated in the interview situation, and an important public relations function is performed. Rejected applicants are particularly likely to leave with very negative attitudes toward the company, if they have not talked with a responsible representative.

Even when the focus is directly on the selection process, the interview appears to possess certain unique values, which may account for its continued widespread use. For one thing, the great flexibility of the technique, which can contribute to limited validity in some selection situations, may represent a major asset at other times. The interview is the method *par excellence* for filling in the gaps between other selection techniques—gaps that could not have been foreseen until the other techniques were actually applied. Responses on the application blank may make it clear that further information regarding the circumstances surrounding certain previous employment and separation decisions is needed. An interview can be of considerable help in providing such information.

It is also clear that the interview is widely used to determine whether an applicant is the type of person who can be expected to fit in and get along in the particular firm. Its use with reference to such organizational maintenance considerations is probably much more widespread than its use in predicting productivity. This is not to imply that other selection techniques cannot be used to predict maintenance criteria, but that, for various reasons, they often are not given the same emphasis as the interview. Something about the process of personal judgment produces a strong feeling of validity, even when validity is not present. It is not surprising, therefore, that many companies place heavy emphasis on interviewing when attempting to predict whether a man will be a source of conflict, will have a negative impact on others, or will be an extremely unhappy employee.

Finally, there are situations, especially when managerial and professional positions are involved, where the interview is the only major selection technique that realistically can be used. When a man who already has a good job, who gives every evidence of being a good prospect, and who does not have a strong initial incentive to make a move is faced with extensive psychological testing, a physical exam, and an application blank (above and beyond the resume he has already submitted), he may shy away. If this seems likely, it is often wiser to rely on the interview, reference checks, and the like, in spite of their short-comings, than to face the prospect of losing the man entirely.

WHAT IS KNOWN ABOUT THE SELECTION INTERVIEW

A great deal has been written regarding the techniques of interviewing for various purposes (1,8,15,19). Much of this, however, derives from the expertise and opinion of specific individuals. What is really known, in the sense that it is based on studies using selection models of the kind discussed in the previous chapter and on other scientific research procedures, is considerably less.

The discussion here will be restricted to that which is known in this scientific sense. Unfortunately, when this is done, a great deal is left to the discretion of the individual interviewer. Yet there is little point in continuing to perpetuate much of the existing lore, which in many instances has been developed out of situations far removed from the company employment office, and which may therefore be quite erroneous when applied to a selection interview in the business world.

Consistency of Interviewer Judgments. There is considerable evidence that, lthough an interviewer will himself exhibit consistency in successive evaluations of the same individual, different interviewers are likely to come to quite disparate conclusions (20). When two employment interviewers utilize their idiosyncratic interview procedures on the same applicant, the probability is that they will come to different decisions. They normally will elicit information on different matters, and even when the topics covered do overlap, one man will weigh the applicant's responses in a way that varies considerably from that employed by the other.

These problems can be overcome. Interviewers can be trained to follow similar patterns in their questioning and to evaluate responses using the same standards. When more structured interview techniques are used, when the questions asked are standardized and responses are recorded systematically, the consistency of the judgmental process increases markedly. Within limits, it does not matter which interviewer is used; the results tend to be similar. Unfortunately, however, structuring of a kind that will increase the consistency of judgments appears to be the exception rather than the rule in most personnel offices. Where strong reliance is placed on the interview, the final selection decision often depends as much on which interviewer is used as on the characteristics of the applicant. On the other hand, agreement does not guarantee accuracy of prediction; there can be great consistency in picking the wrong people.

Accuracy of Interview Information. Studies aimed at determining the accuracy of statements regarding work history made in the interview indicate that reporting errors may occur. In one instance, when a check was made with employers, information given by the interviewees regarding job titles was found to be invalid in 24 per cent of the cases. Job duties were incorrectly reported by 10 per cent, and pay by 22 per cent (36). In general, the tendency was to upgrade rather than downgrade prior work experience.

Other research suggests that, in most employment situations, interview distortion is probably not so prevalent as the preceding figures suggest (33). Yet, in any given instance an interviewer may be faced with an applicant who deliberately, or perhaps unconsciously, falsifies his report. The tendency is for the man to make his record look better than it is. It can be assumed, also, that many applicants will avoid discussing previous instances of ineffective work performance. Where valid data are essential, it is usually desirable to check interview statements against outside sources.

Accuracy of Interviewer Judgments. The inevitable conclusion derived from a number of investigations is that interview judgments, as they are usually made in the employment situation, are not closely related to independent measures of the characteristics judged nor to measures of success on the job. In an over-all sense, the evidence regarding the validity of the selection interview yields a distinctly disappointing picture (20).

There are conditions under which the interview exhibits considerable strength as a selection device, and there are some characteristics capable of being judged more effectively than others. Studies dealing with the relationship between interview estimates of intelligence and test scores indicate that the interview can be quite valid in this area. In addition, the interview would appear to have good potential as a predictor of self-confidence, the effectiveness with which a man can express himself, certain types of attitudes, sociability, and a variety of mental abilities. Such characteristics as dependability, creativity, honesty, and loyalty seem more difficult to estimate correctly in the normal interview situation.

The evidence regarding the value of the interview as a selection procedure is certainly not all negative. Where the interview approach is planned in advance and a relatively structured format is followed, so that much the same questions are asked of all interviewees, relatively good validities have been obtained against job performance criteria (10,37). The results of one such study, which utilized the concurrent model, are presented in Table 6–3. Clearly these interview judgments constitute quite adequate predictors in certain instances. Others among the attitude estimates are considerably less effective.

In another series of studies, rather sizable predictive validities were reported for over-all interviewer estimates of suitability for employment, when a highly structured, patterned interview approach was followed (21). When validated against duration of employment for the 587 people who left the company within an eighteen-month period, the interviews yielded a correlation of .43. The men rated higher initially in the employment interview stayed longer. The 407 employees who were still on the job eighteen months after hiring were rated for performance effectiveness

TABLE 6–3. Correlations Between Attitude Evaluations from Interviews and Supervisors' Performance Ratings

Attitudes	Group 1 (N = 12)	Group 2 (N = 14)
Formulation of goal	.14	.60
Strength of job interest	−.13	.40
Strength of general interests	.42	.85
Self-regard	.67	.63
Acquisitive perseverance	−.13	−.30
All five attitudes combined	.45	.71
Formulation of goal, strength of general interests, and self-regard combined	.54	.66

Source: Adapted from K. A. Yonge, "The Value of the Interview: An Orientation and a Pilot Study," *Journal of Applied Psychology*, Vol. 40 (1956), p. 29.

by their superiors, and the results were compared with the earlier interview judgments. A predictive validity coefficient of .68 was obtained. Subsequent studies using the same patterned interview format produced correlations with success criteria consistently in the .60's.

It is evident that when the selection interview is used in a relatively standardized manner and individualized interviewer approaches and biases are controlled, the interview can be quite effective. Under such standardized conditions, the interview takes on certain characteristics of the application blank or a psychological test. It becomes in many respects an oral version of the common written selection procedures, although still with greater flexibility. There is nothing in what has been said to imply that less structured (and less directive) interviews may not yield equally good validities under certain circumstances and with certain interviewers, but without further research it is not possible to specify exactly what these requisite conditions are.

The McGill University Studies. Certain other conclusions regarding the decision-making process in the interview are derived from a series of studies carried out at McGill University over a 10-year period (35). As a result of this research, it is now clear that in the actual employment situation most interviewers tend to make an accept-reject decision early in the interview. They do not wait until all the information is in. Rather, a bias is developed and stabilized shortly after the discussion starts. This bias serves to color the remainder of the interview and is not usually reversed.

Second, interviewers are much more influenced by unfavorable than by favorable data. If any shift in viewpoint occurs during the interview, it is much more likely to be in the direction of rejection. Apparently, selection interviewers tend to maintain rather clear-cut conceptions regarding the role requirements of the jobs for which they are interviewing. They compare candidates against these stereotypes in the sense of looking for deviant characteristics, and thus for negative evidence with regard to hiring. Positive evidence is given much less weight.

These findings suggest certain guidelines for maximizing the effectiveness of employment interviewing. For one thing, if it is intended that the interview should make a *unique* contribution to the selection process, the interviewing ought to be done with relatively little foreknowledge of the candidate. Contrary to common practice, application blanks, test scores, and the like should be withheld until after the initial selection interview. Personal history data should be obtained directly from the candidate in oral form even if written versions are available. This approach will serve to delay decision-making in the interview with the result that information obtained during the latter part of the discussion can be effectively utilized in reaching a judgment. If data are needed to fill in the gaps between the various selection techniques, these can be obtained from a second interview. Thus, the interview as an independent selection tool should be clearly differentiated from the interview as a means of following up on leads provided by other devices. The interviewer should be clear in his own mind as to which objective he is seeking.

When the interview is used as an independent procedure, information obtained from the various sources should be combined and evaluated subsequently to reach a final selection decision, rather than during the interview proper. When the interview is used to supplement application blank, medical history, and psychological test data, it should be as an information-gathering device only, not as an ideally constituted selection procedure. In neither case should it assume the proportions of a final arbiter superseding all other techniques and sources of information.

TYPES OF EMPLOYMENT INTERVIEWS

It is evident that the content of the selection interview may be varied. Different interviewers may ask different questions, concentrate on different parts of the man's prior experience, and attempt to develop estimates of different characteristics. It is also true, however, that the basic technique or procedure may be varied.

Patterned, or Structured, Interviews. The patterned, or structured, interview already has been noted in connection with the discussions of the consistency and accuracy of interviewer judgments. Often a detailed form is used, with the specific questions to be asked noted and space provided for the answers. The form is completed either during the interview or immediately afterward, from memory. In other cases, only the areas to be covered are established in advance, the order of coverage and actual question wording being left to the interviewer. Either way the more structured approach offers distinct advantages over the usual procedure, where different interviewers may go off in completely different directions depending on their own and the candidate's predilections. On the other hand, it should be recognized that information loss may occur because of a lack of flexibility.

Nondirective Procedures. The nondirective approach derives originally from psychotherapy and counseling. It permits the person being interviewed considerable leeway in determining the topics to be covered. The basic role of the interviewer is to reflect the feelings of the other person and to restate or repeat key words and phrases. This tends to elicit more detailed information from the interviewee, especially with reference to his emotional reactions, attitudes, and opinions. Because the candidate actually controls the content of the interview, this procedure may take the discussion far afield. It frequently yields a great deal of information about the prior experiences, early family life, and interpersonal relationships of the individual, but much of this often has no clear relationship to the employment decision. For this reason, the nondirective technique is usually mixed with a more directive, questioning approach when it is used in the selection interview.

Multiple and Group Interviews. Another procedure, which has proved to yield good validity (20), involves the use of more than one interviewer. Either the candidate spends time talking to several different people separately or he meets with a panel or board whose members alternate in asking him questions. This latter approach can easily be integrated into a patterned or structured format, and when this is done the resulting decisions and evaluations appear to maximize prediction of subsequent performance. Normally, the group evaluation is derived after discussion among the various interviewers, but independent estimates can be obtained from each man, and these then are averaged to achieve a final decision. The major disadvantage of any multiple interviewer procedure, of course, is that it can become very costly in terms of the total number of man-hours required. For this reason, it is usually reserved for use in selecting people for the higher level positions.

Stress Interviews. The stress approach achieved some acceptance in the business world after World War II as a result of its use during the war to select men for espionage work with the Office of Strategic Services. As used in industry, this procedure usually involves the induction of failure stress. The interviewer rather suddenly becomes quite aggressive, belittles the candidate, and throws him on the defensive. Reactions to this type of treatment are then observed.

Because it utilizes a sample of present behavior to formulate predictions, rather than focusing on past behavior, the stress interview is in many ways more a situational test than a selection interview. It has the disadvantage that rejected candidates who are subjected to this process can leave with a very negative image of the company, and even those whom the company may wish to hire can become so embittered that they will not accept an offer. This does not happen often, and usually a subsequent explanation can eradicate any bad feelings. When the fact that there is little positive evidence on the predictive power of the stress interview is added to these considerations, it seems very difficult to justify its use under normal circumstances. The selection situation itself appears to be anxiety-provoking enough for most people.

THE INTERVIEW AND SELECTION MODELS

It seems absolutely essential, if a company is to make effective use of the selection interview, for the interviewer to receive some systematic feedback on the validity of his decisions. In order to accomplish this, written evaluations of each candidate must be recorded at the conclusion of the interview. These interview ratings can then be compared at a later date with criterion information provided by the man's immediate superior or derived from some other source. In this way, the interviewer can modify his technique over time to maximize his predictive validity (7).

This approach suffers in that no follow-up can be made on those applicants who are not hired. However, in most companies, personnel recommendations are not followed religiously. For various reasons, those recommended for rejection are hired on occasion. In addition, other selection procedures may outweigh an original negative interview impression. Thus, there will be individuals in the follow-up group who have received rather low ratings, although the preponderant number will have had generally favorable evaluations in the interview.

One should not expect perfect success from these studies, of course. Yet, an interview should contribute something above what might be obtained by chance alone, and from the use of other techniques. Also, if a standardized interview form is used, individual questions can be analyzed to see if they discriminate between effective and ineffective employees. If certain questions appear not to be contributing to the predictive process, others can be substituted and evaluated in a similar manner.

Application Blanks and Biographical Inventories

Probably the most widely used selection device is some type of written statement regarding the applicants' prior experiences and behavior. This may take the form of the conventional application blank or an extended biographical inventory utilizing a great variety of multiple choice questions. On occasion, the form and content of the statement are determined by the applicant rather than the company. Such résumés are particularly likely to be used when the applicant is at the professional or managerial level.

APPLICATION BLANKS

The actual items included on the application blank vary considerably from company to company (25). Many firms maintain several different versions for various positions. It is particularly common to have a separate blank for professional and technical employees, but it may be expedient to develop special forms for any group of jobs similar in their requirements and for which applications are received frequently.

In addition to such routine matters as name, address, telephone number, date of birth, social security number, marital status, children, and citizenship, most forms request information on arrest history, education, and previous employment. Although many applicants will not report arrests and convictions when requested to do so, it is nevertheless desirable to include a question in this area, merely because important information is sometimes obtained. Items dealing with education normally emphasize the extent of training rather than the quality of the work done. Information on grades, if it is desired, is better obtained from the educational institution itself.

Work history data may be requested in a variety of forms. Usually, it is desirable to determine not only job title, but also duties and the level of the position within the employing organization. Salary data can be helpful in negotiating a salary figure with those who will be entering positions that do not have a set starting rate. Questions regarding the reasons for leaving previous employers are often unrevealing, but on occasion they do yield valuable information.

It is important in constructing an application blank to obtain only data that will be used. There is a tendency for these forms to grow in length over the years, to the point where they can well discourage applicants who, at least initially, are not strongly motivated for employment. It is also important to be sure that the information requested is not in violation of federal and state fair employment practices legislation. In general, it is desirable to avoid any questions dealing with race, nationality, and religion.

WEIGHTING APPLICATION BLANK ITEMS

The scoring of application blanks in accord with the demands of the selection model dates back to the early 1920's. The basic requirement is that responses to the various items on the blank be related to some criterion of job success. Studies have been done using job tenure, success ratings, salary increases, and a variety of other indexes. Application blank data appear particularly useful in predicting turnover (28). One advantage of this approach is that, because application blanks are almost universally filled out by all applicants, it is possible to carry out weighting studies at any time. All that is required is a search of the files for the application blanks of people hired for a given type of work during a specified period. These blanks may then be related to available measures of success or turnover.

A variety of techniques for weighting application blank items have been developed, some of them quite statistically complex (13). In general, however, the more involved procedures do not add a great deal as long as the number of cases used in the analysis is sufficiently large. The much simpler horizontal per cent method, as illustrated in Figure 6–1, appears

Response Categories	Low Group	High Group	Total Number	Percent High	Weight
Marital Status					
Single	35	19	54	35	4
Married	52	97	149	65	7
Divorced	25	8	33	24	2
Separated	15	6	21	29	3
Widowed	13	10	23	43	4
	140	140	280		
Education					
Grade School	13	14	27	52	5
High School Incomplete	28	23	51	45	5
High School Graduate	56	46	102	45	5
College Incomplete	18	16	34	47	5
College Graduate	16	25	41	61	6
Graduate Work	9	16	25	64	6
	140	140	280		
Most Recent Work Experience					
None	18	5	23	22	2
Production	40	30	70	43	4
Clerical	38	28	66	42	4
Sales	8	35	43	81	8
Managerial	5	17	22	77	8
Professional	13	16	29	55	6
Other	18	9	27	33	3
	140	140	280		
Military Service					
Yes	77	86	163	53	5
No	63	54	117	46	5
	140	140	280		

Figure 6–1. Form for Weighting Application Blank Responses by Horizontal Percent Method (Hypothetical Data)

to be perfectly adequate for most purposes. All that is needed is an employee sample that may be divided, usually at the median, into a high and low group on some criterion index. Application blanks filled out previously, at the time of employment, are then checked to determine how many in the low and high groups selected each alternative on a given item. The per cent of those responding in a particular way who also fall in the high group on the criterion is then computed. This percentage is converted to a weight by rounding to a single number. High values are associated with the desired performance, low values with that which is not desired. A total score for the blank is obtained by adding up the weights on the individual items.

In the hypothetical example of Figure 6–1, it is clear that the married group tends to produce more than its share of effective employees. Accordingly, this response on the application blank receives a high score. The divorced and separated responses, being associated with less effective performance, receive a low score, whereas those who report themselves as single or widowed receive only a slightly negative weight. Education does not serve to discriminate very well between the high and low groups, although there is some slight advantage associated with the very highest levels of educational accomplishment. A sales or managerial background, on the other hand, appears to be highly desirable, whereas no previous work experience, or employment in areas other than those listed, perhaps farming, yield low weights. Military service does not matter one way or the other. Using these four questions only, a married man with college education, immediately preceding experience as a salesman, and military service would have a total score of twenty-six. This is well above the fourteen obtained by a divorced high school graduate with no previous work experience and no military service.

It is important, once weights have been developed in this manner, that the scoring be cross-validated on another sample drawn from the same employee group. This is absolutely essential in constructing a weighted application blank, because many of the differences in weights may not reflect real differences, but only chance fluctuations. When a large number of items are weighted in this manner, cross-validation may very well yield validity coefficients well below what the analysis of the original sample seemed to suggest.

Additional cross-validations should also be conducted at periodic intervals after the weighting procedure has actually been introduced into the selection process, especially if any major changes in the jobs involved or in the labor market have occurred in the interim since the weights were originally established. Continuing studies of the relationship between weighted scores and job performance should also be made when the weights used are widely known in the company. In at least one instance, an initially satisfactory validity shrank to zero over a three-year period, because field managers, who were anxious to find replacements and who were familiar with the weights, guided applicants into the desired responses (14). This situation can develop with any selection instrument if there are acute shortages in the labor market or if recruiting is very difficult.

It should be emphasized that studies done to date do not support the view that certain responses on an application blank are universally predictive of future success, irrespective of the job and the situation. In fact, the responses contributing most to the relationship with a criterion are often difficult to explain in any manner. In one study, the factors found to be predictive were an average of at least ten months service with all previous employers, no unfavorable employment references, leaving the last job to seek advancement, living on the north side of the city, living in the city rather than the suburbs, and being over twenty-four years of age (29). Other studies on different groups produce very different results.

BIOGRAPHICAL INVENTORIES

The distinction between a weighted application blank and a biographical inventory is by no means clear cut. However, the typical biographical inventory contains a somewhat larger number of items, utilizes a multiple choice format exclusively, and deals with matters not normally covered in an application form. Often, there are questions dealing with early life experiences, hobbies, health, social relations, and so on, which go well beyond the application blank in their detailed coverage of prior experiences. In some instances, questions on attitudes, interests, values, opinions, and self-impressions are included. When this occurs, the biographical inventory begins to approximate a test. Selection instruments of this kind, although placing primary emphasis on the past as a predictor of the future, can also serve to sample present behavior and functioning to achieve their predictive purpose. Examples of the various kinds of items currently in use are presented in Figure 6–2.

Biographical inventories are usually constructed specifically to predict success in a given type of work. The items included are those that the psychologist believes have some potential as predictors. The mechanics of weighting are essentially the same as those described for the weighted application blank. Usually, however, items that do not discriminate between high and low performers are dropped out of the final measure. Thus, the validation and cross-validation process serves as a means of item selection.

Although biographical inventories have been developed for a great variety of purposes, some of the most interesting recent applications have been in the prediction of scientific accomplishments, especially in the pharmaceutical industry. In one such study carried out with the research staff of G. D. Searle & Co., a correlation between biographical inventory responses and ratings of research competence of .57 was obtained. The more creative researchers had a positive self-image, a need for independence, broad interests, a background of parental permissiveness, a tendency to become overinvolved in their work, a positive reaction to challenge, a desire for unstructured work situations, and an interest in contemplative pursuits (2). Similar results were obtained from a study carried out at Richardson-Merrell, Inc. (3,34). This latter study suggests that items dealing with the early years and with the parental family have

Classification Data
What is your present marital status?
1. Single
2. Married, no children
3. Married, one or more children.
4. Widowed.
5. Separated or divorced.

Habits and Attitudes
How often do you tell jokes?
1. Very frequently.
2. Frequently.
3. Occasionally.
4. Seldom.
5. Can't remember jokes.

Health
Have you ever suffered from:
1. Allergies
2. Asthma
3. High blood pressure
4. Ulcers
5. Headaches
6. None of these

Human Relations
How do you regard your neighbors?
1. Not interested in your neighbors.
2. Like them but seldom see them.
3. Visit in each others' homes occasionally.
4. Spend a lot of time together.

Money
How much life insurance, other than company group insurance, do you carry on your own life?
1. None
2. $1,000 to $7,500
3. $7,500 to $12,500
4. $12,500 to $25,000
5. Over $25,000

Parental Home, Childhood, Teens
During most of the time before you were 18, with whom did you live?
1. Both parents.
2. One parent.
3. A relative.
4. Foster parents or non-relatives.
5. In a home or institution.

Personal Attributes
How creative do you feel you are?
1. Highly creative.
2. Somewhat more creative than most in your field.
3 Moderately creative.
4. Somewhat less creative than most in your field.

Figure 6–2. Typical Biographical Inventory Questions

much less value in predicting creativity than do those in such areas as academic background, adult life, and adult interests. There is also evi-

Present Home, Spouse, and Children
Regarding moving from location to location, my wife:
1. Would go willingly wherever my job takes me.
2. Would not move under any circumstances.
3. Would move only if it were absolutely necessary.
4. I don't know how she feels about moving.
5. Not married.

Recreation, Hobbies, and Interests
Have you ever belonged to:
1. A high school fraternity or its equivalent.
2. A college fraternity.
3. Both a high school and a college fraternity.
4. None of the above.

School and Education
How old were you when you graduated from high school?
1. Younger than 15.
2. 15 to 16.
3. 17 to 18.
4. 19 or older.
5. Did not graduate from high school.

Self Impressions
Do you generally do your best:
1. At whatever job you are doing.
2. Only in what you are interested.
3. Only when it is demanded of you.

Values, Opinions, and Preferences
Which one of the following seems most important to you?
1. A pleasant home and family life.
2. A challenging and exciting job.
3. Getting ahead in the world.
4. Being active and accepted in community affairs.
5. Making the most of your particular ability.

Work
How do your feel about traveling in your work?
1. Would enjoy it tremendously.
2. Would like to do some traveling.
3. Would travel if it were necessary.
4. Definitely dislike traveling.

Source: J. R. Glennon, L. E. Albright and W. A. Owens, *A Catalog of Life History Items.* Washington, D.C.: Division 14, American Psychological Association.

Figure 6–2 (cont'd.)

dence that the biographical inventory responses that work for pharmaceutical company scientists are very similar to those that predict the accomplishments of physical scientists engaged in space research.

PROJECTIVE PERSONALITY ANALYSIS OF
APPLICATION BLANKS

A final variation on the application blank theme involves the collection of information on previous experience and behavior, but this information is analyzed for the leads it may provide on present personality functioning.

The basic rationale is that an applicant will reveal much of his personality by the unique way in which he answers the questions—whether he writes out his full name or uses initials, the specific type of vocation he would prefer, and so on.

This approach to personality assessment has been most fully developed by the authors of the Worthington Personal History Blank. This four-page questionnaire, to be filled out in pencil, contains items dealing with family, physical condition, education, activities, U. S. service experience, business experience, and aims. The questions allow a variety of forms of response and are interpreted in accordance with the dictates of personality theory. The result is a personality description, which may be used as a basis for predicting success on the job. These descriptions appear to be relatively accurate (26). In addition, they have exhibited some validity in predicting the job tenure of salesmen, a constantly recurring selection problem (31). However, the universal validity of the technique has not been demonstrated. In certain situations, it does not appear to be a very effective selection tool.

References and Background Checks

A final method of obtaining information on an applicant's prior behavior utilizes not the individual himself, but those who have associated with him and been in a position to observe him. Usually a written evaluation is obtained, but sometimes telephone or even face-to-face interviews with informants are conducted.

Although the use of references, usually individuals named by the applicant, is widespread in the business world, the available research does not provide much basis for optimism insofar as this approach to the selection problem is concerned. One study related scores obtained from a standardized recommendation questionnaire to subsequent supervisory ratings of performance (23). The questionnaire contained items on occupational ability, character and reputation, and employability. On the average, two completed questionnaires were returned on each individual included in the study, and the scores on these were averaged for the purpose of computing validity coefficients. The recommendations come from previous employers, supervisors, personnel managers, coworkers, and acquaintances. The men evaluated were all civil service employees working in various skilled trades. Results are presented in Table 6–4.

Only the correlations in the .20's have any predictive significance, and these are still low. Since only five of the twelve values reach even this level, the findings cannot be interpreted as providing much support for the use of recommendations. The major difficulty is that the responses were almost without exception very positive. Thus, the range of scores was narrow and discrimination between applicants minimal. This appears

TABLE 6–4. Correlation of Employee Recommendation Scores with Supervisors' Ratings

Trade	N	r
Carpenter	51	.01
Equipment repairman	40	.23
Machinist	100	.24
Machine operator	108	−.10
Ordnanceman (torpedo)	125	−.01
Radio mechanic	107	.29
Aviation metalsmith	94	.24
Highlift fork operator	108	.21
Auto mechanic	98	.09
Painter	70	.07
Ordnanceman	100	.10
Printer	116	.11

Source: J. N. Mosel and H. W. Goheen, "The Validity of the Employment Recommendation Questionnaire in Personnel Selection," *Personnel Psychology*, Vol. 11 (1958), p. 484.

to be a typical difficulty with recommendations. However, there is some evidence that when references are obtained in letter form, rather than by standardized questionnaire, different types of positive statements can have differential significance (27). When only positive statements regarding such characteristics as cooperation, consideration, and urbanity appear in the letter, there is a good chance that the person writing the reference has some doubts regarding the man's qualifications. If, on the other hand, there are positive statements in the areas of mental agility, vigor, dependability, and reliability, it can be assumed that a favorable opinion regarding performance potential really exists.

A question may arise concerning the source of the recommendations, however. It is possible that certain types of people, having had particular kinds of relationships with an applicant, will provide more valid information than other types. A study to check on this hypothesis has been conducted, again with civil service employees in various skilled trades (24). Employment recommendation scores of the kind previously described were correlated with performance ratings given by superiors subsequent to employment. The results are given in Table 6–5.

The correlations for supervisors and acquaintances are reliably different from zero, and therefore meaningful. The others are not. In general, friends tend to be the most lenient, previous subordinates are next, previous coworkers next, and previous employers and superiors the most critical. This would suggest that if one does use letters of recommendation as a selection tool, the letters will discriminate most effectively and at the

TABLE 6–5. Correlation of Employee Recommendation Scores for Different Respondent Types with Supervisors' Ratings

Respondent type	N	r
Personnel officers	102	.02
Supervisors	188	.19
Co-workers	311	.09
Acquaintances	182	.20
Relatives	12	−.16

Source: J. N. Mosel and H. W. Goheen, "The Employment Recommendation Questionnaire: III. Validity of Different Types of References," *Personnel Psychology*, Vol. 12 (1959), p. 474.

same time yield the highest validity when they are obtained from previous supervisors.

A final question involves the relationship between written recommendations and more intensive field investigations, which attempt to develop a picture of a man's background from personal interviews with a variety of people who have known him. A study in this area dealt with government employees hired to fill positions as economists, budget examiners, and training officers (12). Field interviews were conducted with from three to six people who knew the applicant, and the results of these interviews combined into an over-all field evaluation. These latter investigation report ratings were then correlated with previously obtained ratings on a standardized recommendation questionnaire dealing with the applicants' personality, skill, knowledge, human relations competence, and occupational development.

As Table 6–6 indicates, there was a positive relationship between the

TABLE 6–6. Correlation of Employee Recommendation Scores and Investigation Report Ratings

Position	N	r
Economist	41	.22
Budget examiner	21	.54
Training officer	47	.45

Source: H. W. Goheen and J. N. Mosel, "Validity of Employment Recommendation Questionnaire: II. Comparison with Field Investigations," *Personnel Psychology*, Vol. 12 (1959), p. 300.

written recommendations and the more intensive field investigations. What the table does not indicate is the amount of information that came out in the interviews but not in the letters. Such matters as gross incompetence, alcoholism, and homosexuality were practically never mentioned in writing. Yet, the field interviews often led to the identification of such factors. It seems clear, therefore, that the more effort one puts into an investigation of an applicant's background, the greater the probability that meaningful results will be obtained. Letters to friends identified by the applicant are in all probability not even worth the cost of mailing. Intensive interviews with former superiors and others who know the man well can, however, be well worth the effort.

It should be emphasized that field investigations of the type described are not restricted to government employees. Bonding and security clearance investigations are frequently carried out on industrial employees. Many firms regularly obtain credit evaluations on applicants, and the credit agencies often provide detailed information on other matters as well. For a rather nominal fee, checks are carried out on court records, educational credentials, prior work experiences, and places of residence. Detective agencies are used on occasion to investigate managerial candidates. It is common practice to speak either on the phone or in person with mutual acquaintances, especially those with occupational skills similar to the applicant's. Although the evidence on the matter is sparse, it seems very likely that all of these techniques, if they are used in a systematic manner with cross checks between sources, will be more valuable and valid than written references. Nevertheless, it is still important to maintain an ongoing validation effort to determine whether all types of pre-employment information are related to subsequent success.

REFERENCES

1. Bellows, R. M., and M. F. Estep, *Employment Psychology: The Interview.* New York: Holt, Rinehart & Winston, 1961.
2. Buel, W. D., "Biographical Data and the Identification of Creative Research Personnel," *Journal of Applied Psychology,* Vol. 49 (1965), 318–321.
3. Cline, V. B., and M. F. Tucker, *The Prediction of Creativity and Other Performance Measures Among Pharmaceutical Scientists.* Salt Lake City, Utah: Univ. of Utah, 1965.
4. Cronbach, L. J., and G. C. Gleser, *Psychological Tests and Personnel Decisions.* Urbana, Ill.: Univ. of Illinois Press, 1965.
5. Curtis, E. W., *The Application of Decision Theory and Scaling Methods to Selection Test Evaluation.* Eugene, Ore.: Univ. of Oregon, Ph.D. Dissertation, 1965.
6. Dunnette, M. D., *Personnel Selection and Placement.* Belmont, Cal.: Wadsworth, 1966.
7. England, G. W., and D. G. Paterson, "Selection and Placement—The Past Ten Years," in H. G. Heneman *et al.* (eds.), *Employment Relations Research.* New York: Harper & Row, 1960, pp. 43–72.
8. Fear, R. A., *The Evaluation Interview.* New York: McGraw-Hill, 1958.
9. Forehand, G. A., "A Note on Executive Selection and the Decision Model," in R. Tagiuri (ed.), *Research Needs in Executive Selection.* Boston, Mass.: Harvard Univ. Graduate School of Business Administration, 1961, pp. 99–104.

10. Ghiselli, E. E., "The Validity of a Personnel Interview," *Personnel Psychology*, Vol. 19 (1966), 389–394.
11. Glennon, J. R., L. E. Albright, and W. A. Owens, *A Catalog of Life History Items*. Washington, D.C.: Division 14, American Psychological Association, n.d.
12. Goheen, H. W., and J. N. Mosel, "Validity of the Employment Recommendation Questionnaire: II. Comparison with Field Investigations," *Personnel Psychology*, Vol. 12 (1959), 297–301.
13. Guion, R. M., *Personnel Testing*. New York: McGraw-Hill, 1965.
14. Hughes, J. F., J. F. Dunn, and B. Baxter, "The Validity of Selection Instruments under Operating Conditions," *Personnel Psychology*, Vol. 9 (1956), 321–324.
15. Kahn, R. L., and G. F. Cannell, *The Dynamics of Interviewing*. New York: Wiley, 1957.
16. Katkovsky, W., "Personality and Ability Changes over Eight Years," in D. W. Bray (ed.), *The Young Business Manager*. New York: Personnel Research Division, American Telephone and Telegraph, 1965, pp. 24–36.
17. Lawshe, C. H., "Employee Selection," *Personnel Psychology*, Vol. 5 (1952), 31–34.
18. Lawshe, C. H., and M. D. Steinberg, "Studies in Synthetic Validity, I. An Exploratory Investigation of Clerical Jobs," *Personnel Psychology*, Vol. 8 (1955), 291–301.
19. Lopez, F. M., *Personnel Interviewing—Theory and Practice*. McGraw-Hill, 1965.
20. Mayfield, E. C., "The Selection Interview—A Re-evaluation of Published Research," *Personnel Psychology*, Vol. 17 (1964), 239–260.
21. McMurry, R. N., "Validating the Patterned Interview," *Personnel*, Vol. 23 (1947), 263–272.
22. Miner, J. B., *The Management of Ineffective Performance*. New York: McGraw-Hill, 1963.
23. Mosel, J. N., and H. W. Goheen, "The Validity of the Employment Recommendation Questionnaire in Personnel Selection," *Personnel Psychology*, Vol. 11 (1958), 481–490.
24. Mosel, J. N., and H. W. Goheen, "The Employment Recommendation Questionnaire: III. Validity of Different Types of References," *Personnel Psychology*, Vol. 12 (1959), 469–477.
25. National Industrial Conference Board, *Forms and Records in Personnel Administration*, Studies in Personnel Policy, No. 175. New York: The Board, 1960.
26. Peck, R. F., and R. E. Worthington, "New Techniques for Personnel Assessment," *Journal of Personnel Administration and Industrial Relations*, Vol. 1 (1954), 23–30.
27. Peres, S. H., and J. R. Garcia, "Validity and Dimensions of Descriptive Adjectives Used in Reference Letters for Engineering Applicants," *Personnel Psychology*, Vol. 15 (1962), 279–286.
28. Schuh, A. J., "The Predictability of Employee Tenure: A Review of the Literature," *Personnel Psychology*, Vol. 20 (1967), 133–152.
29. Shott, G. L., L. E. Albright, and J. R. Glennon, "Predicting Turnover in an Automated Office Situation," *Personnel Psychology*, Vol. 16 (1963), 213–219.
30. Smith, R. D., and P. S. Greenlaw, "Simulation of a Psychological Decision Process in Personnel Selection," *Management Science*, Vol. 13 (1967), 409–419.

31. Spencer, G., and R. E. Worthington, "Validity of a Projective Technique in Predicting Sales Effectiveness," *Personnel Psychology*, Vol. 5 (1952), 125–144.
32. Spitzer, M. E., and W. J. McNamara, "A Managerial Selection Study," *Personnel Psychology*, Vol. 17 (1964), 19–40.
33. Tiffin, J., and E. J. McCormick, *Industrial Psychology*, 5th ed., Englewood Cliffs, N.J.: Prentice-Hall, 1965.
34. Tucker, M. F., V. B. Cline, and J. R. Schmitt, "Prediction of Creativity and Other Performance Measures from Biographical Information among Pharmaceutical Scientists," *Journal of Applied Psychology*, Vol. 51 (1967), 131–138.
35. Webster, E. C., *Decision-Making in the Employment Interview*. Montreal, Can.: Industrial Relations Centre, McGill Univ., 1964.
36. Weiss, D. J., and R. V. Dawis, "An Objective Validation of Factual Interview Data," *Journal of Applied Psychology*, Vol. 44 (1960), 381–385.
37. Yonge, K. A., "The Value of the Interview: An Orientation and a Pilot Study," *Journal of Applied Psychology*, Vol. 49 (1956), 25–31.

QUESTIONS

1. What are the differences between concurrent and predictive validity? Under what specific circumstances can the concurrent model lead to erroneous selection decisions?
2. What is cross-validation? Why is it an essential ingredient of the selection process? Does cross-validation become increasingly important as the number of predictors tried is expanded?
3. How would you evaluate the use of predictors in personnel selection? What are their shortcomings and their strengths? Under what conditions are they most effective?
4. Discuss the various uses of the interview both within and outside the selection situation. What do you feel will be the future of the technique in the selection context? Why?
5. What do stress interviews, biographical inventories containing items asking for self-impressions, and projective questions in application blanks have in common?
6. How might you construct a biographical inventory using the horizontal per cent method to weight and select items? Write five biographical inventory items and carry out the weighting process using hypothetical data.
7. What do we know about the value of recommendation questionnaires and letters of reference in the selection process?

7

Selection:
Psychological Testing

In this second chapter on the selection process, the coverage will be restricted to those methods of regulating the human input to an organization that stress *current* activity. Both psychological testing and the physical examination are essentially of this nature. Because, however, the physical examination is not generally a matter of psychological concern, the discussion here is limited in large part to psychological testing.

Tests will be classified in terms of the aspects of human functioning that they measure—abilities, personality, skills, and achievements. This is in line with customary practice. In addition, a section at the end of the chapter will discuss some of the criticisms of psychological testing, especially those that view it as unethical in certain respects.

The general approach is to note a number of tests of each kind, which have had considerable application in industry, and then to describe one or two of these in some detail. These latter tests have been selected to illustrate some particular point, rather than because they are presumed to be the most outstanding. At the end of each section, a general review of the validities obtained with each type of test in various business positions will be attempted. More detailed information on the tests noted can be found in *The Sixth Mental Measurements Yearbook* (4).

Abilities

GENERAL INTELLIGENCE TESTS

Tests of general intelligence are heavily weighted with material of the kind that is normally learned in school. The majority of items tend to be verbal in nature and to deal with learning in such subjects as reading, spelling, English, literature, and the like. A secondary emphasis is in the numerical and arithmetic area, and a few of these tests stress symbolic reasoning. The more widely used measures in industry are the Wechsler Adult Intelligence Scale, Otis Self-Administering Test of Mental Ability, Wonderlic Personnel Test, Adaptability Test, Miller Analogies Test, Thurstone Test of Mental Alertness, Wesman Personnel Classification Test, and Concept Mastery Test.

Wechsler Adult Intelligence Scale. This is an individually administered test with questions asked orally by the psychologist and the answers recorded on a special test form. Because it is time-consuming and costly to administer, the Wechsler is not widely used for personnel selection, except at the higher levels. It has, however, been shown to have satisfactory validity within management, especially the strictly verbal subtests (1). There are eleven subtests in all:

Verbal
- Information. A series of open-ended questions dealing with the kinds of factual data people normally pick up in their ordinary contacts.
- Comprehension. Another series of open-ended questions covering the individual's understanding of the need for social rules.
- Arithmetic. All the questions are of the story or problem type. Scoring is for correctness of solutions and time to respond.
- Digit Span. A group of numbers is read and the subject repeats them from memory, sometimes backward.
- Similarities. Pairs of terms are read and a common property or characteristic must be abstracted.
- Vocabulary. A series of words that must be defined in the subject's own terms.

Performance
- Picture Completion. A number of pictures are presented in which the subject must identify the missing component.
- Picture Arrangement. Items require that a series of pictures be arranged in the order that makes the most sense as rapidly as possible.
- Object Assembly. Jigsaw puzzles that must be put together within a given time limit.
- Block Design. Working with a set of small blocks having red, white, or red and white faces, the subject attempts to duplicate various printed designs as quickly as possible.
- Digit Symbol. The subject is given a series of paired symbols and numbers as a code. He is then to write as many correct numbers as he can for each of a series of scrambled symbols within a set time period.

Wesman Personnel Classification Test. A test devised specifically for industrial use, the Wesman is completed by the subject himself, but has a strict time limit. The total score is the number of correct answers written down in the period allowed. There are two types of items that may be scored separately to provide indexes of verbal and numerical abilities, if desired. The verbal items are of the analogy type (—— is to —— as —— is to ——) with both the first and last components left blank. The correct words must be selected from a number of choices. The numerical items are varied, but all require a certain amount of computation. There is less emphasis on the story or problem format than in the Wechsler Arithmetic subtest. Because a person's speed has a very marked influence on his score, tests of this kind characteristically yield relatively low scores among older people. Where rapid thinking is not required in the job itself, an untimed test is probably more appropriately used, especially if many applicants are in the mid-forties or older.

Concept Mastery Test. This specially devised test is intended to discriminate among individuals at the very highest intellectual levels. It was developed for use in connection with a continuing research study of a large group of individuals, originally selected because of their extremely high intelligence in grade school (33). The hope was that by concentrating on very difficult items it would be possible to identify differences among members of this group in adulthood. As Table 7–1 indicates, this goal was achieved. The highest possible score is 190. Very few, even among the Ph.D.'s, came close to this level.

TABLE 7–1. Concept Mastery Test Scores According to Educational Level for Gifted Group

Educational level	*N*	*Mean score*
Ph.D.	51	159.0
M.D.	35	143.6
LL.B.	73	149.4
Master's degree	151	144.3
Graduate study without degree	122	143.0
Bachelor's degree only	263	135.7
College study without degree	163	128.7
No college	146	118.4

Source: L. M. Terman and M. H. Oden, *The Gifted Group at Mid-Life.* Stanford, Calif.: Stanford Univ. Press, 1959, p. 58.

The test contains two types of items. The majority are pairs of words that must be identified as either the same or opposite in meaning. In addition, there are a number of analogies, primarily of a verbal nature. Generally, a considerable background of information is required to do very well on the test. For this reason, it should be used as a selection device only when the job specification calls for a bachelor's or higher degree.

Short Vocabulary Tests. Although, where time is available, it is certainly desirable to use longer tests of the type just described, there are situations where a quick, rough screening is desired. Under such circumstances, a short vocabulary test may approximate the larger measures very closely. Evidence on this point is given in Table 7–2.

TABLE 7–2. Correlations Between General Intelligence Tests in a Sample of 108 Sales Employees

Test	Mean score	Vocabulary Test G-T		Concept Mastery	WAIS Verbal Score
		Form A	Form B		
Vocabulary Test G-T, Forms A & B (40 items)	27.64	.89	.89	.73	.56
Vocabulary Test G-T, Form A (20 items)	13.03		.59	.64	.47
Vocabulary Test G-T, Form B (20 items)	14.61			.67	.54
Concept Mastery Test	61.50				.54
WAIS Verbal Score	67.22				

Source: J. B. Miner, "On the Use of a Short Vocabulary Test to Measure General Intelligence," *Journal of Educational Psychology*, Vol. 52 (1961), p. 158.

The test used in this study contains a series of multiple-choice items that are scaled from very easy to quite difficult. The test appears to meet all requirements for a satisfactory measure, although it can be completed in fewer than ten minutes. It correlates with the Concept Mastery Test better than the Wechsler Verbal Score does. The group of men studied were all above average intelligence. When a correction is made for this restriction of range, both twenty-item tests yielded correlations with the more extensive general intelligence measures of at least .75 (24).

TESTS OF SPECIAL INTELLECTUAL ABILITIES

These measures tap a variety of special abilities. Among the more widely known are the Minnesota Clerical Test, Bennett Test of Mechanical Comprehension, Revised Minnesota Paper Form Board, AC Test of Creative Ability, Watson-Glaser Critical Thinking Appraisal, Miller Survey of Mechanical Insight, and Miller Survey of Object Visualization. In addition, there are several multiability test batteries that provide separate measures of a number of abilities. In this category are the Differential Aptitude Tests, Flanagan Aptitude Classification Tests, General Aptitude Test Battery, and Employee Aptitude Survey. The following treatment will concentrate on these multiability measures, because they provide the best opportunity to illustrate the various item types.

Differential Aptitude Tests. One of the most carefully constructed sets of tests currently available, the Differential Aptitude Tests (DAT) take about four hours to administer. There are eight separate aptitude measures included. With the exception of the clerical test, all have liberal time limits, with the result that older applicants are not unduly penalized. For most purposes, it would probably not be necessary to administer the entire battery, but only those tests with clear relevance for the particular position under consideration. The aptitudes measured are:

1. Verbal Reasoning. These are a series of verbal analogies of the same type as those employed in the verbal part of the Wesman Personnel Classification Test. A good background of general information is required.
2. Numerical Ability. Arithmetic computations with a multiple-choice format. The choices are structured so that the answers must actually be computed.
3. Abstract Reasoning. The items are made up of sets of four "problem figures" that constitute a logical sequence of some kind. A fifth figure must then be selected from among five "answer figures" to complete the sequence.
4. Space Relations. A series of items requiring visualization of forms in space. A key pattern must be matched in some way with one or more of five multiple-choice forms.
5. Mechanical Reasoning. Pictures are shown depicting various mechanical problems. A number of questions then determine if the subject understands the mechanical processes involved. This is the typical item type in mechanical ability measures.
6. Clerical Speed and Accuracy. Five pairs of numbers and/or letters are shown, one of which is underlined. On an answer sheet the same pairs are shown, but in a different order. The task is to pick out the underlined pair on the answer sheet. The test is timed, and the score is based on the number of items completed correctly.
7. Language Usage, Spelling. A series of words, some spelled correctly and some not. The subject must indicate which are right.
8. Language Usage, Sentences. A measure of the degree to which an individual understands the formal rules of grammar.

General Aptitude Test Battery. This battery, constructed by the U.S. Employment Service, has had wide distribution because of its use in the state employment offices. It is aimed primarily at the lower job levels and contains twelve separately timed tests. Scores from these tests are combined to yield measures of nine aptitudes, plus an index of general intelligence.

The tests have been used extensively in occupational research conducted by the U.S. Employment Service. The results of one such study are presented in Table 7–3. In this instance, the aptitude scores were

TABLE 7–3. Correlations Between General Aptitude Test Battery Scores and Piece-Rate Earnings for 65 Radio Tube Mounters

Aptitude	Mean score	r
G—Intelligence	106.9	−.08
V—Verbal Aptitude	102.2	−.06
N—Numerical Aptitude	105.8	.06
S—Spatial Aptitude	109.3	−.01
P—Form Perception	111.8	.02
Q—Clerical Perception	106.2	.10
A—Aiming	107.1	.23
T—Motor Speed	103.6	.19
F—Finger Dexterity	109.5	.44
M—Manual Dexterity	98.7	.35

Source: U.S. Department of Labor, *General Aptitude Test Battery Manual*, Washington, D.C.: the Department, 1958, Section III.

validated against piece-rate earnings. The highest validities on this type of assembly task were obtained with the measures of finger and manual dexterity. In addition, aiming, or perhaps better, motor coordination, and motor speed come close to significance. These measures of so-called *psychomotor* abilities depend on muscular speed, strength, and coordination. Interestingly, the various measures of special intellectual abilities do not yield significant validities for this type of work, nor does G—the general intelligence index.

In another study of fifty file clerks, using supervisory ratings of work output as a criterion, the measures producing significant validities were Verbal, Clerical Perception, and the comprehensive score—G (10). It is clear that the aptitudes related to success in one type of work are not always those associated with success in another. Furthermore, evidence from other sources indicates that special abilities are more effective in predicting quality and quantity of work output, i.e., productivity criteria, than in predicting contributions to organizational maintenance.

PSYCHOMOTOR TESTS

The psychomotor tests of the General Aptitude Test Battery have already been mentioned. Other measures of a similar type are the MacQuarrie Test for Mechanical Ability, O'Connor Finger and Tweezer Dexterity Tests, Purdue Pegboard, Minnesota Rate of Manipulation Tests, and the Crawford Small Parts Dexterity Test. In addition, there are a number of special coordination measures and apparatus tests that tap muscular skills of a grosser nature.

MacQuarrie Test for Mechanical Ability. Although most psychomotor tests require some special equipment, the MacQuarrie utilizes only pencil and paper. There are seven subtests:

- Tracing. The subject draws a continuous line from a start through gaps in a series of vertical lines to a finish point.
- Tapping. The subject makes dots on a paper as quickly as possible.
- Dotting. Dots are made within small irregularly placed circles.
- Copying. Simple designs are copied by connecting the appropriate dots from among a much larger number.
- Location. The subject is required to locate specific points in a smaller version of a large stimulus.
- Blocks. Piled blocks are shown in two dimensions and the total number in the pile must be determined.
- Pursuit. The subject visually traces lines through a maze.

This type of test appears to measure something rather different than the psychomotor tests utilizing special equipment. There is also reason to believe that the latter are more likely to yield adequate predictions in the selection situation (15). Yet, tests such as those in the MacQuarrie have proved valid for such occupations as aviation mechanic and stenographer.

O'Connor Finger and Tweezer Dexterity Tests. These tests require a board with 100 small holes in rows of ten and a shallow tray in which a number of pins are placed. The subjects' job is to fill the holes with the pins using either his fingers or tweezers. The score is the amount of time required to complete the task. This is the traditional measure to obtain an index of finger dexterity. Similar pegboards with screws, nuts, bolts, and so on provide a measure of more comprehensive psychomotor skills of the kind subsumed under the title "manual dexterity."

The O'Connor measures have proved valid as predictors of success among power sewing machine operators, dental students, and on a variety of other manipulative tasks. The pegboard format is, in fact, the most widely used among the psychomotor tests. It has, in general, proved to be highly effective in the selection situation.

Coordination Measures. The most typical measure, probably, in the coordination area is the pursuit rotor, which establishes aiming skill or motor coordination. The task here is to follow a dot on a rotating disk, using a stylus. The best measures electronically record the number of seconds the stylus is actually on the moving point.

Much more complex apparatus tests requiring a subject to pull levers, push pedals, and so on when a given pattern of lights appears were used in selecting pilots during World War II (5). Such apparatus techniques, although they have not been widely used in industry, do appear to possess considerable potential. Unfortunately, separate procedures must be developed for each job, or on occasion, for a job family. This is costly and requires considerable research. In fact, research seems to be very much needed in the area of psychomotor abilities generally. The various tests are not closely related, and a measure that will predict for one job often does not do so for what would seem to be a very similar job. Thus, specific psychomotor predictors must be established separately in each instance.

GENERAL PATTERN OF VALIDITIES: ABILITIES

The most comprehensive and up-to-date summary of previous research available at the present time breaks the ability measures into intelligence, spatial and mechanical, clerical, and psychomotor types (13). Under intelligence are placed not only all the studies involving the use of general intelligence tests, but also those employing specific measures of numerical and verbal abilities. This seems appropriate in that the more general tests are heavily weighted with arithmetic problems, verbal analogies, and vocabulary.

In general, the various measures of intelligence, spatial, and mechanical abilities seem to achieve their greatest predictive effectiveness when used to select individuals for training programs. Used in this capacity they far excel other types of ability measures. However, when prediction goes beyond the training period and moves to actual on-the-job performance, tests of intelligence, spatial, and mechanical abilities appear to do only as well as the clerical and psychomotor measures. This would suggest that, generally, where there is particular concern about selecting people who will be able to get through a training period, emphasis can best be placed on intelligence, spatial, or mechanical measures, as appropriate to the particular jobs under consideration. Tests of this kind deal with the capacity to learn and thus are particularly suited to predicting success in training or educational programs. Job effectiveness, on the other hand, requires these "learning" abilities no more than abilities of other kinds.

When attention is focused on specific types of occupations, and the tests that will predict success in training for these occupations, the differential significance of the various abilities begins to appear. Success in training for clerical positions is best predicted with the intelligence measures and with the job-specific clerical ability tests. In addition, the indexes of spatial and mechanical abilities also yield good validities.

In selecting people for training to perform in the service occupations, it seems best, in view of the validities obtained, to concentrate on intelligence, spatial, and mechanical tests. These measures are also effective in predicting training success for the skilled industrial occupations, as are measures of clerical ability. At the semiskilled level, this picture shifts drastically. The highest validities against training criteria have been obtained with the psychomotor ability tests. The superiority of these measures is so great that there seems little point in using anything else. Yet, training success for unskilled occupations is best predicted with intelligence, spatial, and mechanical tests.

Job Performance. When we shift from success in training to effectiveness on the job, a greater number of studies are available and more occupations have been investigated. At the managerial level, measures of intelligence and also those of a clerical nature appear to work well. With industrial foremen, however, the clerical tests lose their effectiveness, whereas measures of spatial and mechanical abilities have proved to be valuable selection techniques.

Success in clerical work is predicted about equally well by intelligence and clerical indexes. Because spatial and mechanical measures are also effective with clerical employees, it appears that in this area, at least, a test battery constructed to select people for training should be valid in the actual job situation.

In the sales occupations, abilities are not generally very important. An exception to this generalization can be made, however, in the case of the highest level jobs, such as industrial and insurance sales, where intelligence, and to a lesser degree clerical ability, are important. In lower level positions, especially among sales clerks, ability tests do not seem to carry any validity at all.

Effective performance in the protective service occupations, such as policeman and fireman, is about equally well predicted by all types of ability measures, with some slight superiority accruing to the intelligence tests. Performance in the personal service occupations, however, appears to be almost totally unrelated to the abilities. None of the tests discussed has consistently produced satisfactory validities for these jobs.

Success in various industrial positions at the skilled, semiskilled, and unskilled levels can be predicted with ability measures, although generally the validity coefficients tend to be lower than those obtained with managers, foremen, clerical workers, and higher level salesmen. Spatial and mechanical measures are of increasing significance as the skill level ascends, with very little validity for unskilled jobs. They are the most effective at the skilled level, although clerical indexes come close. Among semiskilled workers, all the abilities have much the same significance. Clerical tests have the highest validities among the ability measures in the unskilled occupations. Generally, the intelligence measures are not the most helpful in selecting for performance effectiveness in these industrial occupations. Also, a battery of tests that will predict training success for these jobs may have to be expanded, if predictions of on-the-job success are desired as well.

Personality

This discussion of personality measures will develop more fully some of the distinctions made in Chapter 5, where the various methods of attitude measurement were presented. The available tests fall into two categories, depending on the measurement rationale employed. The majority of the personality tests currently on the market ask the respondent to describe himself in some way, and these self-reports are either taken at face value or related to some group with known characteristics in order to obtain a score. A second approach utilizes the projective rationale. Tests of this kind obtain descriptions or reactions, not with reference to the self in the here and now, but to some far removed situation or stimulus. Inferences are made back to the individual's personality pattern.

As with attitude measurement, the major problem in personality testing is the tendency to portray oneself in the most favorable light. This problem becomes acute in the selection situation. Although the desire to make a good impression may represent a positive contribution when abilities are measured, because it ensures that the applicant will do his best on the tests, such a desire may only produce a distorted and atypical picture in the personality area. Much work done in the field of personality testing over the past twenty years has been concerned with solving this problem.

SELF-REPORT TECHNIQUES

Perhaps the most widely used self-report measures are those that provide information on the degree of interest in various types of activities, primarily those of an occupational nature. The major titles are the Strong Vocational Interest Blank and the Kuder Preference Record-Vocational. There are, in addition, a number of tests that yield scores on several personality characteristics, usually at least four and, in some instances, as many as eighteen. Among these self-report tests are the Minnesota Multiphasic Personality Inventory, Bernreuter Personality Inventory, Guilford-Zimmerman Temperament Survey, California Psychological Inventory, Activity Vector Analysis, Thurstone Temperament Schedule, Gordon Personal Profile and Personal Inventory, Edwards Personal Preference Schedule, and the Study of Values. All have seen considerable use in the industrial situation, and a number have produced at least adequate validities for managerial selection (35).

Kuder Preference Record-Vocational. The Kuder contains groups of three statements descriptive of various types of activities. The subject indicates which of the three he would most like to do and which least. These choices are totaled to obtain various interest area scores, based on the particular activity described. The ten regular scores obtained from the test are listed in Table 7–4. Also noted is a special supervisory interest score developed for the specific purpose of predicting success in managerial work (23).

TABLE 7–4. Correlations Between Kuder Preference Record-Vocational and Management Appraisal Ratings for 420 Managers

Interest area	Mean score	Ratings	
		Present performance	Potential
Outdoor	34	.02	—.12
Mechanical	40	—.01	—.01
Computational	62	.05	.04
Scientific	65	—.15	—.08
Persuasive	64	.09	.20
Artistic	48	—.05	—.12
Literary	69	.04	.11
Musical	59	.04	—.01
Social Service	46	.02	.02
Clerical	35	—.03	—.10
Supervisory		.14	.24

Source: J. B. Miner, "The Kuder Preference Record in Management Appraisal," *Personnel Psychology*, Vol. 13 (1960), pp. 191–192.

As Table 7–4 suggests, the Kuder does not generally achieve very impressive validities when used to select people for initial hiring or promotion. The Scientific and Supervisory scores do yield values significantly different from zero when correlated with the managerial performance ratings; the Outdoor, Persuasive, Artistic, Literary, Clerical, and Supervisory indexes do the same when validated against potential ratings. However, the correlations are not high. Even the Supervisory measure has not always proved effective in subsequent studies (32).

The major difficulty seems to be that an applicant, or a manager seeking promotion, can, and often does, make his choices in accordance with what he feels would be expected in the desired position, rather than on the basis of his real feelings. Job applicants tend to obtain different scores on the test than would be obtained under less stressful, research conditions (14). A tendency of this kind may very well account for the low scores obtained by the managers of Table 7–4 on the Outdoor (or agricultural), Mechanical, and Clerical measures. The managers in all probability consider these to be rather low-status activities in which as managers they *should not* have much interest.

More recently the Kuder Preference Record-Occupational has been developed, which, although it uses an item format similar to the Vocational, is scored in a different manner. Keys for a variety of occupations have been constructed based on the specific choices made by people working in the occupations. It is the response pattern characteristic of actual job performers, rather than the particular type of activity described that determines scoring. This approach is used in the Strong Vocational Interest Blank as well. Validities should be higher under these circumstances, although as long as the applicant is in a position to guess how those in an occupation might respond, there would appear to be a chance of bias in the selection situation.

Edwards Personal Preference Schedule. Another approach to the elimination of bias is reflected in the Edwards Personal Preference Schedule. This is a forced-choice procedure (see Chapter 5) requiring the subject to choose between paired alternatives, the majority of which have been selected so as to be matched in terms of their social desirability. On most items, the subject cannot respond so as to present a "good" image, because he must choose between two equally "good" alternatives. The test measures some fifteen motives, the need or desire for achievement, deference, order, exhibition, autonomy, affiliation, intraception, succorance, dominance, abasement, nurturance, change, endurance, heterosexuality, and aggression. It takes approximately forty minutes to administer.

The Edwards has rather consistently yielded reliable correlations when studied in relation to various indexes of occupational success (16). Yet, there is reason to believe that the use of forced-choice alternatives equated for general social desirability does not entirely overcome bias (34). In the selection situation, applicants seem to bring certain specific conceptions of what answers will be valued with them. Although these preconceived answers are influenced by social desirability considerations, there is more to it than that. There is also the matter of specific desirability for the job under consideration. Two alternatives may be entirely equal in their social acceptability, but one may be clearly more desirable in relation to a given position. The result can well be a response that looks good when compared against the job, but that is not truly descriptive of the individual.

Activity Vector Analysis. Activity Vector Analysis (AVA) is a unique measure, not in its technique of measurement or in its approach to bias, but in the way that it is merchandised. The test is available only to those who have completed a special training course given by the consulting firm that publishes it. This means that independent validity studies conducted by individuals other than members of the consulting firm are few and far between, especially in proportion to the widespread use the test has had in industry.

The measure itself consists of a list of eighty-one adjectives, all generally favorable in nature. The subject is to check those he believes have been used by others to describe him, and also those he truthfully feels are descriptive of him. The words checked are then scored to yield indexes of aggressiveness, sociability, emotional control, social adaptability, and activity. This is, of course, a self-report technique *par excellence.* Unfortunately, it is also one that does little to control job-related bias. In the selection situation, the applicant can easily emphasize those adjectives that appear to be associated with success in the particular job under consideration. If he is right, he will be hired; if not, he will not be. In either case, very little information is obtained about the kind of person he really is.

AVA has failed to correlate with performance criteria in a number of instances, but there have also been some very good validities reported. The research underlying these validities has been severely questioned (9,19). These studies, however, are no more deficient relative to the longitudinal prediction model than are those carried out with several other widely used tests, ability as well as personality. Perfectly controlled, predictive validity studies are not easy to conduct in industry, and AVA has not really proved itself one way or the other. Thus, it is not possible to say whether AVA can be a valuable selection tool, although on the surface it would appear to be rather bias-prone. Unfortunately, this sense of uncertainty is unlikely to be lifted as long as the test and the research on it continue to be rigidly controlled by a single consulting firm.

PROJECTIVE TECHNIQUES

The projective procedures approach the problem of bias very differently than the self-report techniques. A projective test is constructed so that the uninformed person cannot determine what is being measured. The subject simply does not know what he is revealing about himself when he responds to a test item. As a consequence, he cannot bias his response so as to present a socially desirable picture or a picture congruent with job expectations.

In theory, at least, this would appear to be the ideal solution to the bias problem. The subject does not describe himself; he reacts, and by reacting in a particular manner reveals what type of person he is. In practice, however, this approach has encountered sizable difficulties. The very procedures that keep the subject from understanding his own responses also make it difficult for the test administrator to understand them. The projective approach in conquering the bias problem introduces the new problem of interpretation. Work with techniques such as the Rorschach Test, the Thematic Apperception Test, the Rosenzweig Picture-Frustration Study, the various sentence completion measures, the Tomkins-Horn Picture Arrangement Test, and the Worthington Personal History has resulted in some real progress in this area recently. Yet, there is no question that more must be learned about the various ways people reveal themselves through their test responses before the projective tests can achieve their full potentiality as personnel selection techniques.

The Thematic Apperception Technique. The Thematic Apperception Test (TAT) as originally developed contained twenty pictures, many of them quite ambiguous. In many instances, however, fewer pictures are employed, especially in the industrial situation. Furthermore, a number of special versions of the TAT have been conceived, often using pictures of a much clearer and more structured nature than those in the original test. In all instances, however, the subject is asked to tell a story using the picture as a starting point. He is to describe the people, tell what is happening, and develop both the past and the future of the scene depicted. Because he must go beyond the picture itself, his own personal imaginative and fantasy processes are brought into play.

Very little evidence is available regarding the relationship between the TAT in its original form and job performance. Furthermore, although the test may be given in a group situation with the subjects writing their stories, analysis remains a time-consuming process. For these reasons, the original TAT cannot be recommended as a selection technique under most circumstances.

On the other hand, research has been done with certain special versions of the technique, and relatively simple objective scoring systems have been developed. A set of pictures selected to measure a desire for achievement has been found to produce responses that can be scored rapidly, with minimal error. This achievement motivation measure yields consistent relationships with various indexes of managerial success in this country and abroad, but it does not appear to be a valid predictor of sales performance (21).

Another approach closely related to the TAT is the Tomkins-Horn Picture Arrangement Test (PAT). In this test, the subject is presented with three pictures at a time, which he must arrange to produce a sequence that makes a logical story. The brief story describing this pattern of events is written below the pictures. There are twenty-five such items.

As indicated in Table 7–5, the PAT can yield very satisfactory validities. In the case of the petroleum product salesmen, success was associated with such characteristics as perennial happiness, dependence, self-confidence, and a desire for social interaction (26). Among the tabulating machine operators, whose performance was measured by paired comparison ratings made some nine months after testing, the major predictors were measures of conformity and strong work motivation (25).

The Rorschach Technique. Like the TAT, the Rorschach has emerged in a variety of forms over the years, although still retaining its essential character (the ink blot). In its original version, it contained ten cards, each with a single ink blot in black, white, and gray or in various colors. The subject is to describe what he sees in the blot, and as many responses are recorded as produced. Normally, testing is done individually and a so-called *inquiry* is appended, during which the subject goes back over his responses and indicates his reasons for selecting the particular descriptions—i.e., what about the blot led him to a given conclusion. The test

TABLE 7–5. Validity Data for the Tomkins-Horn
Picture Arrangement Test

Criterion measures	Concurrent validity (65 petroleum product salesmen)	Predictive validity (58 tabulating machine operators)
Sales figures		
Gasoline	.56	
Motor oil	.46	
Tires, batteries, and so on	.33	
All products	.58	
Supervisory ratings		
Cooperation		.43
Application		.50
Accuracy		.69
Speed		.40
Overall effectiveness		.61

Source: J. B. Miner, "The Validity of the PAT in the Selection of Tabulating Machine Operators: An Analysis of Predictive Power," *Journal of Projective Techniques*, Vol. 25 (1961), p. 331; and J. B. Miner, "Personality and Ability Factors in Sales Performance," *Journal of Applied Psychology*, Vol. 46 (1962), p. 10.

may also be administered on a group basis with the subjects writing their responses.

Because of the ambiguous nature of the stimulus forms, an almost infinite variety of descriptions is possible, depending on what the subject projects into the blots from his own personality. Bias, in the sense of consciously predetermining the personality portrait that will emerge, is almost impossible. However, because of the ambiguity of the blots, interpretation is also extremely difficult. For this reason, it is easy for the inexperienced person to reach incorrect conclusions about an applicant from his Rorschach responses. The individual making the interpretations has only a limited amount to go on.

With lower level employees, the Rorschach technique has not proved very effective, but recent studies involving managers suggest that validity can be quite good. In one instance, company officers who had continued to progress in their careers were compared with a group who had been demoted or fired (30). The successful executives were found to possess strong power motivation, foresight, self-confidence, a desire to cooperate and compete within the rules, the ability to integrate their activities toward a specific goal, a capacity for rapid mental productivity, and controlled aggressiveness. Research conducted with managers at lower levels suggests that many of these characteristics are associated with success there also (17).

The Sentence Completion Technique. Sentence completion tests, of which there are a number available, present a series of verbal stems, or beginnings of sentences, that the subject is asked to complete. Usually, there is an additional request that in finishing the sentences the subject express his real feelings. Although some of the items may elicit completions of a self-report nature, the tests are usually constructed so that inferences regarding personality characteristics can be made in terms of the symbolic significance of the responses. Thus, the self-reports are not accepted at face value.

Although validity studies are not extensive, there is reason to believe this technique may prove very valuable as a selection device. Unlike the other projectives discussed, it is both easy to administer and to score. In one instance, as indicated in Table 7–6, a sentence completion measure

TABLE 7–6. Relationships Between Sentence-Completion Indexes and Accident Rates ($N = 34$)

Sentence-completion variable	r
Optimism	−.34
Trust	−.51
Sociocentricity	−.76
Pessimism	−.19
Distrust	.02
Anxiety	.09
Egocentricity	.19
Resentment	.29
Negative employment attitude	.70

Source: A. Davids and J. T. Mahoney, "Personality Dynamics and Accident-Proneness in an Industrial Setting," *Journal of Applied Psychology*, Vol. 41 (1957), p. 304.

yields very good concurrent validity when related to accident rates. The industrial workers with frequent accidents were significantly less optimistic, trusting, and sociable. They also had a more negative employment attitude (7). Other studies with the Miner Sentence Completion Scale, which has been devised specifically for use with management personnel, have indicated consistently that this instrument has both predictive and concurrent validity when used with managerial groups (27,28). This test, like a number of other projective measures, may be scored so as to eliminate any tendency to give socially desirable responses.

GENERAL PATTERN OF VALIDITIES: PERSONALITY

Studies relating personality measures, whether self-report or projective, to indexes of success during the training period have almost uniformly yielded disappointing results (13). In those groups where any sizable amount of research has been done, which includes clerical, protective service, skilled, and semiskilled occupations, the reported validities have consistently been well below those obtained with certain types of ability measures.

When the focus shifts to on-the-job performance, this picture changes. Managerial success is best predicted by clerical and general intelligence tests, but personality measures are nearly as effective. With foremen, however, the personality measures do not do so well as those tapping various abilities.

Among clerical employees, the personality measures again come right behind the intelligence and clerical tests. Whereas personality factors appear to make little difference, relatively, in clerical training, they contribute to actual job performance in almost as great proportion as the most relevant abilities. It is in the sales area, however, that personality tests have proven most useful, primarily because here their contribution is almost unique. Ability measures appear to have little relationship to sales success, except for the intelligence measures among those in higher level sales positions. Personality measures, on the other hand, have consistently turned out to be good predictors at all levels of sales employment. Among sales clerks, they are the only kind of test that yields positive relationships at all.

Within the various service occupations, personality tests, although not nearly so effective as in the sales area, achieve validities generally superior to those reported for ability measures. They offer the best prospects as selection instruments (with the exception of intelligence tests for the protective service occupations), although still failing to achieve desired predictive levels, especially in the personal service area.

Job performance in industrial occupations generally is no better predicted by personality measures than ability measures, with one major exception. At the unskilled level, personality tests are by far the most valid selection techniques. This is probably because emotionally disturbed individuals tend to gravitate to unskilled jobs, if they remain in the labor force at all (29). The personality tests presumably pick out those who have little prospect of continued employment within this group, i.e., those who are the most severely disturbed.

In general, personality measures can make a valuable contribution to the selection process. When ranked in terms of validity levels, along with the four types of ability measures, across the ten occupational groups compared, they vie with the intelligence tests for first place (13). Among sales clerks, personal service workers, and the unskilled, they are the best predictors; the validities obtained with managers and salesmen generally recommend their use there as well.

Skills and Achievements

Measures of this kind are derived directly from the job and thus tend to be specific to the occupation for which selection is to occur. Either a job sample is developed as with the various typing and stenographic tests, or a series of questions are asked regarding the job. In some instances, tests of this type are available on a commercial basis, but it is also common practice to construct home-grown measures specifically suited to the needs of a particular company.

JOB SAMPLING PROCEDURES

Tests of this kind are feasible only where the role prescriptions for a job form a rather homogeneous unit. If the job is complex, requiring a great many different types of activities, all of which are equally important to success, any truly inclusive job sample test would be so lengthy and cumbersome that its use in a selection battery would not be expedient. Even with the more homogeneous jobs most such tests tend to be only similar to the actual work situation and not exact duplicates of it (18).

In addition, job sample testing must be restricted either to positions designed with rather simple role requirements or for which only previously trained or experienced applicants are hired. Testing a group of inexperienced individuals on a complex job sample is of little value, because all will obtain low scores. Under such circumstances, ability measures are much more likely to discriminate within the group and predict which individuals will learn rapidly and achieve job success.

A number of firms have developed job sample tests for skilled and semiskilled positions. In some instances, special equipment simulating that used on the job has been constructed. In other cases, a standardized test situation utilizing actual equipment is employed. In any event, it is crucial that all those tested be required to perform the same tasks under the same conditions in the same period of time. Job samples of this kind have been developed for a variety of positions in such areas as punch press operation, inspection, packaging, fork-lift operation, truck driving, and certain kinds of special machine operation (34).

Job sampling procedures have also had widespread use in the clerical field. Here, where jobs tend to be highly standardized across a great many firms, regular commercial tests are much more common than for blue-collar workers. Among those available are the Blackstone Stenographic Proficiency Tests, the Thurstone Examination in Typing, and the Seashore-Bennett Stenographic Proficiency Tests. These require that applicants take dictation and/or type, using materials that are the same for everybody. Scoring procedures have been worked out, and the scores obtained by a given applicant can be compared with those for a large number of clerical workers who have taken the test.

Although managerial work is generally less suitable for job sampling, certain aspects of the job have been simulated with some success. Typical is the In-Basket Test, which requires that various items in an in-basket be handled under controlled conditions. Scores derived from the test are positively correlated with over-all managerial effectiveness (2,20).

Although the job sampling approach is used most widely to screen initial applicants, especially those who have gone through apprenticeship, vocational, or secretarial training programs, it is also used in connection with promotions. Job sample tests have proved particularly valuable in those instances where the union contract limits the promotion process. If, for instance, the contract says seniority shall govern, provided the senior man is qualified to perform the higher level job, it is important to determine whether he is qualified. Job samples can be very helpful in this regard. In other cases, management has more freedom of action and can promote the most qualified man provided, however, that where capability is equal the senior man will be moved up. Here, also, the level of qualification can best be demonstrated with a job sample test. The advantage of using job samples in these situations is that they are predictive of subsequent performance, *and* are usually acceptable to the union. An equally valid projective personality measure, on the other hand, would normally be of much less value for this purpose, because of the *apparent* disparity between the test and the job.

ACHIEVEMENT TESTS

Achievement tests differ from job samples in that they deal with the knowledge or information required to perform a job. Instead of demonstrating his skill, the applicant answers written or oral questions about the work. There is, of course, considerable overlap between the two procedures.

Measures of this kind are useful in discriminating between those who are and are not qualified to perform a given type of work. Because they are relatively easy to construct and administer, they are usually more appropriate for this purpose than job samples. It is not at all uncommon for a job applicant to claim prior work experience as a carpenter, machinist, engineer, or accountant when he has performed in a less skilled capacity. Either the man intends to bluff his way into a higher level position or there is some ambiguity in the true meaning of the occupational title. In any event, a test of job knowledge can be very helpful.

So-called *trade tests* have been developed along these lines by the U.S. Employment Service for a number of skilled occupations. These are oral tests, usually containing fifteen questions. The questions are selected by administering a much larger number of questions to three groups of workers: journeymen, apprentices and helpers in the trade, and individuals employed outside the trade in positions that are part of the same job family. A good question, one that is retained in the final test, should yield consistently correct responses in the first group, and practically no correct responses in the third group. When a number of questions of this kind are put together in a test, experienced journeymen can easily be identified, because they will obtain total scores at a level almost never obtained by those in the other two groups.

Tests of this type have also demonstrated considerable validity as predictors of the degree to which an individual's role behavior actually matches the role prescriptions for a job. In one such study, a test containing twenty-one questions, selected from an original pool of ninety-five as being most discriminative, was found to yield good predictions against supervisory ratings of machinists in a shipyard (22). Among those rated above average, 75 per cent had thirteen or more questions right. Among those rated below average, only 10 per cent achieved this score.

Achievement testing need not be restricted to short oral tests. Written tests have been developed by a number of firms for a range of positions. In addition, tests of accounting knowledge, policies and procedures, human relations, business law, economics, and so on, which cover segments of a job rather than the totality of information required, have been constructed.

Although, in general, achievement measures are constructed to fit the company's own needs, some commercial tests are available. The Occupational Research Center at Purdue University has developed a number of these for the skilled trades. These measure information regarding such occupations as electrician, lathe operator, carpenter, sheet-metal worker, and welder. In addition, more specific tests deal with industrial mathematics, blueprint reading, and scale reading.

Ethical Considerations in Human Measurement

Throughout this chapter, a considerable amount of evidence regarding the validity of various measurement procedures has been presented. There is little doubt that selection tools of the type described can regulate the human input to an organization in such a way as to make a very sizable contribution to goal attainment. A recent review of the literature indicates that validity coefficients on the order of .60 for training criteria and .45 for job performance criteria can be anticipated when an appropriate fit between some test and job requirements is established. These figures apply when a single measure is used. If multiple predictors are employed and combined to yield a multiple correlation coefficient, values of a considerably higher order can be obtained (13). Thus, given adequate research both in the area of test construction and in test selection, it is possible for management to contribute a great deal both toward productivity and to organizational maintenance through the use of psychological tests. The tests do work; not perfectly, but they still work.

Further evidence on this point, in dollar and cents terms, comes from a study carried out on the selection of telephone operators in the San Francisco area (31). A test battery containing numerical and clerical ability measures was used as a predictor. The training savings for operators who would have failed if they had been hired were calculated. The figures presented below correct these training savings for the additional recruiting costs the tests introduce. Scores on the test battery may range from 0 to 80, and the minimum score for hiring could, of course, be set at any point between, depending on the availability of applicants in the labor market and the degree of selectivity desired. This study was published in 1956, and it can be assumed that the savings would be greater today.

Minimum Score for Hiring	Net Saving
30	$ 8,000
40	35,000
50	47,000
60	50,000

It is apparent from these data that good selection procedures developed with reference to organizationally meaningful criteria can yield very sizable savings. The strength of human measurement techniques in selection is that, when correctly validated, they place primary emphasis on merit rather than on the biases and moods of the person doing the selection (8).

It is true, of coure, that measurement may contribute to a selection process that emphasizes conformity, as some people have contended. Whether this is the case depends on the role prescriptions for the job under consideration. In some instances, perhaps among such people as inspectors, typists, and certain kinds of machine operators, conformity may well be a valued quality contributing to success. In other cases, it is clear that it is not. There are, in fact, studies providing clear evidence that nonconformity can be valued in some occupations—within certain managerial groups (11,27) and among research scientists (6). Psychological tests, correctly used, can predict success and contribution to company goals. If success in certain jobs requires conformity, then the tests may well select conformists. If success requires nonconformity, they will select nonconformists.

THE INVASION OF PRIVACY QUESTION

In spite of these obvious contributions to profitability, industry generally has been under considerable pressure to give up selection testing. Several major companies have actually done so, usually as a result of policy decisions made outside the personnel function. Several congressional investigations have been conducted with a view to constraining the use of psychological tests, although no legislation has been passed. A number of books and articles, in recent years, also have attacked the use of tests.

A major concern in all these instances is that selection testing, especially personality testing, represents an invasion of privacy. Individuals are asked to reveal things that they might not wish to reveal. They often do not even known what they are revealing about themselves. Information obtained through selection testing is not held to a confidential psychologist-applicant relationship, but imparted to a third party, the company's management. These actions are felt to be unethical. Those who attack testing and who feel that perhaps legal constraints should be imposed believe that individual freedoms are being violated.

On the other side, employers do need information about applicants. We would certainly not expect companies to hire at random from among those in an applicant pool. We consider it proper that those who will contribute the most to an organization should be selected for membership. To do this, information must be collected so that the potential contributors can be identified.

In some ways, it is surprising that psychological testing has aroused such heated controversy when other selection tools, often with much less evidence of validity, have been accepted with very little question. The interview, application blanks, reference checks, and physical examination all are subject potentially to the invasion of privacy criticism. Yet only the physical examination has been questioned, and that only on the grounds that there is in the pre-employment physical examination situation a violation of the confidential physician-patient relationship, because the results are given to management.

What seems not to be clearly understood is that the selection situation is not synonomous with the physician-patient or lawyer-client relationship. It is not the applicant who wants information or assistance, but the company. Furthermore, the applicant is aware of the purpose of the various selection procedures. If he takes a test, he recognizes that this experience is germane to his being considered for employment. In this sense, selection testing is a far cry from such activities as wire-tapping, searching a home without a warrant, or opening personal mail, with which it has been compared (12). The applicant presumably wants something from the potential employer and understands quite clearly that he must provide certain information in order to get what he wants. He trades information about himself for the opportunity of being hired. This is a long way from coercion, and it is coerced invasion of privacy, where the individual has no choice, that is normally considered unethical.

This is not to say that information obtained from psychological tests, or physical examinations, or other selection tools, cannot be misused by unscrupulous individuals. There are important security problems here, and there can be a major ethical problem as well, if information is used for some purpose other than that anticipated by the applicant, i.e., the evaluation of his qualifications for employment. To protect the public against such misuse of tests, psychologists have devoted considerable time and energy to the formulation and the enforcement of appropriate ethical controls (3). There is reason to believe that these efforts have achieved a considerable measure of success.

REFERENCES

1. Balinsky, B., and H. W. Shaw, "The Contribution of the WAIS to a Management Appraisal Program," *Personnel Psychology*, Vol. 9 (1956), 207–209.
2. Bray, D. W., and D. L. Grant, "The Assessment Center in the Measurement of Potential for Business Management," *Psychological Monographs*, Vol. 80 (1966), No. 17, 1–27.
3. Brayfield, A. H., "Testimony Before the Senate Subcommittee on Constitutional Rights of the Committee on the Judiciary," *American Psychologist*, Vol. 20 (1965), 888–898.
4. Buros, O. K. (ed.), *The Sixth Mental Measurements Yearbook*. Highland Park, N.J.: Gryphon, 1965.
5. Cronbach, L. J., *Essentials of Psychological Testing*. New York: Harper & Row, 1960.
6. Crutchfield, R. S., "Conformity and Creative Thinking," in H. E. Gruber, G. Terrell, and M. Wertheimer (eds.), *Contemporary Approaches to Creative Thinking*. New York: Atherton, 1962, pp. 120–140.
7. Davids, A., and J. T. Mahoney, "Personality Dynamics and Accident-Proneness in an Industrial Setting," *Journal of Applied Psychology*, Vol. 41 (1957), 303–306.
8. Dunnette, M. D., "Critics of Psychological Tests: Basic Assumptions: How Good?", *Psychology in the Schools*, Vol. 1 (1964), 63–69.
9. Dunnette, M. D., and W. K. Kirchner, "Validities, Vectors, and Verities," *Journal of Applied Psychology*, Vol. 46 (1962), 296–299.
10. Dvorak, B. J., "Development of Occupational Norms," in W. L. Barnette (ed.), *Readings in Psychological Tests and Measurements*. Homewood, Ill.: Dorsey, 1964, pp. 132–144.
11. Fleishman, E. A., and D. R. Peters, "Interpersonal Values, Leadership Attitudes, and Managerial Success," *Personnel Psychology*, Vol. 15 (1962), 127–143.
12. Gallagher, C. E., "Why House Hearings on Invasion of Privacy," *American Psychologist*, Vol. 20 (1965), 881–882.
13. Ghiselli, E. E., *The Validity of Occupational Aptitude Tests*. New York: Wiley, 1966.
14. Green, R. F., "Does a Selection Situation Induce Testees to Bias Their Answers on Interest and Temperament Tests?" *Educational and Psychological Measurement*, Vol. 11 (1951), 503–515.
15. Guion, R. M., *Personnel Testing*. New York: McGraw-Hill, 1965.
16. Guion, R. M., and R. F. Gottier, "Validity of Personality Measures in Personnel Selection," *Personnel Psychology*, Vol. 18 (1965), 135–164.
17. Hicks, J. A., and J. B. Stone, "The Identification of Traits Related to Managerial Success," *Journal of Applied Psychology*, Vol. 46 (1962), 428–432.
18. Lawshe, C. H., and M. J. Balma, *Principles of Personnel Testing*, 2nd ed. New York: McGraw-Hill, 1966.
19. Locke, E. A., and C. L. Hulin, "A Review and Evaluation of the Validity

Studies of Activity Vector Analysis," *Personnel Psychology*, Vol. 15 (1962), 25–42.

20. Lopez, F. M., *Evaluating Executive Decision-Making: The In-Basket Technique*. American Management Association Research Study No. 75, 1966.

21. McClelland, D. C., *The Achieving Society*. Princeton, N.J.: Van Nostrand, 1961.

22. McCormick, E. J., and N. B. Winstanley, "A Fifteen-Minute Oral Trade Test," *Personnel*, Vol. 27 (1950), 144–146.

23. Miner, J. B., "The Kuder Preference Record in Management Appraisal," *Personnel Psychology*, Vol. 13 (1960), 187–196.

24. Miner, J. B., "On the Use of a Short Vocabulary Test to Measure General Intelligence," *Journal of Educational Psychology*, Vol. 52 (1961), 157–160.

25. Miner, J. B., "The Validity of the PAT in the Selection of Tabulating Machine Operators: An Analysis of Predictive Power," *Journal of Projective Techniques*, Vol. 25 (1961), 330–333.

26. Miner, J. B., "Personality and Ability Factors in Sales Performance," *Journal of Applied Psychology*, Vol. 46 (1962), 6–13.

27. Miner, J. B., *Studies in Management Education*. New York: Springer, 1965.

28. Miner, J. B., "The Prediction of Managerial and Research Success," *Personnel Administration*, Vol. 28 (1965), No. 5, 12–16.

29. Miner, J. B., and J. K. Anderson, "The Postwar Occupational Adjustment of Emotionally Disturbed Soldiers," *Journal of Applied Psychology*, Vol. 42 (1958), 317–322.

30. Piotrowski, Z. A., and M. R. Rock, *The Perceptanalytic Executive Scale*. New York: Grune & Stratton, 1963.

QUESTIONS

1. You have been asked to develop selection test batteries for the occupations listed below. What specific tests would you try out initially in each instance in your search for valid predictors of on-the-job performance? Explain why you would select each test in each battery.
    1. File clerk
    2. Insurance salesman
    3. Plant manager
    4. Retail sales clerk
    5. Plant guard
    6. Laborer
2. What are the strengths and weaknesses, the advantages and disadvantages, of the following as selection tests?
    1. Wechsler Adult Intelligence Scale
    2. A short vocabulary test
    3. MacQuarrie Test of Mechanical Ability
    4. Activity Vector Analysis
    5. Thematic Apperception Test
    6. Thurstone Examination in Typing
3. Are psychological tests a "good thing" insofar as personnel selection is concerned?

8

Management
Development

Chapters 8 through 13, discuss the various personnel techniques that mediate between the human inputs to a firm and the behavioral outputs that contribute to goal attainment. The primary intent in using these techniques is to change and improve the input so as to maximize the amount of productivity and profit and, at the same time, to ensure the stability of the organization. In some instances, however, mediators merely sustain the effective functioning of the input against forces that otherwise might reduce drastically the level of output. Thus, the most efficient company is the one that selects the best applicants; introduces mediating techniques that, at least, maintain and, ideally, improve on the quality of this input, while also inducing members to devote their greatest efforts toward achieving the organization's goals. Mediators, along with selection procedures, at least partially overcome the constraints imposed by individual differences.

Chapter 3, in dealing with organization planning and job analysis, was concerned with mediators just as much as the following chapters. Organization structures and job descriptions define role requirements. These requirements are constituted to produce a maximal total effort for the organization by its members. Thus, role prescriptions are established to improve or maximize the manner in which those who are selected for employment contribute. This, of course, is what any mediating technique is expected to do.

The only difference between organization planning or job analysis and the mediators to be discussed now is that the former two are basically *structural* in nature. They deal with the way in which the organization is put together. In this and subsequent chapters, on the other hand, we will be concerned with what might best be called *functional* mediators. These latter are processes or subfunctions within the total personnel process, which are carried out on a continuing basis in order to ensure that role behaviors match the role prescriptions established by organization planning and job analysis to the maximum degree.

Chapters 8 through 11 discuss the functional mediators oriented primarily toward the productivity goal. Chapters 12 and 13 discuss the functional mediators oriented toward organizational maintenance. Payment systems, however, are probably more appropriately considered as primarily productivity oriented. Although the classification in terms of the type of company goal served is generally appropriate, there are instances where the categorization must be considered somewhat arbitrary. For example, management development activities are in most cases intended to increase the over-all productivity of the organization, but there are certain types of management development procedures that appear to be directed primarily toward the reduction of conflict within managerial ranks, thus ameliorating internal stresses.

Chapters 8 and 9 are concerned with the various educational techniques used to raise the level of performance of organization members. This may be achieved either by providing new knowledge and information relevant to a job, by teaching new skills of a psychomotor nature, or by imbuing an individual with new attitudes, values, motives, and other personality characteristics. Often these techniques are utilized with segments of a work force irrespective of the existing performance level. A given work group or managerial component may be given a particular course with a view to improving the role behavior of all members, the outstanding as well as the less effective. On occasion, however, training is focused on those who, because they are new to the type of work or for other reasons, are not immediately in a position to achieve a successful level of performance.

As has been the custom previously, with discussions of procedures for developing role prescriptions and of methods used to evaluate organization members, a split will be made in terms of the company hierarchy. The present chapter deals with training techniques normally used with managerial and other employees in the upper segment of the organization. Chapter 9 directs itself to employees at lower levels.

Evaluation of Change Models

When a new selection procedure is introduced it should be validated against existing criteria of success in the organization; so too a new training program should be studied to determine whether it really is contributing to improved performance. There is a strong temptation to avoid this step, because there is a possibility that the program will turn out to have been worthless, thus wasting a good deal of time and money. Yet, from an over-all, company viewpoint, evaluation is essential, if there is any prospect that the same or a similar course might be repeated in the future. As with validity studies in selection, however, there are cost considerations. Validation makes sense only if enough people are to be hired for the particular type of work to justify the expense of the research. Similarly, training evaluation is warranted only when a sufficient number of people are to be trained in a particular way.

It is important, in any event, that a personnel psychologist be capable of carrying out change evaluation studies on his own programs when appropriate and that he be familiar with the studies that have been done by others on the various types of courses that he may be considering. This necessitates a sufficient knowledge of the logic of evaluation to permit discrimination between a good study and a bad one. The discussion that follows should provide this knowledge. In addition, it introduces a basis for determining the effectiveness of the various development techniques to be considered later in this chapter.

THE BEFORE-AFTER MODEL

The basic question that may be asked with regard to any training effort is whether it, in fact, yields a change in the people exposed to it. Normally, an experimental design for answering this question would involve a pretest, exposure to training, and a posttest. The pre- and post-measurements are made using indexes related to what the course is expected to accomplish. An attempt to improve understanding of company policies would presumably be evaluated by using a test of knowledge regarding policy before the course started, and the same or a similar test afterward. Should there be a statistically reliable increase in score for the group as a whole from pretest to posttest, this would provide the type of evidence for change that permits generalization to other applications of the same course.

It would still remain, however, to demonstrate that such a change had been caused by the course itself, and not by some external factor. For instance, it might be that the change in knowledge of policy actually resulted not so much from the training as from the fact that a revised policy manual was issued to all management personnel shortly after the course started. To check on this possibility, one would have to carry out the same pretest-posttest procedure on a *control group,* consisting of managers like those exposed to training, but different in that they did not take the course in company policy. Should this control group increase in knowledge of policy as much as the *experimental group,* who had had the course, this would support the view that some extra-training factor such as the new manual was the major cause of change. On the other hand, a statistically reliable increase in knowledge in the experimental group coupled with a complete lack of change in the control group would support the position that the training was achieving its objective.

In selecting a control group, it is important to use people as similar to those in the experimental group as possible and with the same types of experiences over the period of training. The only difference should be that one group is exposed to the course and the other is not. To demonstrate that the training has been effective, one must show that the addition of this single factor to one of two otherwise similar groups is sufficient to create a real difference at some later point in time. This before-after model is outlined in Figure 8–1.

Group   Time 1   Intervening Period   Time 2

Experimental   Pretest ⟶ Course ⟶ Posttest

Control   Pretest ⟶ Posttest

Figure 8–1.

THE AFTER ONLY MODEL

An alternative approach that offers certain advantages, as well as disadvantages, is outlined in Figure 8–2. Here the experimental and control groups are selected as with the before-after approach, but only posttests are administered. Change is presumed to have occurred if there is a statistically significant difference between the two groups at the time the measurement occurs. This assumes, of course, that the two groups were identical originally.

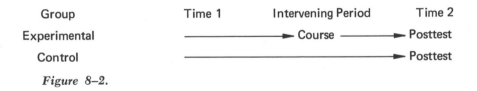

Group   Time 1   Intervening Period   Time 2

Experimental   ⟶ Course ⟶ Posttest

Control   ⟶ Posttest

Figure 8–2.

The problem is that in most ongoing business situations it is extremely difficult to determine whether identical groups have been selected, without employing a pretest to be sure. There is always the possibility, when the after only model is used, that any differences between the two groups established after training might have been present before. What appears to be change might only be a long-standing group difference.

The simplicity of the after only design is appealing, and there are circumstances under which one can feel reasonably confident that relatively good initial matching has occurred. Thus, this approach is used on occasion, although probably not so frequently as the before-after model. It has the additional advantage that there is no possibility of a pretest sensitizing those who take the course to certain specific aspects of the training. Managers may learn certain things only because they get the impression from a pretest that they should learn these particular things. The posttest reveals a change. But in subsequent administrations of the course, without a pretest (or posttest either for that matter), this learning does not occur, and the change can well be negligible. The after only design avoids this source of error.

This pretest sensitizing effect seems to be a real problem primarily when knowledge changes are being evaluated (17), and when the measures used contain items practically identical to material covered in training. In such cases, the ideal evaluation design is a combination of the before-after and after only approaches using at least three groups. This permits the identification of any pseudochanges, resulting from the sensitizing effects of a pretest, through a comparison of the two experimental groups taking the course. Unfortunately, studies that eliminate practically all sources of error are rarely conducted. They are too complex and require more subjects for inclusion in the various experimental and control conditions than are normally available.

THE RETENTION AND ORGANIZATIONAL
RELEVANCE FACTORS

Although the demonstration of a change caused by the educational process is the first step in any evaluation study, this is not all that is required. To be of value to a company, the change must be retained, and it must clearly contribute to goal attainment.

Retention is normally determined by taking a third measurement well after training has been completed, perhaps as long as a year later. Or the posttest itself may be delayed so that retention and change are measured at one and the same time. In the latter instance, if a pretest-posttest change is not found, there is no way of knowing whether the course was totally ineffective or a real change was vitiated by events occurring subsequent to training.

It is clear that such vitiation of change does occur. The consequence is what has been termed *encapsulated training* (11). Within the education situation itself, considerable change occurs, but none of this is actually carried back to the job. Because the training process eventually is terminated, all change will inevitably disappear.

This type of encapsulation seems to be particularly frequent when there is a disparity between the actual role prescriptions for the job and those taught in the course. Management development may emphasize being kind and considerate toward subordinates, whereas the established role prescriptions for a manager, which are enforced by his superiors, emphasize pressure for production and the frequent use of negative sanctions. One solution to the dilemma thus produced is to accept the training values, but only for purposes of training—not back on the job. Because the whole reward structure built around the job is calculated to obtain a close match between role behavior and the established role prescriptions, and because the training emphasis if incorporated in behavior would tend to widen this gap and thus reduce the chances of being considered a success, the manager is careful not to let any training effects manifest themselves in the actual work situation.

Another type of reaction may occur, however, when the role requirements presented in the training situation are distinctly different from those characterizing the job situation. On occasion, the two sets of expectations are carried into the work environment together, with the result that the manager does not know what he is supposed to do and what kind of behavior will be considered as evidence of success. The result is *role conflict* (14). Under such circumstances, the changes produced by training are retained, but at considerable cost to the individual in terms of anxiety and confusion. The consequence for the organization is likely to be internal conflict and, in many cases, the eventual loss of a potentially valuable manager.

The solution to problems of encapsulated training and training-produced role conflict is to be sure that the role requirements taught in the course and those existing in the job situation do not diverge. This can be accomplished by synchronizing the course with existing role prescriptions. When this is done, it can be assumed that the training will be reinforced by subsequent work experiences and changes will be retained. If, on the other hand, the training is intended to introduce alternative role prescriptions and thus move managerial behavior toward a new pattern of expectations, the new role prescriptions should be made part of the job context as well. The changes should be organizational in nature and not restricted to a given management development experience. For this reason, most training directors first attempt to expose the company's top management to any course emphasizing new role prescriptions. They work down through the successive levels of the hierarchy. In this way, a climate favorable to the new behaviors is created from the outset, and retention of change is fostered.

Measuring Organizational Relevance. The final step in the evaluation model, and one that is far too often neglected, ties the change to organizational goals, or to the role prescriptions that mediate goal attainment. Thus, if a knowledge change is produced, it must be demonstrated that the knowledge actually helps those who possess it to perform more effectively. If a change in attitudes occurs, there must be reason to believe these attitudes are associated with job success.

Methods of accomplishing this final step vary considerably. The ideal procedure is to use various judgmental or objective appraisal measures at pretest and posttest. The profit performance of cost centers or the turnover rate in work groups pre- and post-training might be compared. Or ratings might be obtained from superiors at the two points in time. Unfortunately, obtaining comparable objective measures for all members of both experimental and control groups is often difficult. When ratings are obtained from superiors who know the composition of experimental and control groups, the possibility of bias is pronounced. The wish, even though entirely unconscious, to justify the decision to invest in a training program may well distort the posttest evaluations in favor of the experimental group.

For these reasons, it has become common practice to use various tests, attitude measures, and the like as pretest and posttest measures. These must, however, have a positive relationship with success on the job. Validity studies, in many cases predictive validity studies, must be carried out. (The models discussed in Chapter 6 are appropriate for this purpose.) The point is that there must be good reason to believe that the development procedure has moved a number of individuals along some dimension that is known to yield positively valued role behavior.

Human Relations and Sensitivity Training

Although the human relations programs had their origins in the Hawthorne studies of the post-World War I period, research on democratic leadership, during and immediately after World War II, actually sparked their widespread application. Since these beginnings, the programs have consistently emphasized the crucial significance of consideration and kindness as part of the supervisory process.

Originally, the view was that through human relations training a more satisfied employee group could be achieved, with the result that productivity would increase. In basic conception, the programs were intended to foster productivity and profit. In all probability, they do contribute to this goal indirectly through a reduction in strikes, slowdowns, and the like. But it is also true that there is no necessary direct relationship between job satisfaction and productive output. Recognition of this gradually has led to a reconceptualization of the role of human relations training. Increasingly, such programs are viewed as valuable for their specific contribution to reduced conflict within the organization and thus to the maintenance objective alone. At the same time, however, other more productivity-oriented subject matter has been added to the specifically human relations content.

The "human relations package" now may include such topics as safety, production control, union contract administration, company policies, cost control, economics, company organization, job evaluation, methods improvement, and incentive payment, as well as the more typical material on employee motivation and attitudes, group dynamics, communications, counseling and democratic leadership. In this comprehensive form, the human relations program is clearly directed toward both productivity and maintenance considerations.

The Results of Evaluation. Rather consistently, training of this kind has been effective in producing change—in knowledge, in attitudes, and in leadership behaviors (25). However, such research as has been done suggests that there is a very considerable risk involved. There is no question that human relations training can become encapsulated or can produce role conflict. The emphasis on consideration and democratic procedures may be inconsistent with existing role prescriptions.

Evidence of the change-producing potential of these courses is contained in Table 8–1. On both the knowledge measures, the Personnel

TABLE 8–1. Pretest-Posttest Changes for Groups that Did (Experimental) and Did Not (Control) Take a Human Relations Course

Measure		Experimental group means (N = 94)	Control group means (N = 24)
Personnel Relations	Pretest:	21.2	24.1
Test	Posttest:	25.0	25.3
How Supervise?	Pretest:	58.5	62.5
Test	Posttest:	64.4	61.9
Leadership Opinion Questionnaire			
Initiating Structure	Pretest:	54.8	52.0
	Posttest:	52.0	48.5
Consideration	Pretest:	56.3	58.0
	Posttest:	60.0	56.5
Prediction of Human Reactions	Pretest:	47.7	48.6
Test	Posttest:	50.0	47.2

Source: F. J. DiVesta, "Instructor-Centered and Student-Centered Approaches in Teaching a Human Relations Course," *Journal of Applied Psychology*, Vol. 38 (1954), p. 331.

Relations Test and How Supervise?, the experimental group showed a statistically reliable increase, whereas the control group did not. On the Leadership Opinion Questionnaire, both groups decreased in Initiating Structure. Presumably, this indicates that the school environment, to which both the experimental and the control subjects were exposed, produced a less favorable attitude toward a directive approach in supervision. But there was nothing unique about the human relations course per se in this regard. On the other hand, the course did induce more favorable attitudes toward kindness and consideration in the handling of subordinates. Also, on the Prediction of Human Reactions Test, which is primarily oriented toward judging how an individual would react given certain characteristics of individuals and circumstances in a supervisor-subordinate relationship, the experimental group experienced a reliable increase, whereas the controls did not.

This study contained one other aspect of considerable significance (8). Some who took the human relations course were taught by the lecture method, some through group discussions. The various measures noted in Table 8–1 indicated that almost identical changes occurred under both conditions. The two methods were equally effective. Other research suggests that under certain circumstances, discussion techniques can be somewhat more effective in producing personality change, but that this is likely to be achieved at some cost to learning. In the particular study referred to, those taught by the discussion method did not do so well on a knowledge test as those taught by lecture (2).

In spite of this possible deficiency, discussion techniques are widely employed in industry. The method uses a small group that works with a leader to discuss human relations problems. Usually there are ten to twenty people in each group, all of whom must have practical experience with the subject being considered to be able to participate actively.

Actual practice differs considerably insofar as the role of the discussion leader is concerned (7). In some instances, the leader has the conference content outlined in advance and the major conclusions to be reached already clearly established in his mind. He guides the group by questions and comments so that the pre-established points are covered. In other cases, the approach is much more nondirective, with the group developing its own framework for discussion. Here the leader encourages members to participate and is a resource person. Which procedure is best depends on the goal of the training and on the skill of the leader. To effectively guide a discussion to a predetermined conclusion is a difficult art.

Changes resulting from a week-long course in the human relations tradition taught by line managers are presented in Table 8–2. The ap-

TABLE 8–2. Pretest-Posttest Changes for Groups that Did (Experimental) and Did Not (Control) Take a Human Relations Course

Measure		*Experimental group means* $(N = 44)$	*Control group means* $(N = 13)$
Management Practices	Pretest:	33.8	34.9
Quiz	Posttest:	37.9	40.2
Case Analysis	Pretest:	.8	1.0
	Posttest:	1.9	.4
Attitude Scale	Pretest:	91.9	90.2
	Posttest:	98.9	91.1

Source: T. A. Mahoney, T. H. Jerdee, and A. Korman, "An Experimental Evaluation of Management Development," *Personnel Psychology*, Vol. 13 (1960), p. 94.

proach was primarily discussion, although there were a few lectures and some reading assignments. It is interesting to note that although significant attitude shifts were produced and the managers did improve their ability to solve human relations problems, there was no training-produced change in knowledge. Both experimental and control groups increased their performance on the management practices quiz to an almost equal degree. Apparently, this increase was a result of practice with the test; certainly it was not specifically the result of learning in the course (20).

This lack of knowledge change occurs sufficiently often with management development programs to constitute a problem. In this case, the line managers who did the teaching were very poorly informed regarding the subject matter and the reading assignments were rarely completed by participants. This finding argues for the use of training specialists to conduct human relations programs, specialists who are qualified in the subject matter and who can teach effectively. It also suggests that management development programs should be presented as an important aspect of the total job with rewards for good performance, rather than as a semivacation from work. Unfortunately, the latter view does prevail in some companies.

The Prediction of Change. Although little work has been done to predict which managers will change with human relations training, this appears to be a fruitful area for study. If those most likely to change can be identified prior to training, a company will be in a position to save itself considerable money. By selecting only men who exhibit change-potential to undergo management development, it is possible to maximize the return on investments in this area.

One study of this kind has been completed in Switzerland, with favorable results (26). The data are contained in Table 8–3. The Maudsley

TABLE 8–3. Attitude Change with a Human Relations Course Related to Initial Scores on a Personality Test

Groupings based on Maudsley Personality Inventory scores	N	Mean attitude change
Neurotic-introverted	18	+2.89
Neurotic-extroverted	18	−.89
Normal-introverted	23	+1.57
Normal-extroverted	28	+5.32

Source: A Papaloïzos, "Personality and Success of Training in Human Relations," *Personnel Psychology*, Vol. 15 (1962), p. 426.

Personality Inventory, a self-report measure, was administered to the managers before human relations training. Change on an attitude measure did occur for the group as a whole; the results were statistically reliable.

But when the group was split up on the basis of personality test scores, it became clear that this change had been largely restricted to those men who had above average scores on the indexes of normality-neuroticism, *and* extroversion-introversion. Had all efforts been concentrated on this particular group, a maximum return on the investment in training would have been achieved.

LABORATORY, SENSITIVITY, OR T-GROUP TRAINING

The terms laboratory, sensitivity, and T-group training tend to be used interchangeably, although in a technical sense the T-group is a special technique within the broader context of a laboratory or sensitivity program. The approach is closely allied to human relations training, but increasingly has taken on certain specific objectives and procedures that distinguish it from other types of training.

Laboratory training originated with a workshop conducted at the New Britain, Connecticut State Teachers College in 1946 by staff members from the Research Center for Group Dynamics, then located at Massachusetts Institute of Technology (3). In this early period, the major focus was on group discussions of various job related problems brought in by the participants. The discussions were supplemented with lectures, demonstrations, and role playing.

Very soon, however, the emphasis shifted from back-home problems to the processes occurring in the here-and-now group situation. It is this technique of learning about oneself and others through observing and participating in an ongoing group situation that is properly designated as T-group training. Programs of laboratory training containing this element have been conducted at Bethel, Maine, under the auspices of the National Education Association since 1947. Similar training is now offered at a number of universities and in other locations. Increasingly, companies have set up family-group programs, containing only individuals from their own managerial ranks, often managers who are closely associated in their everyday work. Such efforts have been directed at the top-management group of a company (1) and at the total managerial component of a large refinery (5). The more typical approach, however, is to group ten or twelve individuals from a variety of occupations and organizations.

Although lectures, role-playing, problem-centered discussions, special projects, and the like have remained a part of the total laboratory experience, the major aspect is the T-group. This meets for two or three hours daily over a period of a week, or in most cases longer. There is a leader, but he does not impose a structure on the group and its activities; there is no specified task to be performed. At first, the members tend to be frustrated and embarrassed. They cannot see why they are there and want someone to tell them what to do. Gradually, however, the conversation turns to the group itself and its members. The leader encourages frankness in the expression of feelings and reactions to others. Such matters as the effects of authority, the motives of others, and the need to be understood are discussed. The participants gradually open up. Frequently, the ties between them become quite strong, and the group eventually develops its own structure (30). At points during this process, certain participants may become quite anxious. Whether there is likely to be a real threat to psychological adjustment remains a matter of some controversy (13,23).

The Results of Evaluation. A number of studies have now been conducted to identify the impact of laboratory training. These have consistently indicated that change does occur. The findings presented in Table 8–4 are typical.

TABLE 8–4. Proportions of Experimental and Control Subjects Reported as Changed Subsequent to Laboratory Training

Area of change	Proportions changed	
	Experimentals, N = 229	Controls, N = 112
Receiving Communication—more effort to understand, attentive listening, understands	.34	.16
Relational Facility—cooperative, tactful, less irritating, easier to deal with, able to negotiate	.36	.21
Increased Interdependence—encourages participation, involves others, greater leeway to subordinates, less dominating, lets others think	.38	.27
Self-Control—more self-discipline, less quick with judgment, checks temper	.26	.15
Awareness of Human Behavior—more conscious of why people act, more analytic of others' actions, clear perceptions of people	.34	.16
Sensitivity to Group Behavior—more conscious of group process, aware of subcurrents in groups	.24	.09
Sensitivity to Others' Feelings—more capacity for understanding feelings, more sensitive to needs of others	.34	.10
Acceptance of Other People—able to tolerate shortcomings, considerate of individual differences, patient	.49	.29
Tolerance of New Information—willing to accept suggestions, considers new points of view, less dogmatic, less arbitrary	.42	.23
Comfort—relaxed, at ease	.36	.23
Insight into Self and Role—understands job demands, more aware of own behavior, better adjusted to job	.36	.24

Source: D. R. Bunker, "The Effect of Laboratory Education Upon Individual Behavior," in G. G. Somers (ed.), *Proceedings of the Sixteenth Annual Meeting.* Madison, Wisc.: Industrial Relations Research Association, 1964, pp. 225 and 231.

In this instance, individuals who had attended the Bethel program were compared with coworkers who had not, some eight to ten months after returning to their jobs (6). A special questionnaire was administered to people who were in a position to observe both the experimental and control subjects in their work. The questionnaires were designed to elicit information on observed changes in behavior and attitude. The approach is an after only one with a delayed posttest. The variables noted in Table 8–4 revealed a statistically significant difference between experimental and control groups in the proportion of individuals exhibiting change. An additional four variables did not yield reliable results. Over all, approximately two thirds of the experimental subjects changed in some respect, whereas only one third of those who did not attend the Bethel sessions changed.

Objectives of Training. The stated goals of the laboratory procedures are to sensitize the manager to emotional reaction and expression in others, to produce greater skill in perceiving the consequences of actions through attention to one's own feelings and those of other people, to develop in the manager values of a primarily democratic and scientific nature, to provide information about interpersonal and group situations, and to foster behavioral effectiveness in dealing with others (4). The approach deliberately attempts to make those exposed to training value science, democracy, and helping others more than they have in the past. These, of course, are exactly the kinds of changes noted in Table 8–4 and in other similar evaluation studies.

Several writers question whether changes of this kind foster the objectives of business organizations (12,22). Is laboratory training really an effective input-output mediator? Or does it contribute primarily to individual and societal goals rather than to those of an organization? Unfortunately, there is little available evidence on this point. Few satisfactory studies that relate training changes to productivity and organizational maintenance objectives have been conducted. The nature of the changes identified suggests, however, that when encapsulation and role conflict are effectively avoided, the maintenance goal may well be fostered. What the impact on productivity is remains a matter for conjecture. A number of those actively engaged in leading laboratory training groups are somewhat more concerned with making a contribution to a better society than they are with the goals of a specific company. This does not mean, on the other hand, that the company inadvertently is not served also.

Performance Appraisal, Coaching, and Conference Leadership Training

These techniques are widely used to enable managers to evaluate and utilize their subordinates more effectively. They are directed primarily at the productivity goal, although other considerations may be involved.

Performance appraisal training is intended to teach the various methods of rating and evaluating employees used by the company. It is the basic method for installing many of the procedures discussed in Chapters 4 and 5. Particular emphasis is usually placed on the elimination of various sources of error that may creep into the rating process. There is evidence that when the training utilizes discussions that eventuate in a group decision to minimize certain types of rater bias, this objective is most likely to be achieved (19).

Closely related are the various coaching training programs that attempt to make a manager more effective in feeding back and utilizing appraisal data for developing subordinates. These programs have gradually shifted in recent years from a primary concern with methods of telling a man how his work is perceived by his superiors to a concern with self-evaluation. Coaching training now often involves teaching a manager how to guide a subordinate in setting his own objectives or targets for future performance. The subordinate is subsequently expected to evaluate himself against these previously established goals with the help of his superior. Thus, coaching training has become a basic part of the *management by objectives* approach with its emphasis on individual and group planning and target setting.

Another method a manager may use to develop and more effectively utilize his subordinates is to conduct problem-solving conferences with them (21). This is part of the *participative management* approach that favors group decision-making and group involvement in the managerial process rather than unilateral command. The essence of this view is that in many instances decisions are never implemented because the subordinates who actually would have to do the work are resistant for one reason or another. To overcome this resistance, it is only necessary to have the subordinates become involved in making the decision so that they will perceive it as their own. It is recognized that this may result in a somewhat lower quality decision, but in many instances this is preferable to not having a decision implemented at all.

To use the participative approach effectively and conduct conferences that lead to meaningful results is very difficult for many managers, especially those who believe strongly that decisions should be made individually by the person in charge. To change attitudes and develop skills in conference and discussion leadership, a number of firms have instituted training programs for their managers. Just as coaching training has come to have a close association with the management by objectives approach, conference leadership training is an integral part of participative management. The two training procedures and managerial approaches can, of course, be used together.

Problem-solving and Creativity Training

A variety of different training programs have been developed to help managers become more original and effective in solving business problems (24). The emphasis tends to be on up-grading decision-making skills so that the manager will be able to reach more rational conclusions and thus make a greater contribution to a firm's profitability. In some instances, the training provides an impetus in the area of research and invention as well.

One such course is offered through a specialized consulting firm (15). The training contains three aspects. First, there is instruction of a more or less conventional type, using lecture and discussion methods aimed at providing a general understanding of the concepts and sequential steps in the problem-solving process. Then, the participants work together on a simulated problem drawn from the business world. The conferences and conversations are recorded. The final aspect of training, and perhaps the most important, is the feedback process. Here the recordings are played back, and the efforts at problem-solving criticized. The manager has an opportunity to see where he may be going wrong and to learn new approaches.

Another course, which has been more extensively evaluated, has been developed at the University of Buffalo (27). The participants are taught to defer judgment both at the problem definition and at the problem solution stages until they have a clear picture of the many alternatives. The approach emphasizes listing all possible ways in which a problem may be stated, and only then selecting *the* problem. This is broken down into as many aspects as possible and alternative solutions developed for each aspect. The manager learns a technique that stresses selecting from among a large number of known possibilities. Evaluation studies, which meet all criteria for adequacy of design, indicate that training of this kind does increase an individual's ability to develop original problem solutions of high quality. Furthermore, these changes are retained.

Role-Motivation Training

This procedure, although not so widely applied as some of the other techniques discussed, has been rather extensively evaluated with consistently favorable results (25). Training is conducted by the lecture method, plus a certain amount of directed discussion. Emphasis is on the individual, his work group, his family, the organizational milieu, the society as a whole, and the physical work situation that may contribute to ineffective performance in a subordinate. In this way, the manager's responsibility for maintaining satisfactory productivity levels among his men is stressed. In addition, the manager's own motivation to meet certain of the role requirements for his own job is increased.

Evaluation data on this course are presented in Table 8–5. The Re-

TABLE 8–5. Pretest, Posttest, and Follow-up Scores on the Miner Sentence Completion Scale for Groups that Did (Experimental) and Did Not (Control) Take Role-Motivation Training

Group	Mean score at pretest	Mean score at posttest	Mean score at follow-up
Research and development managers			
Experimental ($N = 56$)	4.66	6.77	
Control ($N = 30$)	5.60	4.47	
Business school students			
Experimental ($N = 129$)	3.40	6.67	5.90
Control ($N = 54$)	3.67	3.24	

Source: J. B. Miner, *Studies in Management Education*. New York: Springer, 1965, pp. 98, 115, 122, and 127.

search and Development managers exhibited a highly reliable increase in motivation to manage after training. The control group actually decreased in this regard. Although it was not possible to carry out a third follow-up testing on these groups, a follow-up was conducted over the subsequent five years using personnel records as a source of information. Experimental and control managers were compared for the number who achieved success in the company after the training was completed. Success was defined as having at least one promotion in the five-year period or, if the man left the company in the interim, a favorable separation rating in his file. Experimental and control groups were at the same average grade level at the time of training and were considered to have the same potential for advancement. The two groups started the race at essentially the same point, but those who underwent role-motivation training were more likely to win out, as the following data on the per cent achieving success indicate:

- Experimentals   81 per cent
- Controls   51 per cent

The findings suggest that in this instance the training was congruent with existing managerial role requirements and that encapsulation did not occur. Results for business school students are similar. Although there was some drop-off in motivation within the follow-up period, which averaged about a year, a reliable 70 per cent of the initial pretest-posttest change was retained. Unfortunately, the control subjects could not be tested a third time. As indicated in Chapter 7, the change measure employed is a valid predictor of managerial success. Thus, this particular mediator does appear to contribute to company goals.

Simulations

These techniques have in common that the manager is required to think and/or act in terms of role prescriptions differing to some degree from those applying to his own job in the here-and-now. He is forced out of his current mold and exposed to new ways of thinking and acting. The result can be a considerable amount of new learning and attitude change. Simulations can be very close to the present job, dealing with role behaviors that are to be added to the existing patterns; they can also be quite distant, dealing with the role prescriptions for a position for which the trainee may some day qualify.

There are also major differences in the degree of reality inherent in the simulation. In case study, information is presented in written terms and the participant must imagine the situation. At no point does he do any more than think his way through the role. In certain more complex types of simulations, considerable effort is devoted to reproducing the salient aspects of the situation, and the individual actually acts out his solution to the problem presented.

Case Study. In the case approach, a problem is given in written form to a group for solution. Usually, the group members individually assume the role of the manager who is faced with the problem situation. The written statement stops short of a solution, and the participants must think through to the role behavior they feel to be desirable. The leader does not impose a specific solution. The emphasis is on individual or team problem-solving, group discussion, and group critique.

The method is clearly more appropriate for certain purposes than others (29). It teaches managers to identify and analyze complex problems and to make their own decisions. It covers a great deal of ground, in terms of diverse approaches, interpretations, and personalities, very rapidly. Making snap judgments and applying pat solutions to problems are discouraged at the same time that learning is fostered. When the participants are sufficiently sophisticated and knowledgeable in the subject areas involved, it can serve as a basis for the development of general principles that may then be used to solve on-the-job problems. If the trainees do not have the background knowledge to come up with meaningful case solutions, or they lack any real understanding of the role the case requires them to assume, none of these objectives is likely to be achieved and the method should probably be avoided.

The Incident Process. The incident process is a modification of the basic case study procedure, which attempts to move the training somewhat closer to reality (28). The class is initially given a very brief written incident, and a statement of the role to be assumed in viewing this incident. The total case is then developed by means of a question-and-answer process, with the leader supplying information as the trainees ask for it. Once the problem has been established, each trainee writes his own particular solution down. The solutions are sorted by the leader, and their authors assigned to discussion groups on the basis of similarity of opinion. These groups develop the strongest statement of their members' mutual opinion that they can. The statements may then be presented in the form of a debate or the groups may role-play their solutions.

Finally, and here the incident process goes beyond traditional case study, the leader presents what actually was done in the particular instance and, where possible, the consequences. A general discussion follows that focuses on such matters as the factors accounting for accomplishments and difficulties, the possibilities of accomplishing more, methods of surmounting difficulties, and what can be learned from the case for transfer to on-the-job situations.

Role-Playing. Basically, the role-playing approach may be considered as a type of case study in which actual individuals play the various roles of the persons in the case. All participants do not assume the same role, the role of the responsible manager, as with the typical written case. That participants *behave* in roles rather than merely think in them creates a more realistic learning situation.

Usually, role-playing is done in groups of ten to twenty with members taking turns acting and serving as analysts. The leader assigns individuals to roles. An oral or written briefing is given in order to put the audience and actors into the situation. Sometimes, rather detailed role instructions are given; sometimes the actors actually read a skit up to a certain point; sometimes there is practically no structuring of this kind, and the participants largely develop their own roles. In any event, the actors eventually take over on their own, behaving as they see fit in the situation. The leader terminates the session when the audience has been emotionally involved and either the problem is analyzed or an impasse has been reached. A lengthy discussion normally follows, which attempts to point up the objectives of training.

There are many variants in technique, even to the point of employing professional actors to take certain parts in a skit. In addition, the approach has been used in a number of different contexts, although the training of managers in leadership behaviors is most common, usually in conjunction with a human relations program. Specific applications have been made in connection with the handling of discharges, lay-offs, merit ratings, and grievances, as well as in sales training.

Role-playing can help a manager practice role behaviors, provided a sufficient illusion of reality can be produced. Learning by doing is known to be an effective method of developing new skills, although it does not necessarily guarantee against encapsulation. Research evidence is available, indicating that when there is adequate discussion and critique of each role-playing episode, rather sizable changes in sensitivity to others and in employee orientation can be achieved (18). These changes are similar to those produced by laboratory training, and role-playing is often part of the total laboratory experience. It seems apparent, however, that role-playing need not be oriented toward organizational maintenance considerations only. Roles can be constructed to emphasize factors directly related to productivity.

Business Games. Another method of obtaining high levels of participant involvement is the business game, which may be viewed as a case spread out over time with the consequences of decisions made apparent. The usual procedure is first to inform the trainees regarding the business objectives to be sought, the decisions to be made, and the rules that apply. This may be done orally, but it is common practice to provide written instructions as well. Each competing team organizes itself, studies the available information on operations to date, and makes its initial set of decisions. Each decision-period is equal to a unit of time—a day, week, month, or even longer. After the first decisions are turned in, the trainers calculate the operating results, manually or with the aid of an electronic computer, and feed them back to the teams, often with further environmental and competitive data added. This cycle is repeated several times, and the results are then discussed and criticized at length.

Some available games deal with top-level decisions affecting the total enterprise. Others have been constructed with reference to specific functions and problems—personnel assignment, materials management, stock transactions, sales management, production scheduling, collective bargaining, inventory control, bank management, and so on (9,16). The list is constantly increasing. Although the tendency is to deal with generalized and hypothetical business situations, there are a number of games constructed with specific reference to a particular firm or industry. In some instances, the decisions made by one team are *interactive* with the results obtained by other teams, in that constant mathematical probabilities have been built into the game as concomitants of particular types of decisions. This is not always done, however.

Despite business games having won widespread acceptance, both in the universities and in connection with company management development programs, there is practically no evaluative information available. It may well be that playing these games does change a participant and that in doing so it makes him a better manager; in all likelihood, this is the case. But the kind of evidence demanded by the evaluation of change models is lacking.

There is reason to believe that those managers who do well in the game situation will be more effective on the job, whether or not they change during training (31). The data are presented in Table 8–6. The

TABLE 8–6. Relationships Between Business Game Performance and Management Appraisal Ratings for 63 Department Store Supervisors

Management appraisal dimension	Mean ratings for supervisors in various final game positions			Correlation values (for significant first-third differences)
	First	Second	Third	
Advancement potential	3.3	3.1	3.0	
Overall performance	9.7	9.0	8.5	.42
Job knowledge	4.2	4.1	3.9	.35
Judgment	2.9	2.9	2.2	.38
Initiative	3.8	3.5	3.4	.17
Cooperation	4.4	4.2	4.2	
Responsibility	4.0	3.9	3.7	
Leadership	3.4	3.4	3.1	
Personality	4.3	4.4	4.3	
Health	4.7	4.6	4.2	.58
Customer service	4.3	4.3	4.4	

Source: H. P. Teich, *Validity of a Business Game.* M.S. Thesis. Eugene, Oregon: Univ. of Oregon, 1964, pp. 56–57.

game used in this study (32) requires three companies to compete for industry leadership. For research purposes, individuals, rather than teams, were set equal to companies so that each player could be ranked as first, second, or third in his group of three competitors, on the basis of his average score on the various company success indexes. The data of Table 8–6 are the average appraisal ratings, made by the store manager, for the twenty-one supervisors who were first in their respective industries, the twenty-one who were second, and the twenty-one who were last. In the five instances where correlations have been computed, the supervisors coming in last on the game have a reliably lower performance rating than those coming in first. On four additional dimensions, a similar trend is present in the data. Only the personality and customer service ratings, which would appear on the surface to be far removed from decision-making skills, are clearly unrelated to game performance.

University Programs

Some mention should be made of the various general liberal arts programs offered by universities specifically for management personnel. These are not widespread, but they have engendered considerable discussion because of their emphasis on general personal broadening rather than on directly career-related learning.

One such program, which has been extensively evaluated, was conducted for executives of the Bell Telephone System at the University of Pennsylvania for a number of years (33). The course, which lasted ten months, included such subjects as practical logic, business history, world art, history and aesthetics of music, analytical reading, world literature, social science, philosophy of ethics, history and meaning of science, modern architecture, American civilization, political science, and international relations. Comparison of control and experimental groups indicated that a certain amount of knowledge change did occur in the subject matter areas covered.

There was, in addition, a reduction in the value placed on economic considerations and an increase in aesthetic interests as reflected on the Allport-Vernon-Lindzey Study of Values. Various attitude measures indicated a rather marked shift away from conservative views to radical and liberal positions. Although no attempt was made to conduct follow-up studies and to relate these changes to success indexes, there is good reason to believe that some of these changes may have been associated with either encapsulation or role conflict. The nature of the attitude changes induced suggests that the training may not have been organizationally relevant. A similar question can be raised regarding other liberal arts programs of this type. Is the company's investment appropriate in the sense that the changes produced actually contribute to organizational goals? It is interesting to note in this connection that when the participants pay part of the costs, they tend to be more satisfied with this type of training (10).

REFERENCES

1. Argyris, C., *Interpersonal Competence and Organizational Effectiveness.* Homewood, Ill.: Richard D. Irwin, 1962.
2. Asch, M. J., "Nondirective Teaching in Psychology: An Experimental Study," *Psychological Monographs,* Vol. 65 (1951), No. 4.
3. Benne, K. D., "History of the T-Group in the Laboratory Setting," in L. P. Bradford, J. R. Gibb, and K. D. Benne, *T-Group Theory and Laboratory Method.* New York: Wiley, 1964, pp. 80–135.
4. Benne, K. D., L. P. Bradford, and R. Lippitt, "The Laboratory Method," in L. P. Bradford, J. R. Gibb, and K. D. Benne, *T-Group Theory and Laboratory Method.* New York: Wiley, 1964, pp. 15–44.
5. Blake, R. R., and J. S. Mouton, *The Managerial Grid.* Houston, Tex.: Gulf, 1964.
6. Bunker, D. R., "The Effect of Laboratory Education upon Individual Behavior," in G. G. Somers, *Proceedings of the Sixteenth Annual Meeting.* Madison, Wis.: Industrial Relations Research Association, 1964, pp. 220–232.
7. Davis, K., *Human Relations at Work,* 3rd ed. New York: McGraw-Hill, 1967.
8. DiVesta, F. J., "Instructor-Centered and Student-Centered Approaches in Teaching a Human Relations Course," *Journal of Applied Psychology,* Vol. 38 (1954), 329–335.

9. Greenlaw, P. S., L. W. Herron, and R. H. Rawdon, *Business Simulation in Industrial and University Education.* Englewood Cliffs, N.J.: Prentice-Hall, 1962.
10. Gruenfeld, L. W., "The Effects of Tuition Payment and Involvement on Benefit from a Management Development Program," *Journal of Applied Psychology,* Vol. 50 (1966), 396–399.
11. Haire, M., *Psychology in Management,* 2nd ed. New York: McGraw-Hill, 1964.
12. House, R. J., "T-Group Training—Some Important Considerations for the Practicing Manager," *New York Personnel Management Association Bulletin,* Vol. 21 (1965), No. 9, 4–9.
13. House, R. J., "T-Group Education and Leadership Effectiveness: A Review of the Empiric Literature and a Critical Evaluation," *Personnel Psychology,* Vol. 20 (1967), 1–32.
14. Kahn, R. L., D. M. Wolf, R. P. Quinn, J. D. Snoek, and R. A. Rosenthal, *Organizational Stress: Studies in Role Conflict and Ambiguity.* New York: Wiley, 1964.
15. Kepner, C. H., and B. B. Tregoe, *The Rational Manager.* New York: McGraw-Hill, 1965.
16. Kibbee, J. M., C. J. Craft, and B. Nanus, *Management Games.* New York: Rinehold, 1961.
17. Lana, R. E., "Pretest-Treatment Interaction Effects in Attitudinal Studies," *Psychological Bulletin,* Vol. 56 (1959), 293–300.
18. Lawshe, C. H., R. A. Bolda, and R. L. Brune, "Studies in Management Training Evaluation: II. The Effects of Exposure in Role Playing," *Journal of Applied Psychology,* Vol. 43 (1959), 287–292.
19. Levine, J., and J. Butler, "Lecture vs. Group Decision in Changing Behavior," *Journal of Applied Psychology,* Vol. 36 (1952), 29–33.
20. Mahoney, T. A., T. H. Jerdee, and A. Korman, "An Experimental Evaluation of Management Development," *Personnel Psychology,* Vol. 13 (1960), 81–98.
21. Maier, N. R. F., *Problem-Solving Discussions and Conferences.* New York: McGraw-Hill, 1963.
22. McGehee, W., and P. W. Thayer, *Training in Business and Industry.* New York: Wiley, 1961.
23. McGregor, D., *The Professional Manager.* New York: McGraw-Hill, 1967.
24. McPherson, J. H., "Environment and Training for Creativity," in C. W. Taylor, *Creativity: Progress and Potential.* New York: McGraw-Hill, 1964, pp. 129–153.
25. Miner, J. B., *Studies in Management Education.* New York: Springer, 1965.
26. Papaloïzos, A., "Personality and Success of Training in Human Relations," *Personnel Psychology,* Vol. 15 (1962), 423–428.
27. Parnes, S. J., "Research on Developing Creative Behavior," in C. W. Taylor, *Widening Horizons in Creativity.* New York: Wiley, 1964, pp. 145–169.
28. Pigors, P., and F. Pigors, *Case Method in Human Relations: The Incident Process.* New York: McGraw-Hill, 1961.
29. Proctor, J. H., and W. M. Thornton, *Training: A Handbook for Line Managers.* New York: American Management Association, 1961.
30. Tannenbaum, R., I. R. Weschler, and F. Massarik, *Leadership and Organization: A Behavioral Science Approach.* New York: McGraw-Hill, 1961.
31. Teich, H. P., *Validity of a Business Game.* Eugene, Ore.: M. S. Thesis, Univ. of Oregon, 1964.

32. Vance, S. C., *Management Decision Simulation: A Non-Computer Business Game.* New York: McGraw-Hill, 1960.

33. Viteles, M. S., "Human Relations and the Humanities in the Education of Business Leaders: Evaluation of a Program of Humanistic Studies for Executives." *Personnel Psychology,* Vol. 12 (1959), 1–28.

QUESTIONS

1. Design a complete study to evaluate a special management development course intended to produce knowledge changes in the field of economics. Describe all the steps you would go through.
2. What is meant by the term input-output mediator? Why do companies invest in these techniques? How do they relate to the internal constraints imposed by individual differences? How do structural and functional mediators differ? Give examples of each.
3. Discuss the specific nature of the relationship between each of the various management development techniques and the company goals of productivity and organizational maintenance.
4. What do we know about the change-producing potential of the following:
   a. Human relations courses.
   b. T-groups.
   c. Creativity training.
   d. Role-motivation training.
   e. Business games.

9

Skill Training

At this point, it is desirable to differentiate between *training* and *education*. This is not an easy task. Both certainly are concerned with human change and learning, but they do differ considerably in purpose (3,8). Training is basically role-specific. It attempts to make those who are or will be performing a certain job achieve successful role behavior. Education, on the other hand, is tied to the goals of the individual more than to those of the organization, although some overlapping between the two sets of goals can be anticipated. Education takes the individual, his growth, and the multiple roles that he may play in society as its starting point. Training starts with the requirements of a particular type of employing organization and, within that, of a given job.

In general, where the student is expected to pay tuition to obtain a learning experience he himself desires, as in the universities, we tend to speak of an educational process. Training normally is paid for by the employing organization, although this does not deny the existence of concomitant benefits both to the individual and to the company.

These distinctions leave the various management development procedures discussed in the preceding chapter in a realm of considerable uncertainty. Clearly they are intended to be training, or at least they should be. But managerial jobs tend to have rather broad role prescriptions, especially at the top levels where the demand for the generalist is greatest. Furthermore, there are companies that do not clearly delimit the scope of the various managerial positions. The result is that management development can easily become transformed into education, even when paid for by the company. That is, it becomes more individual- than company-oriented.

Such problems of definition do not characteristically arise at lower levels in the organization. In this chapter the focus will be directly on training as a role-specific process. We will be concerned with learning that in the ideal situation is (1) specifically applicable to the job; (2) complete in its coverage of job requirements; and (3) efficient in terms of the time, money, and resources utilized. This latter requirement implies that the training should not be continued beyond the point where perfectly adequate on-the-job performance is possible.

Because training of this kind must be commensurate with what is known about the processes of human learning, we begin with a brief treatment of the implications from learning theory. A second section discusses methods of identifying training needs. Finally, a number of the techniques, procedures, and applications of industrial training will be covered.

Learning Theory and Industrial Training

This section contains a synopsis of what have been called the *principles of learning*. These principles presumably are as applicable to the management development programs discussed in Chapter 8 as to the training procedures to be considered later in this chapter (1). Unfortunately, knowledge regarding specific applications of these principles is far from complete.

Most of these principles were developed originally within the psychological laboratory, often as a result of work with animals. Although subsequent studies have extended into the human sphere, research has not always been conducted in an industrial setting. Thus, what follows must be considered a best estimate as of this point in time. Yet, as a best estimate, it is important for those who must make decisions regarding the content and format of various training programs.

MOTIVATION

Although there is some question whether all learning requires some motive that can be directly satisfied through the learning experience, it does appear certain that greater efficiency is achieved under these circumstances. If a training program represents a means to some strong personal goal of the trainee, maximal learning is more likely to occur.

The training should be directly tied to the various motives known to characterize those who will be exposed to it. Among the motives that most frequently foster learning in the business world are the desires for security, for acceptable working conditions, for social interaction with others, for personal recognition, for intrinsically interesting work, for a sense of accomplishment, for freedom in the workplace (4), and for achievement. To the extent a learning experience can be related to one or more of these motives, as when retraining on a new piece of equipment is presented as a means to increased job security, the over-all goals of training will be fostered. Motivation is more likely to operate in the desired fashion if the material to be learned is meaningful to the trainee, if it has some relationship to things he has experienced previously, also, if it is sufficiently varied to maintain motivation rather than produce satiation and boredom.

REINFORCEMENT

Closely related to motivation is the *Law of Effect*. According to this law, behavior that is viewed as leading to reward, which satisfies a motive, tends to be learned and repeated; behavior that does not produce a reward or that is punished tends not to be repeated. Any event that operates in this way, so as to change the probability of a particular behavior, is said to be *reinforcing*.

In general, rewards (positive reinforcers) appear to be more effective in producing learning than punishments (negative reinforcers). In fact, it may be more desirable to merely fail to reward a behavior that is incorrect in a particular situation than to punish it. Punishment, at least in its more extreme forms, can lead to a mere suppression of the undesired behavior, with the result that the behavior reappears when the punishment is removed. Punishment can also produce so much anxiety and anger that it disrupts all learning. Somewhat less intense punishment can have a favorable effect, especially if it follows closely on the behavior to be eliminated.

In this connection, it is important to remember that the law of effect applies within the context of a particular person's motivational system and what he considers rewarding or punishing. Although praise is generally a positive reinforcer, it may not always act in this manner (16). If a trainer is frequently an object of contempt, praise from him for a particular type of behavior may only produce ostracism and ridicule from the group in training. Desired behavior is suppressed rather than positively reinforced by the praise, with the consequence that learning follows a course differing considerably from that originally anticipated.

KNOWLEDGE OF RESULTS

Learning is more efficient not only when appropriate motivation is present and when adequate reinforcement is given, but also when the trainee has a clear picture of how well he is doing. Feeding back information on the effectiveness of responses is called *knowledge of results*. It helps in part because the trainee can use the knowledge to sort out behavior that he should learn from that which he should not. Without knowledge of results, a person may well spend long periods of time learning to do things that appear at first to be appropriate, but that subsequently turn out not to be (18).

It is also true that knowledge of results affects motivation. When an individual knows whether a given response was right or wrong, whether he is improving or not, he can set goals for himself, thus making a game out of the learning process and maintaining motivation at a high level. There is reason to believe that explicit goal setting in conjunction with knowledge of results can be particularly helpful where the material to be learned is rather difficult and the goals are set at a high level (6,11).

A demonstration of how knowledge of results can facilitate learning is contained in Table 9–1. In this study, textile workers were given con-

TABLE 9–1. Waste Ratios for Textile Workers Over a 145-Week Period Which Included Training with Knowledge of Results

Period	Mean waste ratio for period
Pretraining (10 weeks)	2.50
Training (3 weeks)	1.50
Reinforcement (12 weeks)	.87
Posttraining I (14 weeks)	.94
Posttraining II (20 weeks)	1.05
Posttraining III (20 weeks)	1.03
Posttraining IV (20 weeks)	1.01
Posttraining V (20 weeks)	.71
Retraining (26 weeks)	.52

Source: W. McGehee and D. H. Livingstone, "Persistence of the Effects of Training Employees to Reduce Waste," *Personnel Psychology*, Vol. 7 (1954), p. 36.

siderable training, aimed at reducing material wastage, over a three-week period (15). The knowledge of results aspect of this training was extended for twelve more weeks through on-the-job reinforcement of the original learning: the men were told what their waste rates were. There was a sizable reduction in the amount of waste from pretraining to training and a further reduction with reinforcement. These training effects were maintained over a long period of time. Subsequently, when a second training program similar to the first was introduced, the amount of waste was even further reduced.

ACTIVE PRACTICE

It is almost axiomatic that learning requires repetition and practice. This practice should be active and overt. The man should do and say what he is expected to learn, rather than merely listen to repetitions of instructions. Active practice of this kind maintains attention and concentration. Thus, job skills are most effectively developed by repeatedly performing the task to be learned, and knowledge is best acquired by writing down the material or reciting it orally.

At least in the early stages of learning, it is desirable to guide this practice closely, rather than let a trainee find out by trial and error which are appropriate behaviors and which are not. A great deal of time can be saved if the trainer directs the practice in this manner so that desired responses are produced almost immediately. However, because the individual eventually will have to perform the new tasks alone on the job, it is important not to carry close guidance too far into the learning process. Training should include considerable independent practice of the newly acquired role behaviors at some point before it is terminated.

MASSED VS. DISTRIBUTED PRACTICE

In general, the available evidence indicates that spacing out training sessions is desirable, especially to aid retention. This assumes, of course, that there is a good deal to be learned. Short lists of instructions and the like are probably best learned in a single intensive session.

The principle of distributed practice is widely violated in industrial training. When a decision is made to place a man on a particular job, every effort normally is made to move him to effective performance in as short a time as possible. This means that all of his time is devoted to training in the new role behaviors. Where the job is quite simple, the result is repeated practice of essentially the same activities, and relatively inefficient learning.

In many instances, it is possible to obtain the advantages of distributed practice, if an effort is made to do so. There are a number of approaches that can be used (13). Job training can be alternated with some useful activity that requires minimal skill, such as filing, cleaning, or loading. When men are being retrained to operate some new, possibly automated, equipment, retraining sometimes can be alternated with continued work performance on the old equipment. Another approach groups the various aspects of the total training into separate packages and alternates among these. This is particularly appropriate if the job is complex and contains a variety of tasks to be performed at different times. Finally, some firms employ high school and college students on a part-time basis and use the work periods for training in activities that will be carried out subsequently when full-time employment occurs.

WHOLE VS. PART LEARNING

Another principle, which is somewhat "shaky" in terms of the evidence supporting it, states that whole learning is preferable to part learning. This refers to the size of the units of content employed. According to this, it is desirable to have the trainees deal with large and meaningful wholes, rather than small bits and pieces, which may not be very meaningful in themselves and must be combined eventually before effective job performance is possible.

Unfortunately for those making decisions regarding training content, there is evidence that under certain conditions part learning is preferable. Thus, the guidelines for action are not entirely clear in this area. Yet some statements can be made (10). More intelligent trainees tend to handle large, self-contained units of content well, whereas the less intelligent may require a more segmented approach. Once an individual has become accustomed to the whole method and has become practiced in its use, its advantages become more marked. Whole learning combined with distributed practice represents a particularly advantageous combination. The whole method is desirable only if the material to be learned does form a meaningful, unified grouping. A job made up of a series of disparate activities without logical connection might best be learned in parts. Finally, because of the nature of most job-related learning, there will almost inevitably be aspects of the material that must be handled on a part basis, even if the initial approach is in terms of the whole. When a particular aspect of the total learning is very difficult, training must focus on this aspect even if some segmentation does result.

TRANSFER OF TRAINING

Chapter 7 indicated that psychological tests having considerable validity for the initial training situation often do not predict as effectively when an on-the-job criterion measure is employed. The reverse is also true. Such findings suggest that transfer from the training to the actual work situation may not be perfect in many instances, that what is learned during training may have very little relevance for job performance. This is the *transfer of training* problem: Under what conditions will that which has been learned to do the old job be most relevant for the new job, should the position be redesigned and retraining carried out?

The principle that seems to work most effectively as an answer to these questions is that of identical elements. If the behavior required and the characteristics of a training situation (or of an existing job) have many elements identical to those on the job (or on the redesigned job), a person who performs effectively in the one instance should do so in the other. Thus, to maximize *positive transfer* of the kind that is normally desired, there should be a close resemblance in the behaviors produced and the meaning content of the relevant stimuli in the two situations. This does not necessitate perfect physical identity, as is evident from what has been said about simulation techniques, but it does require psychological identity in terms of the thoughts and emotions aroused in the two situations.

It is also possible, however, for *negative transfer* to occur. What has been learned on one job can be detrimental for another. What has been learned in training can actually hamper job performance, if the training is not effectively designed or if it is designed with reference to goals differing sharply from those of the job situation. For instance, what one learns during college *could* lead to less effective performance in a subsequent business position. Negative transfer of this kind tends to be most pronounced when the new job requires the opposite behavior from that a man has learned to apply in comparable situations. The old behaviors seem to keep forcing their way back and thus disturbing performance. This means that in redesigning jobs and equipment one should make every effort to avoid situations where workers must make opposite or nearly opposite responses to familiar situations (16).

INTELLIGENCE AND LEARNING

A final guide for the industrial trainer derives from what is known about individual differences and the nature of mental abilities. There is good reason to believe that those with higher ability levels will learn more rapidly than those with less ability, when the ability involved is closely related to the material to be learned (17).

Training will be most efficient to the extent the teaching process can be adapted to the mental ability level of the individual. A very intelligent person can absorb new things very rapidly, and the materials to be learned should be presented at an accelerated pace. The less intelligent are likely to require much longer exposure to the same materials before achieving a comparable degree of learning. Ideally, therefore, training experiences should be individualized for maximum efficiency. This is one advantage of the teaching machines to be described later in this chapter. If individualized instruction is not possible and large job-related individual differences are known to be present in a trainee group, it is generally desirable to group the trainees into "fast" and "slow" classes. In this way, it is possible to avoid the wasteful overlearning that may occur among high-ability individuals who are forced to continue practice while waiting for those of lower ability to catch up. In addition, motivation is more easily maintained where *ability grouping* of this kind is carried out.

Establishing Training Needs

For training to operate efficiently as an input-output mediator, it must be focused on those individuals and situations where the need is greatest. Large gaps between role prescriptions and existing role behaviors must be identified. Then a decision must be made as to whether training might significantly reduce the size of the gap. Establishing training needs requires an answer to two questions: Is there a problem in terms of the level or type of performance? Can training be of any value in correcting such a situation?

In terms of sheer numbers, the training-needs problem is usually most pronounced among individuals just starting out on a new job. New employees, employees who have been shifted into a new position, and employees being retrained because the role prescriptions for a position have been changed all can normally be assumed to have rather acute training requirements. Fortunately, requirements of this kind tend to be rather easy to identify, and the level of motivation to learn quite high.

A much more difficult problem arises in the case of existing employees, who have been working on the current job for some time. Here persistent deviations from role prescriptions must be identified on an individual basis. There is no single categorization, such as that of "new man on the job," to make employees with marked training needs highly visible. Furthermore, motivation for new learning may well be minimal. To be singled out for special training and to accept the need for this training is a tacit admission that one has not been performing with maximum effectiveness in the past. The "experienced" employee may go to great lengths to cover up any training needs and may resist such training as he does receive in order to prove that he has been performing his job correctly all along. This is not a universal occurrence, but it is well for a personnel manager to be sensitive to the possibility.

Whether the training-needs analysis is directed toward individuals who are just starting on a job or to those who have been there for some time, it is very important and may well become even more important in the future. Union pressure has produced many job assignment systems based in large part on seniority. Furthermore, a number of companies are firmly committed to the concept of promotion from within. These plus other factors mean that job security is much greater today than it has been in the past, and training is often the only available procedure for correcting deficiencies in selection and placement (9). If this training is to be applied in an efficient manner, it must be directed into areas where clearly identified training needs exist.

SPECIFIC TECHNIQUES IN TRAINING NEEDS ANALYSIS

Inasmuch as the process of identifying training needs depends at least in part on establishing disparities between role prescriptions and role behavior, any of the various appraisal and evaluation techniques discussed in Chapters 4 and 5 can be of value. In addition, achievement tests and job samples can provide information regarding the extent to which knowledge and skill are below expected levels. Historically, training needs have been identified largely as a result of requests for training from line management, or through more protracted discussions with those responsible for the performance of the men considered for training, or through direct observation of actual job performance (12). Probably these latter techniques remain the most common ones today, although group production records, turnover statistics, and the like are also widely used to pinpoint areas of difficulty.

The important thing, irrespective of the approach, is to develop some conception not only as to whether performance deficiencies are present, but also regarding the extent to which training can remedy such deficiencies and the type of training that might be most appropriate for this purpose. A training-needs analysis should come before any attempt at establishing the method or content of training.

In developing a preliminary estimate of training needs in a particular group, it is helpful to utilize a check list along the lines of the one presented in Table 9–2. Answers to the questions posed can be obtained

TABLE 9–2. **Checklist for Needed Training**

Items recorded by training specialist	Is item seen in this production unit?		Possible training need
	Yes	No	
Downward communications to supervisor slow	X		X
Frequent gripes by supervisors about tools		X	
Supervisors use suggestions from workers		X	X
Many rejects returned to production		X	
Customer's complaints from sales ignored		X	
Turnover in shop higher than seems necessary	X		X
Many lost time accidents		X	
Paper work up to date		X	X
Raw material delays		X	
Supervisors use specialists of company		X	X

Source: D. H. Fryer, M. R. Feinberg, and S. S. Zalkind, *Developing People in Industry.* New York: Harper & Row, 1956, p. 41.

using data and information from the various sources already noted. Once possible training needs are established, the training specialist gradually can narrow his analysis until he is able to deal with the specific needs of specific individuals in specific jobs. The content of training is then developed from job analysis data, either that contained in company job descriptions or that collected as a result of a limited job analysis carried out for training purposes only. The latter approach may prove necessary where a job analysis conducted for other purposes is outdated or inadequate (5).

Methods and Approaches in Training

With the discussions of learning principles and training needs as a background, it is now feasible to consider some of the methods and approaches used in industrial training and to evaluate them. This section will be concerned with such matters as on-the-job training, vestibule schools, apprenticeships, system or team training, teaching machines, and programmed instruction.

ON- AND OFF-THE-JOB TRAINING

Undoubtedly, the most common procedure is for training to be carried out on the job, particularly for new employees. The individual becomes accustomed to the machinery and materials he will use in his work, and he learns in the same physical and social environment in which he will carry out his job duties. Usually, the training is done by an experienced employee or by a supervisor. On occasion, however, trained instructors are assigned for the specific purpose of teaching job skills.

Much on-the-job training still utilizes procedures similar to those developed for use in connection with the Job Instruction Training sessions conducted by the Training Within Industry Division of the War Manpower Commission during World War II. The JIT guidelines are given below.

- A. Pre-training Steps
  1. Have a timetable developed in terms of which skills are to be attained. Indicate the speed at which the various levels of attainment may be expected.
  2. Break down the job into its basic components.
  3. Have all materials and supplies necessary for the training process available and ready.
  4. Have the work place arranged in the same way that the worker will be expected to keep it.
- B. Training Steps
  1. Prepare the worker by putting him at ease, i.e., find out what he already knows and show him the relationship of his job to other jobs.
  2. Tell, show, and illustrate the job to be performed.
  3. Have the worker try to perform the job and have him tell and explain why he performs each specific operation of the job. This tends to clarify the key aspects.
  4. Follow-up on the trainee after he has been put on his own by checking him often and encouraging further questions.

On-the-job training of this kind is very attractive in a number of respects. It requires relatively little special attention, no extra equipment, and the man can do some productive work while he learns. Furthermore, it is consistent with several principles of learning. There is active practice, motivation should be maximal owing to the more meaningful nature of the learning materials, and the problem of transfer of training from the learning to the job situation is almost nonexistent.

There are some difficulties. There is a real risk that expensive equipment will be damaged by inexperienced employees, and the accident rate among on-the-job trainees tends to be high. In the absence of specially assigned trainers, the instruction is often haphazard or neglected entirely. The pressures of the work place may leave little time for effective training. Some activities may actually be more difficult to learn on the job because of their complexity or the regulated speed at which the machinery operates.

For these reasons, it seems desirable, in many cases, to carry out a large portion of the training process away from the job. This is a widespread practice in the management development area, but it is considerably less common for skill training. Only in the case of relatively simple production, clerical, and sales jobs does the use of on-the-job training alone seem appropriate. If it is necessary to restrict the learning process to the actual work situation, it is usually desirable to have specific individuals designated as training specialists and to relieve them of other job duties, at least on a temporary basis. This permits a systematic training effort comparable to those obtained with many of the Training Within Industry programs of World War II.

Vestibule Training. An approach that is intermediate between on- and off-the-job training utilizes the vestibule school. Here the trainee uses equipment and procedures similar to those he would use in on-the-job training, but the equipment is set up in an area separate from the regular work place. This special installation is to facilitate learning, not to obtain productive output. A skilled trainer is in charge, and new workers receive detailed instruction while practicing their new skills at a rate appropriate to each individual.

From the learning viewpoint this appears to be an ideal approach. There is evidence that it does reduce training time and yield more skilled work performance (16). But it is also expensive, especially if the number of men to be trained on a particular type of equipment is small, and it is not suitable for many jobs. Unfortunately, some companies have placed obsolete or even broken machinery in vestibule schools in an effort to avoid the expense of purchasing duplicate equipment. This tends to limit severely the value of the training. It may even yield negative transfer effects.

Orientation Training. Orientation programs provide new employees with information on such matters as company organization, the history of the firm, policies and procedures, pay and benefit plans, conditions of employment, safety practices, names of top executives, locations of various departments and facilities, manufacturing processes, and work rules. On occasion, brief orientation programs are offered for experienced employees in order to bring them up to date on current procedures.

In many companies, this kind of orientation is conducted by the personnel department during the first few days of employment. Handbooks, films, and other materials may play an important part in this initial effort to provide the employee with knowledge of his new environment. In those cases where immediate supervision has primary responsibility for these matters, the training tends to become more individualized, more variable, and on occasion more superficial. For most purposes, a standardized program including classroom sessions and group tours of facilities appears to offer major advantages, but these can frequently be integrated with further training by supervision.

APPRENTICESHIP

Apprentice training offers an integration of on- and off-the-job learning that under ideal conditions appears to be extremely effective. It is used to prepare employees for a variety of skilled occupations of the kind noted in Table 9–3. The apprentice agrees to work for a company, at a

TABLE 9–3. Selected Apprenticeable Occupations Classified by Length of Apprenticeship

Two years	Four years	Six years
Baker	Carpenter	Compositor
Barber	Draftsman	Electrotyper
Iron worker	Locksmith	Stereotyper
	Millwright	
Two to three years	Tailor	Seven years
Jewelry engraver		Engraver (bank note)
Meat cutter	Four to five years	
	Electrician	Eight years
Three years	Instrument maker	Die sinker
Commercial photographer	Tool and die maker	
Granite cutter		Five to ten years
Painter and decorator	Five years	Picture engraver
	Plumber	(steel plate
Three to four years	Pottery presser	engraver)
Bricklayer, mason		
Cook, chef	Five to six years	
Roofer	Job pressman	
	Photoengraver	

Source: New York State Apprenticeship Council, 1968.

rate averaging somewhat above half of that paid to fully qualified workers, in return for a specified number of hours of training. In many instances, the conditions of training have been negotiated with the relevant union and are specified in the union contract. Most of the programs are registered with the federal Department of Labor, which promotes apprenticeship training throughout the United States, and with appropriate state agencies.

The actual content of the training usually is established by a local apprenticeship committee that specifies the number of hours of experience for each machine or kind of work. The classroom part of the apprenticeship is conducted at a vocational school, with an experienced journeyman in the trade acting as instructor. These courses emphasize applied mathematics, the physical sciences, and the techniques of the occupation. The classroom instruction may be offered during the work day or after hours. It may also be by correspondence. The on-the-job training also is given by a skilled journeyman, and insofar as possible it is integrated with the classroom material. Thus, the apprentice is given an immediate opportunity to practice what he has been taught.

Evaluation. As indicated, this type of training can be extremely effective where complex skills must be learned. Yet, there is reason to believe that many apprenticeship programs are unnecessarily long, with the result that a good deal of inefficient overlearning occurs. A number of the trades are not so complex and difficult to learn as their members would like to believe. Largely as a result of union pressure extended training periods of the kind noted in Table 9–3 have become accepted. Evidence for the view that overlearning is widespread in apprentice programs comes from the fact that many individuals attain the same skilled positions through considerably less lengthy on-the-job experience. Also, a number of drop-outs from apprentice programs nevertheless enter the same trade, in spite of the abbreviated learning period (20).

It is also true that apprentice training is on occasion subverted by a desire among certain management representatives to obtain as much productive labor as possible at the reduced apprentice rate. Thus, on-the-job learning is de-emphasized, and there is little concern as to whether the man attends classes or not. The major stress is on the amount of work produced, with the result that the training objective is lost.

Perhaps the most difficult problem is that apprenticeships tend to take on a rigidity unsuited to the advent of automation and a shifting technology. Occupations are changing constantly as skills must be combined and recombined to meet the demands of new working environments. There is some question under these circumstances as to whether the traditional skilled trade categories are any longer appropriate. This questioning has extended to the apprenticeships that prepare individuals for these trades. Many personnel managers would prefer to avoid the formal apprentice training programs entirely and utilize a more flexible approach that could yield individuals with the specific combinations of skills needed to do a given job in the most efficient manner. Changes gradually are being introduced into the formal apprenticeship programs. And there is still widespread agreement that carefully integrated classroom and on-the-job training can be very effective, given a satisfactory method of keying learning materials to existing job requirements.

TEACHING MACHINES AND PROGRAMMED INSTRUCTION

The principles of learning described earlier in this chapter find their clearest manifestations in the field of programmed instruction. This individualized procedure utilizes training materials organized into a series of frames, usually of increasing difficulty and with each successive frame building on those that precede. Information, questions, and problems are presented to the learner who either writes in his answer or selects the answer from multiple-choice alternatives. Feedback is then provided on the correctness of the answer. The material is developed so that a high proportion of the questions will elicit the desired response and thus result in positive reinforcement. The frames are frequently presented in a teaching machine using film or sound tapes. Some machines are tied in with computers; almost all have electronic features. There are also a variety of programmed books and other printed materials where the trainee uncovers the successive frames manually (14).

Inherent in all programmed instruction, irrespective of the way in which materials are presented, are such features as active practice, a gradual increase in difficulty levels over a series of small steps, immediate feedback, learning at the individual's own rate, and minimization of error. Thus, a variety of learning principles are explicitly built into the technique. There is reinforcement, knowledge of results, active practice, and guidance. There can be distributed practice, and the material may be learned in a time period suited to the ability level of the trainee. If the material is selected from the job in an appropriate manner, there should be positive transfer. Only whole learning seems to be missing, and that may not be essential. Also the routine nature of the training may on occasion dampen motivation.

Evaluation. Given this degree of synchronization with learning theory, one would expect programmed instruction to provide an extremely efficient method of training. Such evidence as is available certainly confirms this expectation (19). Selected data are presented in Table 9–4.

There are certain cautions. The approach is more suitable for knowledge than for skill training. As a result, it is currently of rather limited value in the case of many production jobs, although some applications have been developed in this area. It is also extremely costly, if a new program must be written. A single frame takes up to an hour to write, and a total program can contain hundreds or even thousands of frames, depending on the complexity of the material and the desired size of the

TABLE 9–4. Examples of Improved Performance and Training Time Savings Associated with the Use of Programmed Instruction

Course and company	Average performance score		Average length of time (hours)	
	Conventional instruction	Programmed instruction	Conventional instruction	Programmed instruction
7070 computer nomenclature (IBM)	86.2	95.1	15	11
Reading engineering drawings (du Pont)	81.2	91.2	17	13
Dermatology and mycology (Schering)	60.1	91.9	No information	
Basic electricity (Bell Labs)				
Facts	64.9	76.8	No information	
Concepts	47.5	66.4		
Analog computation (du Pont)	No information		40	11
Package billing (Spiegel)	No information		40	26

Source: J. R. Murphy and I. A. Goldberg, "Strategies for Using Programmed Instruction," *Harvard Business Review*, Vol. 42, No. 3 (1964), pp. 118–119.

learning steps. The approach is feasible only when a large number of employees must be trained for a given job.

In spite of these considerations, industry is making increasing use of the technique. Programs are being written for new jobs and job components at a rapidly expanding rate. Some of these are noted in Table 9–4. Others are telephone operator procedures, company benefit plan characteristics, computer language, fundamentals of life insurance, telephone relay adjustment, and product characteristics. To date there has been little application at the management level.

SYSTEM AND TEAM TRAINING

The training of groups of individuals whose work tasks interact has developed primarily within the armed services. However, various types of work-unit training are gradually finding their way into industry, especially in the field of air transportation (2).

In general, when the systems concept is applied as a basis for organizing work, the terms system or subsystem training are applied. In other instances, one hears of team or crew training. In either case, complex man-machine interactions may be involved.

Training of this kind normally is introduced relatively late in the over-all learning sequence, when individual workers are reasonably knowledgeable and proficient on their own individual jobs. A task is developed that requires role behavior from a number of employees in interaction. Usually, the task is selected to focus on special problem areas within the total work effort. The training may be conducted in the real-life work situation or in a simulated environment with the salient features built in. At the end of the exercise, knowledge of results on total team performance is provided insofar as this is possible, and the team members discuss their own performance. It is generally considered undesirable to introduce any type of evaluation or criticism from outside the team at this point (21).

The intent is to develop a cooperative effort and over-all levels of effectiveness beyond those obtainable from individual learning. As training progresses through successive trials on various tasks, the individual increasingly becomes aware of how his role behaviors may help and hinder his coworkers. He also begins to view his own work in terms of its place in the total team effort. Team training permits a group to develop solutions to various problems, such as the overloading of a single member that results in a bottleneck in production. Solutions of this kind are rarely learned when the training program relies entirely on individual instruction.

Especially when simulations are used, and simulations can be of considerable value in focusing on specific work problems, this training tends to have much in common with the business games discussed in the preceding chapter. The parallel even extends to the situation where employees are trained in a simulated situation to take over the operation of a man-machine system, the machine components of which are still under construction. Business games also are often used prior to any assumption of actual job duties.

There are, however, several major differences. For one thing, business games characteristically operate in fast time: events occur much more rapidly than in the actual business situation. System training on simulators occurs in real time. Second, business games normally are played with peers. Either all those engaged are students or, if management groups are involved, the tendency is to select individuals from approximately equal levels. Under system concepts, all those engaged in the operation of the system as it relates to the specific problem simulated must participate in the training, irrespective of the level in the organization.

Evaluation. Several arguments have been advanced against the use of this type of team training in the industrial situation (7,22). No doubt these are the major reasons the approach has not been adopted outside the military more rapidly than it has.

For one thing, it is extremely wasteful of time and money. Team training exercises almost invariably require role behavior from only a few members at a given point in time. The others act as observers or await their turn for participation. It is very difficult to maintain alertness and motivation among the nonactive members. Their time is often wasted, and labor costs increase with little return on the investment. In addition, there are the costs associated either with the use of machinery for non-productive purposes or with the construction of adequate simulations.

Second, there are problems related to the identification of individual errors and the over-all evaluation of results. It is often almost impossible to determine exactly what went wrong when difficulties arise. Immediate feedback and knowledge of results may be hard to achieve, and the specific source of an error may not be identified. Also suitable criteria of team performance must be established so that an effective effort can be clearly differentiated from an ineffective one. This can be done, but an adequate backlog of information does not exist as yet in this area, with the result that team standard-setting can become a major problem. Thus, the knowledge of results requirement tends to run into difficulties both at the level of the individual team member and at the level of the total team.

On the positive side, however, where cooperative effort represents a major aspect of the work, clear gains in efficiency above those obtainable with individual training do appear to result from the team approach. There are factors in any actual work situation with its flow of work activities and its patterning of social interactions that cannot be adequately handled through individual training. When considerations of this kind are marked, some group training does seem to be a desirable adjunct to other procedures.

REFERENCES

1. Bass, B. M., and J. A. Vaughan, *Training in Industry: The Management of Learning*. Belmont, Cal.: Wadsworth, 1966.
2. Biel, W. C., "Training Programs and Devices," in R. M. Gagné (ed.), *Psychological Principles in System Development*. New York: Holt, Rinehart & Winston, 1962, pp. 343–384.
3. Crawford, M. P., "Concepts of Training," in R. M. Gagné (ed.), *Psychological Principles in System Development*. New York: Holt, Rinehart & Winston, 1962, pp. 301–341.
4. Dunnette, M. D., and W. K. Kirchner, *Psychology Applied to Industry*. New York: Appleton-Century-Crofts, 1965.
5. Fryer, D. H., M. R. Feinberg, and S. S. Zalkind, *Developing People in Industry*. New York: Harper & Row, 1956.
6. Fryer, F. W., *An Evaluation of Level of Aspiration as a Training Procedure*. Englewood Cliffs, N.J.: Prentice-Hall, 1964.
7. Glanzer, M., "Experimental Study of Team Training and Team Functioning," in R. Glaser (ed.), *Training Research and Education*. Pittsburgh, Pa.: Univ. of Pittsburgh Press, 1962, pp. 397–407.
8. Glaser, R., "Psychology and Instructional Technology," in R. Glaser (ed.), *Training Research and Education*. Pittsburgh, Pa.: Univ. of Pittsburgh, 1962, pp. 1–30.
9. Haire, M., *Psychology in Management*, 2nd ed. New York: McGraw-Hill, 1964.

10. Hilgard, E. R., *Introduction to Psychology*, 3rd ed. New York: Harcourt, Brace & World, 1962.
11. Locke, E. A., "A Closer Look at Level of Aspiration as a Training Procedure: A Reanalysis of Fryer's Data," *Journal of Applied Psychology*, Vol. 50 (1966), 417–420.
12. Mahler, W. R., and W. H. Monroe, *How Industry Determines the Need for and Effectiveness of Training.* New York: Psychological Corp., 1952.
13. Maier, N. R. F., *Psychology in Industry*, 3rd ed. Boston, Mass.: Houghton-Mifflin, 1965.
14. Margulies, S., and L. D. Eigen, *Applied Programmed Instruction.* New York: Wiley, 1961.
15. McGehee, W., and D. H. Livingstone, "Persistence of the Effects of Training Employees to Reduce Waste," *Personnel Psychology*, Vol. 7 (1954), 33–39.
16. McGehee, W., and P. W. Thayer, *Training in Business and Industry.* New York: Wiley, 1961.
17. Miner, J. B., *Intelligence in the United States.* New York: Springer, 1957.
18. Mosel, J. N., "How to Feed Back Performance Results to Trainees," *Journal of the American Society of Training Directors*, Vol. 12 (1958).
19. Murphy, J. R., and I. A. Goldberg, "Strategies for Using Programmed Instruction," *Harvard Business Review*, Vol. 42 (1964), No. 3, 115–132.
20. National Manpower Council, *A Policy for Skilled Manpower.* New York: Columbia Univ. Press, 1954.
21. Porter, E. H., *Manpower Development.* New York: Harper & Row, 1964.
22. Smode, A. F., "Recent Developments in Training Problems, and Training and Training Research Methodology," in R. Glaser (ed.), *Training Research and Education.* Pittsburgh, Pa.: Univ. of Pittsburgh Press, 1962, pp. 429–495.

QUESTIONS

1. Differentiate training and education. Should companies engage in education? Should universities engage in training?
2. Describe the various procedures you might employ in carrying out a training needs analysis among the hourly work force of a large manufacturing plant.
3. Which principles of learning appear to operate most consistently when the following training procedures are used? Which are lacking?
   a. Programmed instruction.
   b. Vestibule school.
   c. System training.
   d. On-the-job training.

10

Accidents
and Safety

The preceding chapters have dealt with input-output mediators that contribute to the productivity or profit goal by changing the human input in some way so as to improve the capacity to produce output. In this chapter, the focus shifts from such maximizing processes to the somewhat more prosaic goal of maintaining organization members in good status as active contributors.

To keep employees producing at least at the level indicated by their potential when hired, it is necessary to prevent anything from happening to them that might result in a temporary or permanent reduction in output. The major causes of such reductions are injuries and illnesses. Thus, it becomes extremely important for business firms to limit accident frequency and severity and to eliminate anything that might contribute to the onset or prolongation of an illness. This is of course a humanitarian responsibility of any management, but it is also a factor in company goal attainment. Injuries and illnesses disrupt output and carry with them sizable costs.

This chapter will focus first on the various techniques that have been developed to prevent accidents, either by changing the environment to make it safer or by influencing the individual to make him less likely to fall prey to the potential danger around him. A second major topic will be the peculiar proclivity some individuals exhibit to have accidents and incur injury.

Safety Procedures

Although it is common practice to administer an accident prevention program from a safety division, usually located within the personnel structure, committees have become an important adjunct in this area. The primary reason for this development appears to be the widespread acceptance and cooperation essential to the success of any safety effort. To the extent a large number of individuals distributed throughout the company can be involved in the program, actual implementation of decisions related to safety is likely to be facilitated. It is particularly important that those at the higher levels of management feel this sense of involvement.

Under normal circumstances, the highest level safety committee is established on an interdepartmental basis and is concerned primarily with policy matters. Such a committee has primary responsibility for establishing safety rules, investigating particularly hazardous situations, making expenditures related to accident prevention, and resolving disputes.

In addition, a number of departmental committees deal with inspection and, to a degree at least, the correction of unsafe conditions. Unlike the policy committee, these groups are not restricted to managerial personnel. In fact, they appear to function more effectively if there is a heavy representation from below the managerial level.

The departmental committees may also handle safety training and publicity, but it is not uncommon to find a separate committee structure devoted to this purpose. These groups develop and carry out programs to promote interest in safety, to obtain compliance with safety rules, and to disseminate safety knowledge. In some companies, these training committees and those concerned with inspection have taken on a joint union-management character. Less frequently, the higher level policy group also has union representation. In some instances, this joint approach is necessary and even helpful, especially if the union leadership is strongly concerned about safety matters, but it may introduce a number of extraneous considerations into a group decision-making process that is often slow-moving and cumbersome even without this additional obstacle. The joint union-management committees can become so bound up in conflict that they are incapable of action.

ACCIDENT STATISTICS

Accident statistics are a valuable aspect of a total safety effort for two reasons. When calculated for the company as a whole, they permit comparison against the national and industry figures provided by such organizations as the National Safety Council and the federal Bureau of Labor Statistics. Thus, a company can determine its position relative to other firms and set its accident prevention goals accordingly. Where comparative statistics suggest that a major problem exists, a sizable total investment in safety procedures would seem to be warranted. Second, when rates are determined separately for the various work units within a firm, it is possible to pinpoint trouble spots and concentrate preventive efforts with these in mind. The accident prevention process may be focused where it will do the most good.

Most statistics use two rate formulas:

$$\text{Injury Frequency Rate} = \frac{\text{Number of disabling injuries} \times 1{,}000{,}000}{\text{Number of man-hours worked}}$$

$$\text{Injury Severity Rate} = \frac{\text{Number of days lost} \times 1{,}000{,}000}{\text{Number of man-hours worked}}$$

The usual practice is to use disabling or *lost time injuries* only in these calculations, although rates for *minor injuries* may be determined separately. Lost time injuries include deaths, partial or total permanent disabilities, and injuries that render a person unable to work for at least a whole work shift. Minor injuries do not meet the above criteria, but do require treatment in a dispensary or physician's office or first aid. Because they are either subject to workmen's compensation claims or reflected in absenteeism statistics, lost time injury data tend generally to be valid. Minor injuries, however, may go unreported. In calculating severity rates, standard time charges are used in the case of deaths and disabilities—actual days lost for temporary conditions.

Over the years, frequency and severity rates have tended to be high or low in the same industries. Communications, electrical equipment, aircraft manufacturing, automobile, rubber, and storage and warehousing are generally low on both indexes, and mining, marine transportation, construction, lumber, quarry, and transit are high. There are some marked exceptions to this generalization. Steel and cement have low frequency rates, but are well up among the various industries in severity. Wholesale and retail trade have a very low severity index, but are above the average in frequency. The electric utilities are high in terms of the severity of injuries, but do not have a particularly high frequency rate. Meat packing is just the reverse, being a high frequency industry with relatively low severity (11).

Motor vehicle accident rates are normally recorded on a separate basis for all company-owned cars or trucks. For purposes of motor safety, an accident is defined as any contact with the company vehicle causing either personal injury or property damage. The rate formula is:

$$\begin{matrix}\text{Motor Vehicle Accident} \\ \text{Frequency Rate}\end{matrix} = \frac{\text{Number of accidents} \times 100{,}000}{\text{Number of vehicle-miles operated}}$$

Usually, an attempt is made to compute separate rates for accidents chargeable against the company employee who was driving and those that are not his fault. There is some question, however, whether such efforts at differentiation are ever entirely successful. Obtaining the required information is often difficult and almost always time-consuming.

SAFETY TRAINING

There is evidence that, where the work situation is relatively hazardous, injuries are particularly likely to occur during the first few months of employment when the man has not yet learned how to protect himself against the dangers in his environment (16). Under such circumstances, it is apparent that any kind of training, whether directed toward orientation, skills, attitudes, or anything else connected with the job, can serve a preventive purpose insofar as accidents are concerned. To the extent such early training makes a new employee more capable of coping with his work environment, it will inevitably contribute to safety.

Actual training programs for new employees characteristically contain considerable safety content. Items covered are special hazards in the work situation, examples of previous accidents, nature and use of safety equipment, availability of medical services, accident reporting, and safety rules. Where the work is particularly hazardous, first aid procedures are often included.

Some firms also introduce discussions of safety off the job into the training process. This is done because many companies, as a result of their safety efforts, have produced a situation where injuries at work are less frequent than during the rest of the day. Factories are often safer than the home. Time lost owing to off the job injuries may well be greater than that resulting from work-connected injuries. Under such circumstances, the tendency has been to include a rather broad treatment of accident prevention within the training context.

Retraining. Another type of safety training is directed to those situations where there has been a deterioration in accident rates. It is not uncommon for experienced employees to develop group norms that sanction the breaking of safety rules and the failure to use protective devices. When this happens, safety training becomes an important antidote. The usual procedure is to review safety procedures in a series of discussions conducted by a safety specialist. Considerable opportunity is given for open criticism of existing rules and procedures, and, on occasion, changes are introduced in response to group decisions. Every effort is made not only to impart safety information, but to get employees personally involved in the safety effort. Some companies carry out this type of retraining on a periodic basis with all workers, irrespective of the accident rate in the group. The procedures used include lectures, reading assignments, films, television, discussions, and programmed instruction (2).

PUBLICITY AND CONTESTS

Safety publicity can take a variety of forms. Among those commonly used are posters, booklets, special memoranda, and articles in company publications. In many instances, these media advertise contests that pit various work groups against one another in an effort to minimize the number of lost time accidents.

Perhaps the major source of posters for industry is the National Safety Council, which provides new material monthly for a special fee in addition to membership. Many companies also print their own posters and notices. Insofar as possible, these should remind employees of safe practices without arousing too much anxiety. Gruesome and disturbing material is simply avoided by many people; they do not look at it at all. The main function of a good poster is to attract attention and keep employees thinking about safety, not to scare them.

There is some scientific evidence that safety posters of this kind are an effective means of reducing accidents. In one such study, the introduction of posters into seven steel mills was found to produce a sizable increase in safety behavior over a six-week test period (6). However, it remains true that many personnel managers and psychologists doubt the value of posters.

Company publications can be used to provide information on accidents that have occurred or on hazardous situations that have been corrected. Running accounts of the results of safety contests are often provided. All these promote safety consciousness, and to the extent the average employee is kept aware of the possibility of injury, he is likely to exhibit safer behavior.

Safety rules and regulations are usually printed in a separate booklet that is widely distributed. Unfortunately, these booklets rarely achieve a readership even approximating their distribution. Furthermore, some create disrespect for safety procedures rather than promote them, because there is a strong temptation for management to absolve itself of responsibility for accidents by proscribing all behaviors that might conceivably prove unsafe. As a result, many of the rules turn out to be entirely unrealistic, and employees break them without thinking, often with the tacit approval of their supervisors. When this happens the entire system of safety regulation becomes denigrated, with little differentiation being made between realistic and unrealistic rules. The only way to protect against this eventuality is to keep safety restrictions to a minimum and to recognize that a rule that no one will obey and that cannot be enforced is of little value to anyone. In fact, it can have a negative impact because of its influence on more appropriate regulations.

Contests. All manner of contests are conducted in the safety area, and apparently in most cases with considerable success. In general, the emphasis is on internal comparisons within a company, but there are some industry-wide contests such as those conducted by the National Safety Council. Perhaps most common is a competition between departments with similar accident potentials as indicated by national rates. These contests may stress a low frequency rate, or they may be concerned with the number of days without an injury. Sometimes, only lost time injuries are counted; sometimes minor injuries as well. Departments may also compete against their own records for certain periods in the past. Awards are often given to employees working in high accident occupations, such as truck drivers, for remaining accident free over an extended time span.

Although contests do appear to have a generally salutory effect on injuries, there are certain negative aspects that should be recognized. One is the tendency to let down when a long accident-free period finally comes to an end. A rash of injuries can occur at such a time, if something is not done to divert interest to some new contest or record. Second, there is some tendency to cover up injuries when they occur in the context of a contest, especially if minor injuries are included. The result can be a failure to obtain needed first aid and dispensary treatment. In addition, accident reports may not be filed when they should be with a resulting distortion of statistics.

CONTROL OF THE WORKING ENVIRONMENT

Design of the work place, and of equipment used in it, is probably the major approach to accident prevention, and the most effective. Safety devices and the like not only reduce accidents, but give employees a sense of confidence and security in the work place. Anxiety levels are reduced accordingly, and thus a potential source of performance disruption and failure is eliminated. This is a particularly important consideration in situations that would be extremely dangerous without accident prevention devices.

Although an extended discussion of safety engineering techniques would take us well beyond the field of personnel psychology as it is usually defined, several points can be made.

Probably most crucial is to construct equipment so as to introduce barriers that make it very hard, if not impossible, for the individual to expose himself to danger. Protective clothing, guards, covers, and the like can often serve to isolate a person from a danger source so that, irrespective of what he does, there is little chance of injury. In addition, controls should be designed and placed so that opportunities for erroneous use are kept to a minimum. Devices that yield information regarding any malfunctioning or breakdown of equipment should be installed wherever possible, and they should be readily visible. Self-correcting mechanisms and automatic shut-offs are ideal, because danger is eliminated without the need of human intervention. But if these cannot be installed, all controls, releases, gauges, and the like should be built so as to mesh to a maximal degree with the capabilities and characteristics of the human operator.

Although equipment design constitutes the major aspect of environmental control insofar as safety is concerned, there are other factors. Floors, stairs, ramps, elevators, and many other features must be constructed initially with safety in mind, and they must be inspected continually. Fire prevention and protection is also a normal safety function, as is protection against such catastrophes as floods, wind storms, and nuclear attack. As previously noted, automobile accidents represent a safety concern even when only property damage is involved. Safety considerations in the design of new products, and such matters as air and water pollution may also contribute to role prescriptions in the safety area. In all these areas, plans must be developed, inspections or tests carried out, and corrective actions taken.

SAFETY AND AUTOMATION

In general, automation seems to have resulted in a decreased injury rate, and it should produce even more impressive results in the future. Ventilation, temperature, humidity, and noise can easily be controlled and kept at an optimal level. Materials need not be handled by the worker, and thus toxic effects are minimized. Also, contact with machinery is almost nonexistent, as is most lifting and loading. Hernia cases decreased by 85 per cent at the Ford Motor Company after the introduction of automated equipment (13).

The result should be that handicapped workers increasingly will find opportunities for employment in the automated industries. Yet, there is reason to believe that during the period of transition to automated equipment, injury rates may well rise. Workers are not used to the new procedures, and unless training is extensive, nervousness and anxiety in the face of the complex electronic and mechanical systems can become acute, so acute, in fact, that the distracted workers may fall prey to accident hazards that they would otherwise avoid (8).

Maintenance work on automated equipment may well prove to be the most resistant to accident prevention efforts. Electrical hazards are considerable, and so is the possibility of falls. Although operating conditions can be largely standardized and the operator isolated from danger, maintenance and repair will invariably introduce unanticipated circumstances. Thus, it is here that injuries are, and probably will continue to be, most frequent and also most serious.

Accident Proneness

Accidents are most frequent in the seventeen-to-twenty-eight age range and decline steadily after that to a low point in the late fifties and sixties (12). Evidence indicates that those individuals who have high injury rates in one year are most likely to have high rates the following year (14). The data of Figure 10–1 are typical. In this instance, there is a steady increase in the number of accidents during the second year as a function of the first year frequencies. Those who had no accidents the first year averaged only .69 the second year. Those who had nine accidents the first year averaged 5.14 the second year. The same trend appears in all of the eleven separate departments represented in the combined data of Figure 10–1. Additional studies to determine whether the hazards associated with specific jobs could account for these results produced

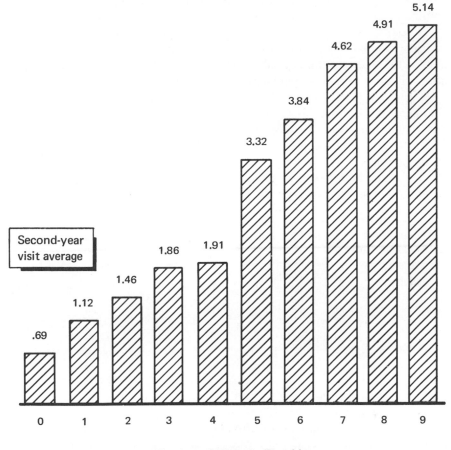

Number of Visits in First Year

Figure 10–1. Frequency of Hospital Visits in Second Year for Steel Mill Workers with Various Rates in First Year

negative results. When differences in job danger were controlled, the same pattern was still present in the data.

Findings of this kind are consistent with the widely held opinion that injuries are not merely a direct function of the degree to which the working environment contains hazardous features. It is true, of course, that training deficiencies and the fact that younger workers are more likely to be new on the job could account for part of the injury-age relationship. But these cannot explain all the findings. For one thing, the increase during the early years is far too marked. For another, the injury rates do not reach their highest level until age twenty-one or twenty-two, even though skill deficiencies are most pronounced among those who are younger.

It seems, then, that contrary to the earlier view that differences in accident frequencies could be accounted for in terms of chance fluctuations (10), certain individuals are consistently more susceptible to injuries than others. This tendency may well be more pronounced during a specific period of a man's life, however. Research into the personality characteristics of individuals with high injury frequency rates supports this conclusion. There do appear to be some consistent differences between these accident repeaters and those who do not have such a high injury potential.

One such study has already been discussed in Chapter 7. The results noted in Table 7–6 are reproduced in Table 10–1. The *accident prone*

TABLE 10–1. Relationships Between Sentence Completion Indexes and Accident Rates ($N = 34$)

Sentence completion variable	r
Optimism	−.34
Trust	−.51
Sociocentricity	−.76
Pessimism	−.19
Distrust	.02
Anxiety	.09
Egocentricity	.19
Resentment	.29
Negative employment attitude	.70

Source: A. Davids and J. T. Mahoney, "Personality Dynamics and Accident-Proneness in an Industrial Setting," *Journal of Applied Psychology*, Vol. 41 (1957), p. 304.

individuals are clearly very negative in their attitudes. They dislike their superiors, their jobs, and work generally. Furthermore, they tend to be almost devoid of optimism and trust, and, in fact, have little positive feeling toward people at all (3).

Another investigation involved the testing of fifty-four individuals with extremely high injury frequency rates (7). The lack of warm emotional relationships with others was again apparent. Most had a number of acquaintances, but they were not really close to these people. In addition, the negative attitudes toward those in positions of authority noted in the study just mentioned were once again present. These accident-prone individuals exhibited a marked, and often unreasonable, hatred of their superiors at work as well as of other authority figures.

There were certain other findings as well. The high accident group was concerned about health matters, although actual illness tended to be rare. There was a strong desire for increased social status coupled with very little accomplishment in this regard. Emotionally disturbing situations were often handled by misperceiving and distorting the world around them so as to make it less threatening. As a result, these people made frequent bad mistakes in judgment. Planning for the future was apparently minimal. They preferred to live from day to day and were, in fact, quite impulsive. This latter finding fits well with data from another study that indicates that people with high injury frequency and severity rates are likely to act with a high degree of muscular speed even though they lack the visual capacity to comprehend a situation with equal rapidity (4). Thus, action often precedes perception and thought, which is a good description of what is meant by impulsiveness. This particular study was carried out in the metalworking department of a large factory.

Taken together, these investigations and others of a similar nature (1,15) yield a rather consistent picture of the accident-prone person, although it must be understood that a great many work injuries, perhaps the majority, involve people who do not have frequent accidents and who do not possess the characteristics found among these accident repeaters. The accident-prone persons seem to be rather socially irresponsible and immature, although not really emotionally ill in most cases. Because their high injury rates are not normally maintained throughout life, but only over periods of a few years, it seems most appropriate to view accident proneness as a transient personality maladjustment that is most likely to develop before age thirty.

The major motivation behind the repeated accidents themselves would appear to be a desire to impress others by resorting to sudden and very risky decisions and behavior. Research has repeatedly demonstrated the very marked "adventuresomeness" of those with high accident frequencies (5). This impulsiveness is usually combined with a strong hatred of people at higher levels in the organization and a consequent defiance of the rules and policies established by these people. Thus, safety regulations are deliberately flouted, not only as a way of impressing others with one's skill or bravery, but as a means of attacking and resisting management. Under such circumstances, exposure to danger becomes unusually frequent for these employees. With an exposure level this high, it is not surprising that they are injured on a number of occasions. By their own actions, they repeatedly place themselves in an extremely hazardous work environment, even though their jobs might not, under normal circumstances, be considered dangerous at all.

In some instances, this pattern may be supplemented as a result of certain additional personality processes. Hatred toward one's superiors on occasion can generate considerable guilt, and a wish, whether conscious or unconscious, to escape this guilt by being punished. To the extent punishment is viewed as atonement for one's sins, it may well be desired. For these people, an accident may be equated with punishment, and a real desire to suffer injury may develop at periodic intervals when guilt becomes too pronounced. Here the accident is not merely a chance event in a personally created hazardous environment, but a desired and directly caused outcome. The need for self-preservation gives way before the need to expiate guilt, just as it often does in suicide cases.

DEALING WITH ACCIDENT PRONENESS

The question remains: What can be done to reduce the frequency of personally created accidents of this kind? To some extent, selection procedures may screen the input on this basis, although this has not been widely done. Such an approach seems particularly desirable in high accident rate industries such as mining and lumber. It seems less appropriate in safer industries, where it may not be economically feasible to screen out a limited number of accident-prone individuals who in all likelihood would not have an extremely high rate of injury in any event because of the lower danger level.

Given the fact, then, that, because of a lack of, or the imperfections of, input screening, accident-prone people are likely to be employed by any company at least in limited numbers, what can be done to deal with the problem? As the age-accident frequency relationship suggests, accident proneness tends to correct itself eventually, but not until a number of injuries have occurred, large sums have been disbursed in disability payments, and in many instances sizable output and equipment losses have accrued.

Thus, some kind of direct action does seem to be called for. One approach is to reduce the danger in the work environment as much as possible. This will have only limited impact on those who really want to injure themselves to reduce guilt, but it will yield results among the high risktakers, because there will be less chance for an accident to occur. In part, danger reduction can be achieved through equipment design; in part through transferring the accident-prone individual to low hazard work. Equipment design is of value, however, only to the extent it removes control of the safety factor from the employee. Protective clothing and warning devices are of little help with the accident prone. Automatic shut-offs and fixed barriers, on the other hand, can be much more effective.

The second point relates to the hatred of people in positions of authority, which is known to characterize the accident prone. It is when they are forced into continuing close relationships with their superiors that these individuals are most likely to be injured. In view of this, managers should, insofar as possible, keep at a distance from those who have had high accident rates. Everything possible should be done to minimize conflict and resentment. To the extent the man can work on his own with only very limited restriction, control, and discipline, the chances of injury will inevitably be reduced. Appropriate supervisory techniques for use with the accident prone can be taught as part of various management development programs (9).

REFERENCES

1. Alexander, F., *Psychosomatic Medicine*. New York: Norton, 1950.
2. Bass, B. M., and J. A. Vaughan, *Training in Industry: The Management of Learning*. Belmont, Cal.: Wadsworth, 1966.
3. Davids, A., and J. T. Mahoney, "Personality Dynamics and Accident-proneness in an Industrial Setting," *Journal of Applied Psychology*, Vol. 41 (1957), 303–306.
4. Drake, C. A., "Accident-proneness: A Hypothesis," *Character and Personality*, Vol. 8 (1940), 335–341.
5. Kunce, J. T., "Vocational Interests and Accident Proneness," *Journal of Applied Psychology*, Vol. 51 (1967), 223–225.
6. Laner, S., and R. G. Sell, "An Experiment on the Effect of Specially Designed Safety Posters," *Occupational Psychology*, Vol. 34 (1960), 153–169.
7. LeShan, L. L., "Dynamics of Accident-prone Behavior," *Psychiatry*, Vol. 15 (1952), 73–80.
8. Mann, F. C., and L. R. Hoffman, *Automation and the Worker*, New York: Holt, Rinehart & Winston, 1960.
9. Miner, J. B., *The Management of Ineffective Performance*. New York: McGraw-Hill, 1963.
10. Mintz, A., and M. L. Blum, "A Re-examination of the Accident Proneness Concept," *Journal of Applied Psychology*, Vol. 33 (1949), 195–211.
11. National Safety Council, *Accident Facts*. Chicago, Illinois: The Council.
12. Schulzinger, M. S., *The Accident Syndrome*. Springfield, Illinois: Charles C Thomas, Publisher, 1956.
13. Shils, E. B., *Automation and Industrial Relations*. New York: Holt, Rinehart & Winston, 1963.
14. Tiffin, J., and E. J. McCormick, *Industrial Psychology*, 5th ed. Englewood Cliffs, N.J.: Prentice-Hall, 1965.
15. Tillmann, W. A., and G. E. Hobbs, "The Accident-prone Automobile Driver," *American Journal of Psychiatry*, Vol. 106 (1949), 321–331.
16. Van Zelst, R. H., "The Effect of Age and Experience upon Accident Rate," *Journal of Applied Psychology*, Vol. 38 (1954), 313–317.

1. Differentiate the following:
   a. Injury frequency rate vs. injury severity rate.
   b. Lost time injuries vs. minor injuries.
2. What negative features are associated with each of the approaches to accident reduction?
3. What is accident proneness, and how might it be minimized as a factor in company injury rates?

11

Industrial Clinical Psychology

The previous three chapters have dealt with a variety of functional input-output mediators, all directed primarily toward the achievement of productivity and profit goals. These have been classified to differentiate between mediators that attempt to improve the quality of the original human input and mediators that work toward the essentially hygienic function of preventing output disruption. One further type of mediator remains to be discussed. An individual may perform below the level of his initial promise, even to the point where a sizable disparity between role behavior and role prescriptions exists; he may fail to perform satisfactorily in one or more respects. At this point, concern tends to focus on the process of performance control and on mediators that may serve a corrective function.

The discussion that follows describes certain details of this control model in its application to human performance. A subsequent section deals with the factors that may cause an individual to perform ineffectively. Finally, the various mediators that may be used for corrective purposes are considered. Special attention is given to such approaches as moving the man to another job, modifying existing personnel policy, discipline, counseling, and medical treatment.

The Control Model and Human Performance

The various procedures used to correct performance deficiencies are best understood when viewed in the context of the control model. This model focuses on those cases where some deviation from an established standard occurs. With regard to performance, this means the employee whose work behavior departs from role prescriptions so markedly that it falls below a minimum acceptable level. In these specific instances of clear-cut ineffective performance, some type of corrective procedure is needed if the man is to make any sizable contribution to company goal attainment. Performance control identifies individuals whose work is consistently below standard and acts to restore performance to an acceptable level. In its major characteristics, it is essentially comparable to production control, quality control, inventory control, and cost control.

ESTABLISHING STANDARDS

Minimum acceptable standards are established using a variety of performance indexes of the kind discussed in Chapters 4 and 5. Any type of appraisal or evaluation variable may be used, with the single proviso that all should be related to organizational goal attainment.

The minimum acceptable level on each performance index or criterion may be established in either of two ways. The most common practice is for the immediate superior to set standards in his own mind on a judgmental basis. Under such circumstances, the minimum acceptable level of performance may vary somewhat from manager to manager and even at different points in time with the same manager. A second approach, which avoids this difficulty, involves a more objective standard-setting process carried out by some such group as industrial engineering on a company-wide basis. Unfortunately, suitable objective measures of this latter kind are not always available.

Performance standards, whether established judgmentally or in a more objective manner, relate to both the productivity and the organizational maintenance goals, although the greatest concern tends to be with productivity, the quantity and quality of output. Other important considerations are the extent of absenteeism, impact on the work of others, contribution to internal stress and conflict, and dishonest behavior.

PERFORMANCE ANALYSIS

Outside the personnel area, the control concept has often been applied without giving detailed attention to determining the specific cause of the deviation from standard. The major concerns have tended to be with (1) establishing the standard, (2) measuring the deviation, and (3) setting up a feedback mechanism or some similar procedure to correct the deviation.

When the control model is applied in the personnel area, however, it becomes clear that corrective procedures cannot be effective unless information is available regarding the *causal* factors that have produced the performance failure. The situation is comparable essentially to that which exists in medicine. A physician must make a suitable diagnosis, which identifies the *cause* of the failure to meet acceptable health standards, before he can select from among the numerous available treatments. He needs to know what specific disease he is dealing with. Otherwise, his treatment will be on a trial-and-error basis, and the chances for cure will be small.

Performance analysis is the name given to this process of identifying contributory causes, of diagnosing the factors that have produced a given instance of performance failure (16). Basically, a series of hypotheses are formulated regarding the possible strategic factors. Each hypothesis is then checked against what is known about the individual, and either accepted or rejected. The result is a list of contributory causes that can guide the selection of an appropriate corrective procedure.

FIRING AS AN ALL-PURPOSE SOLUTION

As indicated in Chapter 6, selection procedures cannot achieve perfection. There inevitably will be some individuals hired who either immediately, or at some subsequent date, fail to perform effectively. Thus, although a judicious use of selection techniques can reduce the incidence of performance failure, the problem will still remain. Performance control cannot be entirely circumvented by concentrating on achieving a high quality of input to the organization.

One other possibility does remain, however. Could not all who become ineffective be fired immediately, thus eliminating any need for time-consuming and costly procedures such as performance analyses and corrective actions? The answer is that although firing is always a possibility, it has become hedged with so many constraints, both internal and external to the organization, that it is often not really feasible. In addition, it can well be as costly as taking corrective action. Thus, it must be considered a last resort in most cases.

That company payments toward unemployment compensation are based on an experience rating procedure that penalizes a firm for high involuntary turnover rates tends to exert pressure against firing. Furthermore, a number of companies have policies requiring severance payments to individuals who are separated against their will subsequent to an initial probationary period. Although these may not always be paid in discipline cases, a unionized firm that utilizes firing extensively as a solution to performance failure can expect to make severance payments in a relatively large number of instances.

This is only one of the pressures related to unionization. If there is a possibility that the dismissal represents an unfair labor practice in that the firing occurred because of union activity, a firm may have to reinstate with back pay. This can be ordered by a Labor Relations Board or by the courts. Even if the company wins such a case, the investment in time and money is likely to be sizable. In any event, formal grievances nearly always are filed in discharge cases, and in many instances, these require outside arbitration. In one series of over 300 discharges appealed to an arbitrator, only 46 per cent were sustained. In 19 per cent of the cases, the man was reinstated with full back pay; the remainder were reinstated but with some pay loss (1).

Strikes in response to an unfair firing are frequent in firms that do not have a clause barring such work stoppages incorporated in the union contract. Even where a no strike agreement applies over the period of the agreement, slowdowns and other types of retaliatory action may occur. The only solution to these varied union pressures may be eventual reinstatement.

Internal pressures against firing need not be mediated through the union. Individuals, or groups of employees, may consider a discharge inequitable and act to make things difficult for the responsible manager, or retaliate against the company in some way. Even where a manager does not view such an eventuality as likely, he may hesitate to fire because of the enmity his action might create or because he himself would feel guilty were he to discharge the man. Especially in the case of long service employees, strong social pressures against firing are characteristic in the business world.

Externally, there is always the possibility that a company that resorts to frequent discharge may create an image for itself in the community that severely restricts the available labor market. The number and quality of applicants may be sharply curtailed, and recruiting costs may rise considerably. In some instances, too, antagonism toward the company resulting from a high discharge rate may influence the sale of products and other types of business dealings. Both the product and the labor markets may suffer.

Finally there are all the costs associated with turnover of any kind:

1. The cost of recruiting and selecting a replacement.
2. The cost of training a replacement.
3. The costs associated with overpayment of the replacement during the period of learning when he cannot produce at full capacity.
4. The cost of breakage and waste during the learning period and of any accidents that may occur.
5. The cost of any overtime work put in by others during the period between firing one man and the achievement of full capacity by another.
6. The cost of production losses owing to the lack of a man to perform the job between firing and replacement, plus the similar costs

attributable to the process of achieving an adjustment between the work group and its new member.

7. The costs resulting from a failure to fully utilize equipment during the replacement's training period (19).

Taken as a whole, this imposing array exerts a strong pressure for performance control rather than discharge. Certainly firing is not an impossibility, but it is often a last resort. As an all-purpose solution to ineffective performance it is clearly inappropriate. As a solution when corrective action is known to be either impossible or inexpedient, it seems preferable to letting an entirely unsatisfactory man stay on indefinitely.

The Schema for Performance Analysis

Intensive study of a large number of cases where performance failures have occurred has resulted in the development of a schema that appears to cover at least the great majority of possibly strategic factors (7,16). The elements of the schema may be treated as hypotheses to be considered either implicitly or explicitly in the process of performance analysis or, to use the medical term, diagnosis. Each hypothesis is checked against all available information and either confirmed or rejected.

The number of confirmed hypotheses or strategic factors that emerge from this process varies considerably from case to case. Job failure is rarely a result of a single cause. Usually, there are about four contributory factors, but in an occasional instance there can be as many as seven or eight. People fail because, with their own particular pattern of abilities and personality characteristics, they become enmeshed in a specific constellation of circumstances. The problem is to spell out exactly which individual and environmental factors have played a causal role.

INTELLIGENCE AND JOB KNOWLEDGE

Insufficient Verbal Ability. As noted in Chapter 2, the further up in the job hierarchy a position is located, the greater its demand in terms of verbal ability or general intelligence. Given this circumstance, it is not surprising that on occasion people attain a level where the role requirements are intellectually beyond them. At such times, failure is likely to be reflected in a high incidence of errors and incorrect decisions.

The available evidence suggests that underplacement on the basis of verbal ability is not generally a problem. At least, it seems clear that a great many people are working in jobs that demand much less intellectually than they could give (14). Yet, under certain circumstances, especially where advancement opportunities are severely restricted, underplacement can be a source of difficulty, although usually in interaction with certain personality factors.

Insufficient Special Ability Other than Verbal. Various jobs, irrespective of their level in the hierarchy, require widely differing types of intellectual abilities. Numerical, spatial, mechanical, clerical, and other abilities are relevant for some types of work, not for others. To the extent an individual lacks whatever abilities may be required, he is likely to fail through an inability to think effectively and learn rapidly. Having abilities that are not utilized in a job constitutes less of a problem, unless the desire to use the ability is particularly strong.

Insufficient Job Knowledge. Here the failure cannot be attributed to any lack of ability. The individual has the intellectual capacity to learn the job, but because of inadequate training or for some other reason he has not done so. In some instances, the difficulty stems from a lack of any real desire to take advantage of learning opportunities or from emotional blocks to learning.

Defect of Judgment or Memory. In most cases, these defects reflect the interference of emotional factors with intellectual processes. On standard intelligence tests, the individual may score quite high, but when it comes to applying his intelligence on the job the results are not so good. Defects of this kind are particularly frequent among those suffering from some type of emotional disorder, but they can also result from a disturbance in brain functioning, such as might occur as a result of a head injury.

EMOTIONS AND EMOTIONAL ILLNESS

Continuing Disruptive Emotion. As noted, emotions can disrupt intellectual functioning to produce defects of judgment and memory. They can also, if intense enough and frequent enough, have a detrimental impact on many other aspects of job behavior. This is particularly true of negative emotional states such as anxiety and fear, depression, shame, and guilt. But failure can also occur as a result of persistent anger, jealousy, and excitement. The individual need not be emotionally ill for a severe impact on the level of work performance to manifest itself. The result may be a number of errors, an inability to concentrate so that output is slowed, a tendency to be constantly emersed in controversy, or, and this is perhaps most frequent, a continuing avoidance of many required job behaviors.

Psychosis. These, like the neuroses to be discussed next, manifest themselves in a variety of symptoms that take on an inflexible character and disrupt many of the ongoing processes of life. In a psychosis, the preoccupation with symptoms, emotions, and the warding off of unpleasant feelings becomes so intense that a real break with reality occurs, at least at certain times and under certain circumstances. Symptoms vary from incessant emotional states, to disorders of physical functioning, to pathological behavior and speech, and even to extreme distortions of perception and belief. Although the various psychotic conditions represent relatively rare phenomena insofar as the work environment is concerned, their impact on performance is generally marked. Often the man cannot continue work at all while in the psychotic state.

Neurosis. The neuroses, although milder in their impact on the personality, may on occasion have just as detrimental an effect on work performance as the psychoses. This appears to depend to a considerable extent on the job level, however.

As Table 11–1 demonstrates, true emotional health is found much

TABLE 11–1. **Mental Health Differences Between Factory Occupational Groups**

Occupational category	*Young (20–29)*		*Middle-aged (40–49)*	
	Proportion with high mental health, %	Number of workers	Proportion with high mental health, %	Number of workers
Skilled			56	45
	58	33		
High semiskilled			41	98
Ordinary semiskilled	35	46	38	82
Repetitive semiskilled	10	30	26	73
Total workers		109		298

Source: A. Kornhauser, *Mental Health of the Industrial Worker.* New York: Wiley, 1965, p. 57.

more frequently at the higher occupational levels. In lower level positions of a repetitive nature, symptoms of emotional disorder, primarily those associated with neuroses, are much more common, and in these particular jobs the detrimental effects appear to be minimal (13). In such positions it cannot be presumed that if a neurosis is present, it will account for any ineffective performance. At higher levels, on the other hand, neuroses are typically quite disruptive. Whether the high incidence of poor mental health in low level factory positions is attributable primarily to the impact of the routine work on the individual (11) or to the fact that the emotionally ill gravitate to such jobs (17) remains an open question. There is evidence for both views. In any event, it seems clear that people *can* be overplaced emotionally, as well as intellectually.

INDIVIDUAL MOTIVATION TO WORK

Strong Motives Frustrated at Work. Probably the most common type of motivationally caused performance failure is the case where an individual wants something very much from his job and is unable to attain it. Among the things desired that seem to be important in this sense are success, the avoidance of all failure, domination of others, popularity, social interaction, attention, emotional support, and freedom from any anxiety that may have become associated with certain job aspects. When such motives are frustrated, the individual may leave his job, he may stay on but make practically no effort, he may become sullen and angry, or he may attempt to achieve what he wants through behavior that is antithetical to effective job performance.

Unintegrated Means to Satisfy Motives. Resorting to behavior that is not job-integrated may occur among individuals who do not actually experience any frustration of a strong motive at work, as well as among those who do. Many people almost immediately develop an approach to a new job that permits motive satisfaction, but at the expense of fulfilling role requirements. A secretary who desires social interaction may make friends rapidly and spend most of her time talking to others, to the detriment of their performance and her own. Similarly, theft and other forms of dishonesty may represent a rapid route to success.

Excessively Low Personal Work Standards. Another possibility in the area of motivation is that an individual may set very low work standards for himself, standards well below those considered minimally acceptable either by his superior or in the company as a whole. There is good evidence that individuals with such low standards, as well as those with unrealistically high standards, tend to be poor workers (9). Apparently, they achieve a sense of personal success and accomplishment with a degree of effort far below that actually required.

Generalized Low Work Motivation. There are individuals whose motivational systems are so structured that their important desires tend to be satisfied outside the work situation, or at least through behavior not included within the role prescriptions for any job. In such cases, there is practically no mesh between the individual and the world of work at all, and, as a consequence, the quantity, and perhaps quality also, of the man's output will be low, quite irrespective of the position held.

PHYSICAL CHARACTERISTICS AND DISORDERS

Physical Illness or Handicap. The major way in which physical disorders contribute to ineffective performance is absence from the job, although quantity and quality of output may also be affected. And there may even be an increase in uncooperative, conflict-producing behavior as occurs with certain kinds of brain disorder. Handicapped employees have generally proved as competent as other workers, if their handicaps do not bar working at all (2), but in some instances, certain disabilities may contribute to failure in specific jobs. There are things that the deaf, the blind, those with heart conditions, epileptics, and other handicapped people just cannot do effectively.

Physical Disorders of Emotional Origin. A number of physical symptoms such as headaches, fainting, ulcers, high blood pressure, hay fever, backache, and skin disorders may be caused by emotional factors. When this is the case, the symptoms and the work disruption are identical to what would exist if no emotional element were present; only the cause is different. In order to select an appropriate corrective action, disorders of this kind must be differentiated from those resulting from physical illness or handicap.

Inappropriate Physical Characteristics. There are features of bodily proportion and aesthetics that, although not widely significant, may become strategic in certain jobs. A large man may have difficulty working in a cramped space, a small man in a truck cab with the seat far removed from the controls, an unattractive woman in a modeling position. Many physical characteristics are less important today, with the advent of human engineering and the consequent emphasis on designing equipment to fit the human operator, but these factors can become crucial at times.

Insufficient Muscular or Sensory Ability. As noted in Chapter 2, a variety of muscular dexterities and abilities, as well as the purely intellectual abilities, may influence job performance. Where there is a deficiency in some ability that is required by the job, ineffectiveness can result. Strength and physical dexterities have decreasing relevance as automation advances, but they still can be a factor in failure on some jobs. Defects and deficiencies of vision and hearing remain a significant source of problems in many cases, also. Competence in driving a truck, for instance, is strongly influenced by such sensory abilities.

FAMILY TIES

Family Crises. A number of significant events in the home environment can affect the personality of certain individuals sufficiently to disturb work performance. Among these are desertion, divorce, threatened divorce, illness of a family member or death, and criminal prosecution. Normally, these effects are transitory, but on occasion the performance decrement is maintained for a considerable period. Unfortunately, such crises do not always come to the attention of a personnel manager, and as a result the frequency with which they are strategic may be markedly underestimated.

Separation from the Family. The mere fact of extended separation from either the parental family or a wife and children can produce a very intense homesickness in some individuals. Business trips, temporary out-of-town assignments, management development programs at universities, and the like can induce considerable anxiety in some people, especially those who have rarely been away from home. The result can be a severe disruption of performance during the period of absence with frequent errors, poor decisions, and difficult interpersonal relationships.

Predominance of Family Considerations over Work Demands. In contrast to family crises, the predominance of family considerations over work demands does not represent a threat to the family's unity or survival. Yet it can, and frequently does, have a considerable impact on performance. A demanding wife can require so much of her husband's time that he has little left for work. Or a wife may become disturbed at leaving her home town, or going to a foreign country, and impose a severe burden on her husband as a result. Certain family situations are little short of chaos, and some carryover into the work situation is inevitable. Competition between father and son or wife and husband may well produce emotional reactions which permeate the job.

THE GROUPS AT WORK

Negative Consequences Associated with Group Cohesion. There is reason to believe that the process of *restriction of output,* within a cohesive group can yield a low level of production that is, nevertheless, socially sanctioned. Although it is common to observe a generally centralizing tendency among group members when restriction occurs, it is also true that some individuals may be forced below the minimum acceptable level of output by the restricted standard. These are typically low producers, who are incapable of gauging their work sufficiently well to remain above the unacceptable level when a low group standard is established.

Also groups with a marked sense of cohesiveness or belongingness can reject members whom they believe to be deviant. Although such ostracism may have no effect on some people, it is extremely threatening to others. The result can be intense anxiety or anger that constantly disrupts work.

Ineffective Management. The discussion of management appraisal techniques in Chapter 4 was preceded by a review of studies dealing with the behavior of effective and ineffective managers. Using the terminology of the Ohio State research, it was found that managers who were inconsiderate of subordinates and those who failed to initiate structure were particularly likely to have low-producing groups (16). It is also apparent that a similar lack of consideration or a failure to establish and enforce standards can contribute to the ineffective performance of specific subordinates. It is not at all uncommon for supervisory action to conflict with subordinate personality patterns and, as a result, actually produce failure, even where the opposite result is desired.

Inappropriate Managerial Standards or Criteria. As previously indicated, the criteria by which subordinates are judged are usually set by their superiors, as are the performance standards used to determine effectiveness. In certain cases, these may be established without any reference to organizational goals. Thus, failure may be embedded in the evaluative process rather than in the individual. Because of supervisory biases, standards may be set at an unrealistically high level. Or the criteria employed may be totally irrelevant to role prescriptions and the company's goals. In such instances, the failure may be by definition only. This is one of the few cases where only one factor may be strategic.

THE COMPANY

Insufficient Organizational Action. Job failure may occur or be perpetuated because the company does not take the kind of corrective action required. Medical treatment, training, and the like may not be provided, either intentionally or through some oversight. In either case, the lack of action on the part of the company, or its representatives in the personnel area, can become strategic.

The decision not to invest in corrective action may be based on various considerations. The cost may be too high. The time required to restore effective performance may be too long, as with certain kinds of education and training. The chances of success, if the best available type of corrective action is applied, may be far from good. This is true, for instance, of psychotherapy with certain kinds of emotional disorders. Finally, potentially effective replacements may be readily available so that any sizable investment in correction that may be required seems to be unwise.

Placement Error. Placement error probably appears in more cases than any other. It is particularly prevalent where random assignment policies, seniority, or union pressures govern the placement process and where accordingly there is little effort to put individuals with known characteristics in appropriate jobs. If intellectual, emotional, motivational, or physical factors are strategic, there is nearly always a placement error as well.

Organizational Overpermissiveness. On occasion, a company will operate under such lax and permissive personnel policies and procedures that employees are actually encouraged not to work. When circumstances of this kind exist, individuals with certain types of motivational patterns may become ineffective.

A company may, for instance, encourage insubordination through a lack of discipline. Excessive training, far beyond what is required for complete learning, can foster a feeling that actual on-the-job production is unimportant. Liberal sick leave policies can result in excessive absenteeism. In all these cases, there is a deficiency in organizational action that interacts with individual motives to produce job failure.

Excessive Span of Control. In some cases, a manager may fail to deal effectively with a particular subordinate, and thus contribute to a performance failure, not because of any inadequacy in himself as a manager, but because there simply is not sufficient time. The number of individuals supervised, the span of control, may be so great that the manager just cannot deal with his subordinates as individuals, carrying out performance analyses and the like. Here the deficiency is not in the manager, and thus a group factor is not strategic. Rather, the organizational structure has been established in such a way as to preclude effective action by a superior aimed at preventing performance failure.

Inappropriate Organizational Standards or Criteria. This is the counterpart of the inappropriate managerial standards or criteria category discussed under the work group heading. In this instance, however, the focus is on standards set as a result of organizational policy or high-level decisions, rather than on those established by individual superiors.

SOCIETY AND ITS VALUES

Application of Legal Sanctions. This category covers those cases where an individual is unable to perform his job duties because he has committed a crime and been sent to jail. Under such circumstances, societal values are strategic in that they form the base for the legal structure.

Enforcement of Societal Values by Means Not Connected with the Administration of the Law. Although society obtains compliance with its values in large part through the agency of the legal process and police action, it is also true that pressure may be exerted outside the law. A salesman may fail because no one will buy from him, after he has committed some act that his potential customers consider unethical or immoral. In cases of this kind, it is the enforcement of the societal value structure that produces the ineffective performance, but the source of enforcement is not connected with the legal process.

Conflict Between Job Demands and Cultural Values. The most frequent type of strategic factor involving societal values is the conflict of an individual's strong convictions with the role prescriptions for his job. Intense commitments to equity and fair play, to individual freedom, and to morality can contribute to job failure, even though all are highly valued in the society as a whole. It is not uncommon for industrial scientists, for instance, with a strong belief in freedom of inquiry, to become incensed at the restrictions of a bureaucratic organization. Similarly, salesmen with a particularly strong sense of honesty are very likely to fail because they view the behavior required of them on the job as basically dishonest (15).

SITUATIONAL FORCES

Negative Consequences of Economic Forces. Negative consequences of economic forces usually occur in conjunction with an emotional or motivational factor. Competing firms, or economic conditions generally, produce a situation where a man cannot achieve at a level consistent with his standards. As a result, he becomes emotionally distressed, and eventually his performance does not come up to what could realistically be expected under the existing circumstances. Problems of this kind are particularly common among salesmen who are assigned to economically depressed territories or who face sharp price-cutting by competitors.

Negative Consequences of Geographic Locations. A similar type of reaction may occur as a result of being forced to work in an inappropriate geographic location. Being sent to a foreign country is very disturbing to some individuals, because of the strangeness of the world and people around them. This reaction may be totally unrelated to the fact of separation from loved ones at home. Some people experience debilitating physical symptoms in certain climates, and a sailor who is prone to seasickness may well never achieve a satisfactory performance level when he is at sea. In all such cases, something associated with the geographic location of the work makes effective performance impossible.

Detrimental Conditions of Work. Many environmental forces impinging on an individual derive from the various groups of which he is a member—his family, the work group, the company, society. Others derive from the aspects of the situational context already noted, other economic organizations and the geographic location. Equally effective as situational forces are the physical characteristics of the actual working environment—the noise level, the amount and type of illumination, the temperature, and various aspects of the design of the work place or the equipment in it. To the extent the working environment contains features that do not mesh with the physical capacities and characteristics of the individual, or on occasion with his intellectual, emotional or motivational make-up, it can contribute markedly to performance failure.

Excessive Danger. One aspect of the physical work context that appears to be sufficiently important to warrant separate attention is the danger level. The preceding chapter dealt with this topic at some length. A work environment with a high built-in accident potential can contribute to excessive absenteeism. It can elicit anxiety, too, and thus interfere with output.

Subjective Danger. An individual may read much more danger into a situation than actually exists. Fears associated with heights, airplanes, closed places, and the like are common. Almost any aspect of the work context can produce such reactions in certain people. When this happens, the individual experiences emotions comparable to those aroused under really dangerous conditions. Subjective danger situations of this kind stimulate sufficient anxiety in some instances to make any work effort impossible. In other cases the emotion serves only to distract, producing errors and reduced output.

THE ROLE OF THE INDUSTRIAL CLINICAL PSYCHOLOGIST IN PERFORMANCE ANALYSIS

Precise answers to the questions noted can be obtained only when there is considerable information available regarding the individual. The more that is known about the man, the better the performance analysis. In large part, the information can be obtained by observing behavior on the job and by talking to the man and to those who know him. This any competent manager can do.

Another source of data, however, normally requires extensive psychological training. A battery of psychological tests combined with an intensive clinical interview can provide much information. To use these tools well requires a background in personality theory and considerable knowledge of the various psychological tests. Projective measures are particularly helpful, but using them effectively in connection with a performance analysis is a complex task (20,23). Graduate work in industrial psychology and clinical psychology is required. An industrial clinical psychologist can make a major contribution in carrying out difficult performance analyses, where the strategic factors are numerous and complexly interrelated. Even in somewhat simpler cases, a psychological evaluation can often expedite the solution.

Corrective Procedures

A number of the input-output mediators discussed in preceding chapters may be used as corrective procedures to restore effective performance. Inasmuch as applications of these mediators in the area of performance control were not noted previously, it seems appropriate to do so now. Subsequent sections discuss corrective techniques that have a more specific connection with the performance control process.

One obvious approach is to redesign the job to more closely approximate the individual's capabilities. Through the processes of organization planning and job analysis, new role prescriptions may be established to fit the intellectual, physical, or personality characteristics of a specific person. Behaviors that the individual finds difficult or impossible are no longer required; new behaviors within his repertoire are introduced. This is feasible, of course, only within certain limits. Beyond these, transfer to a new position is usually more appropriate.

In addition to this application of structural mediators, a number of the functional mediators discussed previously may be used as corrective procedures. Management development and training may overcome knowledge lacks, change an individual's motivation relative to job requirements, and introduce new skills of a physical nature. Furthermore, management development as applied to the ineffective individual's immediate superior may so change the superior that he becomes capable of restoring effective performance in his subordinate. In this way, management development improves the leadership environment.

When motivation is strategic, alterations in the payment process may prove useful. This topic is considered in greater detail in Chapter 13. In general, where motivational problems are present and pay is known to be relevant, providing an opportunity to earn more money in return for effective job-integrated behavior is an appropriate solution.

TRANSFER, PROMOTION, AND DEMOTION

Changing an employee from one position to another may occur for a number of reasons. Because of shifts in technology, new product lines, or a reorganization, certain jobs may have to be eliminated. Expanded or contracted operations almost always involve numerous job changes. The process of *bumping,* whereby men with greater seniority move down to lower level positions when layoffs are required, is commonly provided for in union contracts. Reassignments for training and development purposes are also widespread. Moving a man into a new position is not merely a way of correcting performance deficiencies, although this is a common consideration.

When such a change of job is carried out, it may be done in order to overcome the impact of almost any type of strategic factor. The important thing is that the new position have role prescriptions that the individual can meet. Thus, in the intellectual area, a demotion usually is required if the man has been overplaced on verbal ability, but a lateral transfer will normally be sufficient to overcome deficiencies in other abilities. Jobs with emotional, motivational, and physical requirements more appropriate to the individual can often be located. When separation from the family is a problem, this can be corrected by transferring the man to a job where separation is not necessary. A more suitable work group or type of supervision can be achieved through reassignment. So, too, can a value climate better fitted to the individual, or a more appropriate working situation.

The only strategic factors that cannot under any circumstances be overcome by placement changes are some in the company or organizational category. In these cases, the causal process continues to operate irrespective of the particular job, because it reflects company-wide policies or philosophies as applied to all positions.

In actual practice, however, placement change is not the all-purpose corrective action it appears to be. Most firms, especially the smaller ones, do not have enough kinds of positions available to permit the transfer of all their ineffective workers to more appropriate jobs. The potential value of reassignment as a corrective procedure is limited by the kinds of openings that can be found in any given company.

Transfer. Strictly speaking, a transfer involves shifting an individual to another job at the same grade level. In some companies, such shifts are relatively easy to accomplish, if they appear to provide an adequate means of improving performance. In other cases, they are so restricted by seniority provisions, supervisory prerogatives, and craft demarcations that there is little a psychologist can do, even when he is sure he has a potential solution to a particular failure situation. In any event, it is important that supervisors not be permitted to foist their unsatisfactory workers on unsuspecting colleagues without reference to performance considerations. A transfer will achieve a corrective purpose only if there is good reason to believe the man will succeed in the new position.

Where transfers (or promotions) involve moving the employee's family, help is often provided by the company. Management employees nearly always get monetary assistance. At lower levels, moving expenses may or may not be paid, but they are much more likely to be covered if the transfer is initiated by the company than if it is employee-requested (18). Some firms also assist in the sale of a home.

Promotion. It may seem strange to consider promotion as a solution to problems of performance failure. Yet, in clear-cut cases of underplacement, where the man is strongly motivated to do the things a higher position requires, and perhaps also to achieve the status that goes with such a job, promotion can work. On the other hand, where the man seems hesitant about moving up in the job hierarchy, promotion is not normally a good solution.

In handling any promotion, there is always the problem of the unsuccessful candidates. This difficulty is accentuated in cases where a man who is failing in his current job is selected. Organizational maintenance considerations may weigh so heavily that promotion cannot be applied as a solution, even though clearly appropriate on all other grounds. If the man can be promoted into a different work unit, this may help to minimize conflict somewhat. Certainly the crucial consideration, however, is that he actually make good. Promoting a poor performer who then merely continues to fail will inevitably create long-term dissension and feelings of inequity.

Demotion. Moving a man to a lower level position is a more common solution to performance deficiency than promotion. It is most appropriate when there has been overplacement either on intellectual or emotional grounds. At such times, resistance to the change is likely to be minimal, if the man has actually experienced failure in his current position over a continuing period. In fact, in the writer's experience actual requests for demotion under such circumstances are not at all uncommon. Even when the man does resist, the reaction is normally short-lived, if he is able to perform satisfactorily on the new job and achieve a sense of freedom from the anxieties associated with failure. Should this not be the case, however, continued and often vociferous resistance can be expected. The demotion solution has to achieve its goal.

PERSONNEL POLICY MODIFICATION

Policies are formulated to apply to all employees of a company or, on occasion, to certain clearly defined groups. They limit the discretion of individual managers by serving as commands when certain indicated circumstances arise. They provide decision-making criteria so that consistency of action can be maintained across the company, and they obviate the need for frequent repetition of an extended decision-making process.

In this sense, they foster economy of time and effort. In some cases, they represent abstractions or generalizations that are retrospective recognitions of existing decision guides. But in other cases, policies establish new role prescriptions, and are thus a source of organizational change (10).

A policy can contribute to ineffective performance, either because it is poorly thought out and formulated or because in a given instance it happens to have a negative impact on a specific individual. In the former case, policy modification means changing the policy or perhaps eliminating it entirely. When this is done, it may be possible to act with regard to a man in such areas as placement, discipline, payment, and training that were not previously possible. In those company-caused instances of failure where transfer, promotion or demotion are inappropriate as solutions because all jobs are affected equally by a policy, modification of this kind may be the only answer.

Changing or eliminating a policy is not an easy task, and at times it is clearly not desirable. An appropriate alternative may be to modify the policy only in the sense of permitting an exception. Such an exception can permit the solution of a relatively unique instance of ineffective performance, while leaving the over-all policy structure intact.

THREAT, PUNISHMENT, AND DISCIPLINARY ACTION

One type of corrective action that may be applied in certain instances where motivational factors are strategic is the use of managerial power to threaten or actually invoke sanctions against an individual. In this way, motivation appropriate to job role prescriptions may be aroused, and effective behavior restored. This approach is particularly useful when standards of conduct or productivity are low and new ones must be introduced. Unfortunately, however, threat and discipline are often applied in cases where the failure is not due to motivational causes that can be corrected in this manner. At such times, where the performance analysis has been faulty or nonexistent, punishment may do more harm than good.

A resort to negative sanctions in an effort to restore effective performance may take one of two courses, although in any given case both may be invoked eventually. One approach is for a supervisor or personnel representative to demand improved performance and couple this demand with a threat of future managerial action if improvement does not occur. The threat may be implicit or explicit, but the entire process is relatively informal and usually does not involve any written statement or record.

The alternative to this is a formal disciplinary action carried out in the manner specified in the union contract. In many instances, this results in an appeal through the grievance machinery. Actions of this kind are normally recorded in writing and become a part of the man's personnel file. The approach is strongly legalistic.

The mildest formal action is an official warning. Disciplinary layoff, or suspension without pay, and demotion are also used. The most extreme discipline, which is also an admission of failure, is of course discharge. In actual practice, supervisors do not appear to utilize any of these sanctions as frequently as they could in terms of the number of infractions of company rules that occur (12).

PERSONNEL AND PSYCHOLOGICAL COUNSELING

The history of counseling in industry starts with a department established in the Ford Motor Company in 1914 to advise employees on personal affairs and to assist them with health, legal, and family problems (3). The approach was strongly directive and permeated with Henry Ford's own personal philosophies. The result was considerable employee resistance and an eventual abandoning of the program. Similar large-scale efforts have been initiated in a number of firms, most notably the Western Electric Company, where counseling was introduced as an aspect of the now famous Hawthorne studies (4). In almost every instance, these comprehensive programs have failed to survive.

In recent years, industrial counseling has tended to focus more on specific types of employee problems, has involved the industrial clinical psychologist to a much greater extent, and has been more widely viewed as a corrective procedure for ineffective performance than as a means of increasing employee satisfaction. Under these conditions, limited scale programs have prospered and appear to have made sizable contributions to productivity. It is now recognized that the needs of an individual and the goals of an organization may well be in conflict and that certain kinds of counseling activities involving such matters as career planning and general emotional adjustment should be performed outside the employment context.

Counseling Technique. Although in dealing with some types of problems a counselor must be somewhat directive, in that questions must be answered and information conveyed, the general approach in industry where emotional or motivational factors are strategic has been to stress *nondirective counseling.* This emphasis is particularly prevalent where the counselor has had extensive psychological training. In the nondirective approach, the employee is encouraged to express his feelings, to gain an understanding of himself, and eventually to solve his own problems. The counselor listens and occasionally reformulates what the employee has said to permit greater understanding of the true emotional meaning of certain words. The counselor may also repeat certain phrases or sentences to stimulate the employee to continue and to lead him to concentrate on certain topics.

In the business context, counseling of this kind tends to focus on matters of performance, and on social relationships at work, although family and other considerations may be treated if they prove relevant. Often the counselor serves as an upward communication channel between the man and his organization, correcting distorted communications and misunderstandings (22). The emphasis is on working out relatively mild adjustment problems that may be blocking performance effectiveness. More severe emotional disorders are normally referred to a psychotherapist working outside the company. If the problem appears to require more than ten or fifteen one-hour sessions, the man almost invariably is advised to seek help on a private basis. Some firms, in fact, reject all internal adjustment counseling of this type, on the grounds that such matters are the sole responsibility of the individual (5).

Executive Counseling. At the higher managerial levels, counseling usually is done by an outside psychological consultant rather than by a professional on the company staff (6,8). Although, in some instances, this counseling attempts to cope with a performance failure, it is also true that many top-level men are emotionally alone and thus in real need of someone with whom they can discuss problems. Under these circumstances, an industrial clinical psychologist may continue to counsel an executive at intervals over an extended period of time. The approach, in contrast to that of a regular management consultant, tends to be nondirective, with the executive increasingly learning to understand himself and the motives behind his actions.

Retirement Counseling. Retirement counseling prepares employees for retirement, although on occasion it may be directed toward the rehabilitation of older workers whose performance has fallen off sharply with the approach of retirement. The counseling tends to be rather directive, emphasizing information on pension plans and other benefits. The counselors usually do not have psychological training. Counseling of this kind may be initiated as much as five years before the anticipated date of separation, although the total number of meetings with the counselor is not likely to be large.

MEDICAL AND PSYCHIATRIC TREATMENT

Medical treatment is not likely to be a major aspect of the industrial physician's job. Companies are much more prone to invest in selection through the physical examination and in preventive measures. Thus, although medical treatment is the major corrective procedure in cases where physical illness disrupts performance, the treatment does not represent an organizational function in most cases. It is performed outside the company.

Similarly, psychiatric treatment for psychoses and neuroses is not usually provided by the company, although some firms do have psychiatrists on the regular staff. In certain instances, however, a company will take a very active role in arranging for the treatment of a high-level executive and will pay all bills incurred. Also, there are companies that maintain special facilities for the treatment of alcoholics or contribute to the support of such facilities. It is not at all uncommon for a firm to maintain a close liaison with a local Alcoholics Anonymous chapter and to arrange for a representative of that organization to be constantly available to assist employees.

REFERENCES

1. American Arbitration Association, *Procedural and Substantive Aspects of Labor-Management Arbitration: An AAA Research Report.* New York: The Association, 1957.
2. Barker, R. G., *Adjustment to Physical Handicap and Illness: A Survey of the Social Psychology of Physique and Disability.* New York: Social Science Research Council, 1963.
3. Bellows, R., *Psychology of Personnel in Business and Industry,* 3rd ed. Englewood Cliffs, N.J.: Prentice-Hall, 1961.
4. Dickson, W. J., "The Hawthorne Plan of Personnel Counseling," in S. D. Hoslett (ed.), *Human Factors in Management.* New York: Harper & Row, 1946, pp. 228–250.
5. Dunnette, M. D., and W. K. Kirchner, *Psychology Applied to Industry.* New York: Appleton-Century-Crofts, 1965.
6. Flory, C. D. (ed.), *Managers for Tomorrow.* New York: The New American Library, 1965.
7. Ginzberg, E., J. B. Miner, J. K. Anderson, S. W. Ginsberg, and J. L. Herma, *The Ineffective Soldier: Vol. II, Breakdown and Recovery.* New York: Columbia Univ. Press, 1959.
8. Glaser, E. M., "Psychological Consultation with Executives: A Clinical Approach," *The American Psychologist,* Vol. 13 (1958), 486–489.
9. Heller, F. A., "Measuring Motivation in Industry," *Occupational Psychology,* Vol. 26 (1952), 86–95.
10. Katz, D., and R. L. Kahn, *The Social Psychology of Organizations.* New York: Wiley, 1966.
11. Kornhauser, A., *Mental Health of the Industrial Worker.* New York: Wiley, 1965.
12. Maier, N. R. F., and L. E. Danielson, "An Evaluation of Two Approaches to Discipline in Industry," *Journal of Applied Psychology,* Vol. 40 (1956), 319–323.
13. Markowe, M., "Occupational Psychiatry: An Historical Survey and Some Recent Researches," *Journal of Mental Science,* Vol. 99 (1953), 92–101.
14. Miner, J. B., *Intelligence in the United States.* New York: Springer, 1957.
15. Miner, J. B., "Personality and Ability Factors in Sales Performance," *Journal of Applied Psychology,* Vol. 46 (1962), 6–13.
16. Miner, J. B., *The Management of Ineffective Performance.* New York: McGraw-Hill, 1963.
17. Miner, J. B., and J. K. Anderson, "The Postwar Occupational Adjustment of Emotionally Disturbed Soldiers," *Journal of Applied Psychology,* Vol. 42 (1958), 317–322.
18. National Industrial Conference Board, *Company Payment of Employees' Moving Expenses,* Studies in Personnel Policy No. 154. New York: The Board, 1956.
19. Pigors, P., and C. A. Myers, *Personnel Administration,* 5th ed. New York: McGraw-Hill, 1965.
20. Piotrowski, A. Z., and M. R. Rock, *The Perceptanalytic Executive Scale.* New York: Grune & Stratton, 1963.

21. Stogdill, R. M., and A. E. Coons, *Leader Behavior: Its Description and Measurement.* Columbus, Ohio: Bureau of Business Research, Ohio State Univ., 1957.
22. Tannenbaum, A. S., *Social Psychology of the Work Organization,* Belmont, Cal.: Wadsworth, 1966.
23. Tomkins, S. S., and J. B. Miner, *PAT Interpretation—Scope and Technique.* New York: Springer, 1959.

QUESTIONS

1. What is meant by performance control? How does it differ from other types of control? To what extent does performance control appear to be an important function in a firm? Can it be ignored?
2. How is a performance analysis carried out? Can you analyze an instance of job failure that you yourself have observed in the past?
3. What difficulties do you see associated with the introduction of an employee counseling program in a company? Why do you think a number of these programs have failed?
4. Take each of the possible strategic factors noted in the schema for performance analysis and indicate for each whether a placement change might provide a solution, and if so what specific characteristics should be present in the new position.

12

Internal Communications

This chapter will consider those communications procedures that are part of the personnel process and can be used to foster goal attainment. As will become evident, this is a limited perspective in comparison to what might be covered were the discussion to treat organizational communication processes as a whole. However, the present volume deals with the field of personnel psychology, not organizational psychology, and it is appropriate that the coverage should be restricted accordingly. The focus, then, will be on those internal communications techniques that can be brought directly to bear in utilizing a company's work force effectively. With only a few exceptions, communications procedures of this kind have been directed toward organizational maintenance, not productivity, as with the input-output mediators considered in preceding chapters.

Although the present chapter devotes little space to superior-subordinate communications, as they occur on a day-to-day basis in the work place, it should not be assumed that interactions of this kind are totally unrelated to personnel psychology. As a part of the general management process, they are of concern to all managers in all aspects of the business, including managers in the personnel area. In addition, such topics as semantics in communications, communications skills, barriers to communications, and two-way communications are widely included in management development programs. It is indirectly, through management development, that the personnel function achieves much of its impact on the primarily productivity-oriented superior-subordinate communication process.

Management development is not the only indirect approach that personnel people can use to influence communications within the firm. Role prescriptions characteristically indicate rather specifically who is to communicate with whom and regarding what topics. Organization planning and job analysis both contribute to the establishment of formal communications channels by indicating expected reporting relationships. Thus, through such procedures as organization planning and job analysis the personnel function can influence organizational communications to a considerable degree. There is no guarantee that communications will necessarily follow the patterns thus established in every respect. Role behavior may deviate from role prescriptions. A subordinate manager may "go over his superior's head" to discuss certain matters with a higher level executive, even though such behavior is not generally condoned. Although considerations of this kind involve personnel psychology, through their relationship to organization planning and management appraisal, they can be directly influenced at a point in time only by the particular managers themselves. For this reason, such malfunctioning of formal communications channels is probably best treated in connection with discussions of the managerial process as a whole, and thus as part of organizational psychology.

RUMOR AND THE GRAPEVINE

The rumor transmission process also fails to meet the specifications for extended treatment here. But in this case it is not the lack of *direct* control over the communication process that leads to the exclusion, but the lack of any control at all. There is very little that can be done to utilize the *grapevine* purposefully as a means to goal attainment.

As a result, rumors probably do at least as much to subvert organizational goals as to foster them. They may well stir up dissension. They are frequently contrary to fact. In one study carried out within six companies, sixteen of the thirty rumors checked were found to be false (9). Finally, rumors rarely reach everyone. Research has indicated repeatedly that the grapevine is spotty in its coverage and that a relatively large proportion of employees may not hear the rumor (5,17).

Accordingly, it seems appropriate to conclude that the rumor transmission process is not only unusable as an internal communication technique, but that it is, in fact, so poor as an input-output mediator, and often so harmful in its effects, that every effort should be made to suppress it. A key to this is that rumors become most rampant in departments where the manager in charge deliberately withholds information as a means of exercising power and control (12). It would seem, then, that if employees are given maximal and valid information in those areas that are of major interest to them, the grapevine will have little opportunity to thrive. In fact, under most circumstances, the number of rumors circulating in a particular environment, and the rapidity with which they spread, provide a good index of the effectiveness of other communications procedures.

This view, that the grapevine is the antithesis of effective communications, and that considerable effort should be devoted to minimizing its impact, is reflected in the *rumor clinic* concept. Clinics of this kind provide a specific locus where employees may obtain valid information with regard to rumors they have heard. No doubt, with ideal communications procedures in other respects, techniques of this kind would not be necessary. However, it seems apparent that the rumor process can rarely, if ever, be entirely eradicated.

Communications Downward

This section concentrates on the various techniques that may be used to transmit information from the higher levels of an organization directly to individuals. The objective in using mediators of this kind is to create a sense of belonging. Thus, the over-all cohesiveness of the company as a social unit is fostered; employees will presumably be more satisfied with their work situation. Downward communications should pull the organization together and unite it behind the particular task objectives. To do this may, on occasion, require a concerted effort to subvert the goals of a union, which does or is attempting to represent the company's employees, since unions produce a major devisive force within the firm.

The media used to achieve these goals vary considerably. Among them are company magazines and newspapers; mass meetings, for all or groups of employees; employee letters, sent directly to the home or inserted in pay checks; information racks containing circulars and pamphlets; employee handbooks and manuals; bulletin boards and posters; bulletins and memoranda to management; and tours of company facilities. Annual reports, news items in the popular media and even commercial advertising may communicate with employees. In such cases, external media are used for internal purposes.

Downward communications techniques may rely on oral or written media. They may utilize speeches, television, telephone, teletype, films, public address systems, slides, radio or the various written modes. In any event, it is important that the internal communication system operate rapidly and with maximal validity. To the extent the system produces information that later proves to be incorrect, or lags and so yields its data subsequent to the public or other media, it will be viewed as lacking in value by employees and will lose much of its audience. Without an audience, it can have little impact as an input-output mediator.

THE SELECTION OF MEDIA

There is ample evidence that any medium of communication must meet certain requirements to be effective (18). It must reach all employees for whom it is intended. It must be official, in the sense that the information is perceived as originating with individuals who are in a position to know. It must convey a certain type of information consistently, so that employees will look to this source when they desire to know about a particular matter.

Given these conditions, however, is there any evidence that some media are inherently more effective than others in getting information to employees? Table 12–1 shows the results of three separate studies: one

TABLE 12–1. Mean Accuracy of Recall Scores for Information Transmitted Using Various Media

Method of presenting information	College student sample		Manufacturing employee sample		Retail store sample	
	Mean recall score	Number	Mean recall score	Number	Mean recall score	Number
Oral and written	6.54	281	7.30	30	7.70	102
Oral only	5.31	161	6.38	13	6.17	94
Written only	4.58	279	4.46	28	4.91	109
Bulletin board	3.52	152			3.72	115
Grapevine only	2.88	157	3.00	13	3.56	108

Source: T. L. Dahle, "An Objective and Comparative Study of Five Methods of Transmitting Information to Business and Industrial Employees," *Speech Monographs*, Vol. 21 (1954), pp. 24, 26, and 27.

with a large group of college students enrolled in a public speaking course at Purdue University; one with the production employees of a building materials manufacturing plant; and one with the employees at a single facility of Spiegel's, a mail order chain store organization (4). The same information was transmitted in various ways including oral presentations by professors or supervisors, written hand-outs or letters, and bulletin board postings. Information retention was measured with a ten-item questionnaire administered approximately two days after the original communication. In all cases, a control group was included that could learn only through the grapevine. The bulletin board method was not used in the manufacturing plant.

The results are suprisingly consistent. A combination of written and oral media is clearly preferable. However, oral presentations at a meeting are more effective. Posting an item on a bulletin board appears to accomplish relatively little, being indistinguishable from the grapevine, when standard tests of statistical significance are applied.

The superiority of the oral mode in a face-to-face situation does not appear to be limited to information transmission. At least one large-scale investigation indicates that employees prefer it as well (16). In another instance, comparisons were made between two almost identical plants, one of which relied on regular monthly meetings conducted by foremen to transmit information, whereas the other did not. Not only were the employees in the plant with the meetings much more likely to feel well informed, but also they were more likely to feel that they really belonged in the company (62 per cent vs. 29 per cent), and more likely to be highly satisfied with it as a place to work (45 per cent vs. 20 per cent) (6). The meetings not only served to provide information; in doing so they made a sizable contribution to organizational maintenance.

It should be emphasized that in this instance the meetings involved a two-way communications process. Employees were encouraged to ask questions in the meetings, either to clarify points made by the foremen or to elicit new information. In general, such an approach fosters employee satisfaction (1). A one-way system can create considerable frustration, if the material is at all ambiguous or important aspects are omitted. Providing an opportunity for questioning markedly increases understanding. It also produces greater trust, openness, and a feeling of belonging as regards the company. One major difficulty with the various written media is that it is difficult to integrate communication upward with them in a meaningful way.

In using oral communications, with or without a two-way approach, a great many companies go to considerable trouble to stage and program their presentations. Materials often are prepared in advance, and the manager who is to do the speaking may receive coaching from various training specialists. Presentations involving the company's financial position, in conjunction with the annual report, are particularly likely to involve considerable preparation. In other cases, information may be transmitted to management via various memorandums or bulletins. These serve as a basis for oral communications to appropriate employee groups. During union negotiations, a strike, or an organizing attempt, management bulletins may appear quite frequently.

It is important to recognize that the mere fact that employees have accumulated a large amount of information about their company is no guarantee that organizational maintenance will be fostered. See Table 12–2. In only one instance (Firm D) is the correlation between information level and attitude level significant. The companies surveyed were a public utility, a trucking company, a wholesale distributing firm, a textile manufacturing firm, and an electrical equipment manufacturer (14).

A firm that refused to provide any information, or did so on a very minimal basis, would almost certainly suffer negative consequences. But given that communication is attempted at some meaningful level, the crucial considerations are how and what, rather than how much. The

TABLE 12–2. Correlations Between Information and Attitude Scores for Samples of Employees from Five Firms

Firm	Number of employees	Correlation
A	95	.06
B	59	.12
C	105	.12
D	90	.27
E	108	.12

Source: D. Perry and T. A. Mahoney, "In-plant Communications and Employee Morale," *Personnel Psychology*, Vol. 8 (1955), p. 342.

advantages of a two-way approach have already been noted, and certainly the tone inherent in any communication can influence attitudes. But even more important is the content of what is said. Certain kinds of information may well make employees less satisfied, as for instance the knowledge that the firm has been put up for sale or merger. If no effort is made to utilize the communication system to convince employees that they are part of a worthwhile organization, favorable attitudes are unlikely to result. Neutral communications may increase information tremendously, but have little impact on how employees feel about the company.

Combining oral and written media to convey a piece of information with maximum effectiveness will contribute to goal achievement only if the information creates favorable attitudes. This is not to say that unpleasant information should be withheld or distorted. It is important that employees trust management and its information channels. A communication system that does not yield important information will soon lose its audience. But communication procedures can appropriately be used to encourage pride in the organization; to point up real advantages of employment, such as benefits and services; to state company, as opposed to union, viewpoints; and to demonstrate the advantages of the economic system that makes the company's existence possible.

Given this orientation, a company should utilize those media that convey maximal information and yield maximal recall. Without such a goal-related orientation, there is a question as to whether the expense of a comprehensive internal communication system can be justified. Over the years, a number of firms have failed, for various reasons, to utilize their publications and other media to encourage favorable employee attitudes. This presumably is reflected in the data of Table 12–2. The positive implications of the information transmitted, insofar as the company is concerned, apparently have not been emphasized in four of the five firms. Further evidence on this point will be presented in the next section.

COMPANY MAGAZINES AND NEWSPAPERS

Almost all large corporations and a great many smaller ones publish a company magazine, on a monthly basis or at more frequent intervals, that goes to all employees. Many firms have additional publications for separate departments, geographical regions, or plants. When these internal media are combined with those directed to stockholders and the public, the total journalistic effort is likely to emerge as very comprehensive indeed.

For many years, these publications said practically nothing about the company as an organization and did little to develop favorable employee attitudes. Even when information about such matters as the company's economic position, organization, products, equipment, methods, benefits, and services was included, it was usually presented in an entirely factual manner. There was little attempt to indicate the company viewpoint and thus to encourage cohesiveness and loyalty. This remains largely true today.

The reason often given for avoiding persuasive material, and even information regarding the company as an organization, is that too much stress on such matters will result in a loss of readership. Many company editors have maintained that if an employee does not find frequent mention of himself or people he knows in the pages of the magazine or newspaper, he will cease to read it. In particular, they have argued that "propaganda" should be avoided. The feeling has been that the audience must be held at all costs and that this cannot be done if one moves directly into the realm of organizational maintenance. This viewpoint, of course, involves testable assumptions about the nature of employee readership preferences and patterns. And, in fact, evidence does exist regarding reading differentials for material that is unrelated to company goals, company-oriented material, and material that is persuasive to a company viewpoint.

Readership Surveys. One relevant study dealt with readership patterns among employees of The Atlantic Refining Company (13). Fifteen articles, which proved to be relatively evenly spaced along a scale of company-orientation, were selected from various prior issues of *The Atlantic Magazine* and reprinted in a questionnaire. Scale position was determined by judges. None of the items dealt with economic, political, or union considerations, so that persuasion to a company viewpoint on such matters was not a factor in this particular study. Headlines for typical items judged to be highly company-oriented, in the middle range, and not company-oriented are noted below.

- Company-oriented
  "Retirement System Ends 25th Year"
  "New-Products, Applications, Customers"

"Questions and Answers on Company's Recent $55 Million Issue of Debentures!"

- Middle range
  "Safe Drivers Are Honored"
  "Atlantic Congratulates Its Faithful Employees Who Celebrate Service Anniversaries"

- Not company-oriented
  "Two at Pittsburgh Avid Stamp Collectors"
  "Egg Magic" (four recipes)

In each instance, the employee was asked to indicate whether he usually or only rarely read this particular type of item in the magazine. Questionnaires were sent to a representative sample of 600 employees; 251 were returned. Subsequent follow-up studies of the nonrespondents indicated that had all 600 employees returned questionnaires the readership results obtained would not have differed from those derived with the 251.

The findings presented in Table 12–3 indicate that the employees not only did not object to company-oriented material, they actually preferred

TABLE 12–3. **Rank-Order Correlations Between Scale Values on Degree of Company Orientation for 15 Company Magazine Articles and Extent of Readership of the Articles**

Group	N	Correlation
Total sample	251	.72
Sex		
Male	218	.70
Female	33	.40
Job level		
Supervisory	58	.72
Nonsupervisory	193	.74
Company service		
0–10 Years	92	.79
11–20	65	.68
21+ Years	94	.77
Education		
0–11 Years	67	.63
12 Years	79	.72
13+ Years	96	.79
Unknown	9	

Source: J. B. Miner and E. E. Heaton, "Company Orientation as a Factor in the Readership of Employee Publications," *Personnel Psychology,* Vol. 12 (1959), p. 615.

it. The company magazine was viewed as the primary source of information regarding the firm's level of success. Thus, through such company-related material as appeared, employees could determine whether they were associated with an effective organization that could provide them with both security and opportunity. With the exception of the female employees, most of whom were young and would not stay long, there was a consistent tendency toward more widespread readership of the company-oriented articles. There was no evidence that chit-chat was necessary to maintain readership; quite the opposite. This conclusion has since been supported by other research (19).

A second study goes beyond the matter of company orientation to the use of directly persuasive items (8). In this instance, articles from past issues of the *Illuminator,* published by the Washington Water Power Company, were judged, both as to their degree of company orientation and their degree of persuasiveness to a company view. The readership survey questionnaire contained twenty items, five each in the categories of high company orientation and high persuasiveness, high company orientation and low persuasiveness, low company orientation and high persuasiveness, and low company orientation and low persuasiveness. Examples of the four types of articles are as follows:

- High company orientation and high persuasiveness
  "Extras That Count—Liberal Sick Pay Program Is Protection"
  "Vacation Time; Relax . . . With Pay"
  "You'll Want to Know These Pertinent Facts about Rate Proposal"

- High company orientation and low persuasiveness
  "Branzell Is Now President; Robinson Retains Key Role"
  "Canadian Line to Give WWP Third Gas Source"

- Low company orientation and high persuasiveness
  "Union Magazine Looks at Power"
  "Ideals of Socialists Survive Though Party Declines, Says Writer"
  "What Is Profit? Recent Graduates Didn't Know Answer"

- Low company orientation and low persuasiveness
  "Tight Races Features All Bowling Leagues"
  "Bad Weather Brings These Driving Tips"

In this instance, the persuasive communications related to the company tended to stress what the company was doing in the area of employee benefits, and certain arguments bearing on governmental constraints applied to the utility industry. In addition, the magazine devoted space to matters concerning the economy generally and union activities.

The persuasive material tended to be well written and relevant to company goal accomplishment.

Employees were asked to indicate whether they usually or rarely read items of the kind presented. A "usually" response was given a score of 3, a qualified response a 2, and a "rarely" response a 1. The mean scores for the 230 respondents in the four categories are presented in Table 12–4.

TABLE 12–4. **Mean Readership Scores for 20 Company Magazine Articles Varying in Persuasiveness and in Degree of Company Orientation**

	Company orientation		
Persuasiveness	High (5 items)	Low (5 items)	Combined (10 items)
High (5 items)	2.67	2.36	2.51
Low (5 items)	2.79	2.22	2.51
Combined (10 items)	2.73	2.29	

Source: C. O. Henderson, *The Company Magazine as a Medium for Communicating Persuasive, Management Oriented Subject Matter*, DBA Thesis. Eugene, Oregon: Univ. of Oregon, 1964, p. 46.

The data clearly indicate that, at least with this company's approach, persuasive material does not result in any loss of readership. It appears to be read with a frequency almost identical to the nonpersuasive material. However, the conclusion must be qualified with reference to female employees. Their readership scores were consistently below those for the males, not only on the company-oriented items, but on the persuasive as well. Only in the chit-chat area (noncompany and nonpersuasive) did female readership equal that of the males.

Taking these studies as a whole, it seems that the widespread assumptions regarding loss of readership when company publications are oriented specifically to the goal of organizational maintenance do not meet the test of the research evidence. Articles of the kind described as company-oriented in *The Atlantic Magazine* and company-oriented and/or persuasive in the *Illuminator* can be used. In fact, to a degree at least, this is what employees appear to want from company publications.

There is one important consideration, if employee attitudes are to be influenced. The company magazine must not be viewed as an organ of extremism. It must be considered a trusted source of information; it must be accepted as a legitimate medium for transmitting the particular kind of material it contains; it must have a reputation for moderation (1). Given these conditions, there is every reason to believe that an appropriate selection of content along the lines suggested can make company publications a meaningful factor in organizational goal attainment.

THE PROBLEM OF READABILITY

During the late 1940's and early 1950's, there was widespread concern in the business world regarding the reading level of material published for employees. A number of studies indicated that much of what was produced as part of the downward communication process was far above the comprehension level of the intended audience. Although the stress which this topic received in all likelihood did yield considerable change in readability levels, the matter remains an important one. An employee who is continually exposed to material that he finds difficult or impossible to understand is unlikely to view the source of this material favorably. Such communication is most likely to yield feelings of inferiority and defensive criticism of the publication, perhaps also of the company as well.

An example of the problem is presented in Table 12–5. This study

TABLE 12–5. A Comparison Between Flesch Reading Ease Scores in Terms of Educational Level Required for Eleven Employee Handbooks and Median Educational Level of Unskilled Employees

Corporation	Educational level required by handbook	Educational level
1	Some high school	Fifth grade
2	Some high school	Eighth grade
3	High school or some college	One year of high school
4	Seventh or eighth grade	Seventh or eighth grade
5	High school or some college	Eighth grade
6	Some high school	Four years of high school
7	Seventh or eighth grade	Four years of high school
8	High school or some college	Eighth grade
9	Sixth grade	Sixth grade
10	Some high school	Eighth grade
11	College	Fourth grade

Source: C. Carlucci and W. J. E. Crissy, "How Readable are Employee Handbooks?" *Personnel Psychology,* Vol. 4 (1951), p. 385.

dealt with employee handbooks published by a number of major corporations. These handbooks concentrated on such topics as attendance, safety, health, health insurance, promotion, recreational activities, formal training facilities, financial benefits, grievances, company history, employee services, vacations, holidays, pay, and working hours. Some dealt with other matters as well, such as permanence of employment, suggestion systems, and disciplinary rules (3). From the data presented, it appears that seven of the eleven handbooks were written at a level above that of their intended readers; in some cases, the discrepancy was sizable.

The readability problem appears to arise because employee publications are written by individuals with at least a college education, to be cleared by managers both within and outside the personnel area, who are equally well educated. Thus, handbooks, magazines and practically anything else written for employees can represent difficult reading for those whose education is limited. Fortunately, however, industrial editors have become increasingly conscious of this problem, and at the same time the educational level ot the population has been rising. The gap clearly is narrowing. In all probability, differentials of the kind found in corporation 11 of Table 12–5 are now to be found only in a few isolated instances.

Communications Upward

Communications from the bottom to the top of the organizational hierarchy are of significance for two reasons. First, it is primarily through some type of feedback process that management is able to obtain the information needed to evaluate and perhaps correct its downward communications. Feedback of this kind is needed in order to determine whether employees have received and understood the messages directed to them through the company media and supervisory channels. Second, without some mechanisms through which employees can ask questions, express dissatisfactions, register complaints, or make suggestions regarding company policies and procedures, management may remain completely unaware of major problem areas and threats to organizational maintenance for extended periods of time. The consequence can be a continual festering of problems until open conflict, mass resignations, or even disintegration of the organization occurs.

In contrast to downward communications, techniques of communicating upward are rather limited in number, and it is often difficult to control them, so as to keep the focus on goal-related information. As noted in the last section, the content of items initiated from the top can shift easily to areas, such as bowling leagues and cooking, that have little to do with company goals; this problem is accentuated many times when transmission is initiated at lower levels.

In part, the difficulties of upward communication are inherent in the nature of business organizations, with their stress on hierarchy, and their underlying premise that those at the upper levels should tell individuals below them what to do and how to do it, not the reverse (10). Furthermore, because a manager or supervisor controls the work situation in many of its aspects, employees are not likely to communicate upward anything that might reflect negatively on them. Should an individual complain to his superior, or make a suggestion, he cannot be certain that the matter will go to higher levels. The supervisor may consider it unimportant, or be too busy to take any action, or he may deliberately fail to report it to his superior because it implies that his own performance has been less than perfect. Even within the ranks of management, upward communications may be severely stifled or distorted, particularly where a subordinate has strong aspirations toward advancement in the organization (15).

TECHNIQUES IN UPWARD COMMUNICATION

It is apparent that the barriers and distortions that plague downward communications are magnified many times in the upward situation. Because of the uncertainties associated with the use of the superior-subordinate channel, various techniques permit employees to bypass their immediate superiors in registering complaints or making suggestions. Other approaches, such as gripe boxes, permit employees to express dissatisfactions on an anonymous basis. The existence of these techniques does not necessarily mean that employees will use them extensively.

Table 12–6 is based on a survey of personnel executives (2). It indi-

TABLE 12–6. Most Effective Upward Communications Techniques

	All companies, %	Larger (over 1,000 employees), %	Smaller (1,000 employees or less), %
First-line supervisors	39	48	23
Informal inquiries or discussion	36	25	59
Formal attitude surveys	26	25	33
Formal meetings	23	24	20
Counseling or interviewing techniques	17	9	30
Gripe boxes	13	17	—
Union representatives	13	11	16
Formal grievance procedure	13	14	10
Question-and-answer column in plant newspaper	9	—	25
Grapevine	4	4	3

Source: Bureau of National Affairs, Inc., *Upward Communications,* Personnel Policies Forum Survey No. 76. Washington, D.C.: the Bureau, 1964, p. 4.

cates quite clearly that in the opinion of these individuals the superior-subordinate channel remains the most effective, despite its inadequacies. First line supervision is stressed in more companies than is any other technique, and this emphasis is particularly pronounced in the larger firms. Several of the other approaches to upward communication involve the superior-subordinate channel, also. This is true of both informal discussions and formal meetings, for instance, although both have downward, as well as upward, components in most cases.

Although some companies do rely on union representatives for in-

formation, it is generally conceded that reports from this source need to
to be carefully evaluated. Often, union leaders are more concerned with
promulgating the union viewpoint than with providing an honest appraisal of a situation to the company. Other techniques include gripe
boxes, which seem to have little appeal to the employees themselves, and
question-and-answer columns in company publications. The latter normally involve considerable delay before answers are forthcoming. As a
result, they do not elicit widespread activity in most cases.

Some of the other techniques noted in Table 12–6 have already received considerable attention in other connections.

Attitude Surveys, Interviewing, and Counseling. Employee attitude
measurement, including the use of interviewing approaches, was discussed
at length in Chapter 5 in connection with the treatment of performance
evaluation. This is, in some ways, as much an upward communications
device as an evaluation procedure. The communications aspects become
particularly evident when questions are included to determine the extent
of employee information on such matters as company policies and benefit
programs.

Employee counseling was discussed in Chapter 11 as one of the
corrective procedures used in connection with performance control. Although counselors will rarely transmit specific problems of specific employees to higher management, because in doing so they might create
mistrust and thus prevent other employees from coming to them in the
future, they may provide general impressions of employee attitudes. If a
company does utilize counseling on a wide scale, this can be a valuable
upward communications technique. But counseling is rarely, if ever, introduced for its upward communications value alone. The communications
aspect tends to emerge subsequently, as a by-product.

Grievance and Complaint Procedures. Grievance processes primarily
provide a method of dealing with labor relations problems. Procedures of
this kind may also facilitate upward communications, even though when
used with any frequency, they tend to reflect a breakdown or blockage
within the superior-subordinate channel. The major difficulty, however,
from a communications viewpoint is that the grievance machinery may be
used largely to further union goals. Thus, it may not provide valid information on real sources of employee dissatisfaction.

SUGGESTION SYSTEMS

A rather widely used technique for upward communications, which
has not been considered previously in any other context, is the suggestion
system. In many respects, this approach is unique. It is not characteristically designed to provide feedback with regard to downward communications; those at lower levels must initiate largely in terms of their
own ideas. It is not intended to express complaints, so much as to permit
employees to communicate upward in a positive and constructive fashion.

The ideas communicated may relate to either productivity or maintenance goals; they may deal with more efficient production methods or with procedures for improving job satisfaction. But the existence of an effective suggestion system per se contributes primarily to organizational maintenance. This technique can well yield a considerable feeling of involvement in the organization, a belief that one's contributions count and will be rewarded. Loyalty, cohesiveness and commitment are likely to be fostered. On the other hand, suggestion systems may also provide financial rewards for creative effort. Under these circumstances, they are more than a technique of upward communication.

Suggestion systems take a variety of forms. In some cases, they are tied to specific objectives, as with work-simplification and cost-reduction programs, or they may be built into an incentive payment procedure. The system may be company-wide or it may apply only to a segment of the work force. Some companies maintain entirely independent suggestion systems for production, office, and managerial employees. Usually, operation is continuous, but on occasion a definite time limit is established. In such cases, the scope may also be restricted, to ideas related to safety, for instance.

Operating Procedures. Suggestion systems need to be carefully administered, if they are to make a positive contribution to organizational maintenance. There is always the risk that feelings of inequity and injustice will be aroused, with conflict the only observable consequence. For this reason, most effective suggestion systems have standard forms for employees to use in submitting ideas. They set specific time limits for acknowledging the receipt of suggestions, investigation by the department concerned, and acceptance or rejection by the suggestion committee. They establish procedures to ensure the anonymity of those making suggestions during the review process. The suggestion committee itself is usually constituted primarily from among rank-and-file employees; often the only management representative is someone from the personnel department. However, to the extent top management can be involved, support for the suggestion system is likely to be increased. The union may well have formal representation, although this is by no means a universal practice.

Applicable rules and regulations normally attempt to ensure that the employee who first submits a suggestion receives credit for it and that suggestions are not rejected without a full explanation. The usual practice is to exclude ideas which fall within the normal scope of the individual's job. Thus, if the role requirements are such as to indicate that ideas of a certain kind *should* be produced by a particular individual, such ideas are ineligible for a suggestion award.

Awards. Probably the most difficult aspect is determining the award for an acceptable suggestion. Most plans provide for awards in cash, although some firms award an equivalent amount in savings bonds or company stock certificates. There are also plans that make no formal provision for payment. The employee receives only a certificate of merit or a letter of commendation. But a copy of this goes in his personnel file. Pay raises, promotions and other personnel actions may well be influenced, even though direct payment is lacking.

Where cash awards are made, the minimum payment can vary from $15, or less, to $25; the maximum can be as much as $10,000, or there may be no specified upper limit. Employees whose suggestions yield measurable savings to the company ordinarily receive an award amounting to a percentage, usually 10 or 20 per cent, of the anticipated savings during the year subsequent to adoption. Such awards may well run into thousands of dollars. Some companies conduct a special review at the end of this initial year to determine actual savings. Should these be greater than originally anticipated, a supplemental award is made; should they be less, the employee is permitted to keep all money paid on the estimate.

Determining awards for suggestions, where the value cannot be stated in monetary terms, even though there is some definite intangible value to the firm, is more complex. Unfortunately, in many employment situations, suggestions of this kind are much more frequent than those involving identifiable savings. The usual procedure is to award points to the suggestion in terms of the particular factors considered to be relevant. The approach has much in common with certain types of job evaluation. The points awarded on each of the factors are totaled, and this point score is then converted to a dollar amount using a standardized award scale. An example of a typical form used in evaluating intangible suggestions is provided in Figure 12–1.

Factors in Effectiveness. In spite of their tremendous potential contribution, many suggestion plans are in a semidormant state. Few suggestions are submitted, and the contribution to goal attainment probably is not sufficient to justify the cost of maintaining the machinery. This is particularly likely where monetary awards are minimal or nonexistent, but it can occur under other circumstances as well.

The major factor in effectiveness appears to be the attitude of first-line supervision (7). Does the supervisor create the impression that good suggestions are desired and important? Or does his attitude imply that submitting suggestions is merely a troublesome currying of favor? Yet, even in departments where supervision actively promotes the suggestion system, it may not operate very effectively. In a study of office workers in a large corporation, numerous suggestions were submitted by employees in a department with poor productivity, but the level of monetary awards was quite low. In another, high productivity department fewer suggestions were submitted, but awards averaged almost three times as high as in the department with low productivity (11). Apparently supervisors must transmit attitudes related to both quantity and quality for maximal results to be realized.

Suggestion No. _____

Nature of Benefit	Points
1. Has definite therapeutic value	16 to 20
2. Results in a definite improvement in safety	16 to 20
3. Produces a marked improvement in operations	16 to 20
4. Improves employee relations	6 to 15
5. Improves working conditions	6 to 15
6. Of only limited importance-minor improvement	1 to 5

Distribution of Value of Benefit |
--- | ---
1. Company-wide application | 21 to 25
2. More than one department or installation | 16 to 20
3. Single department or installation | 6 to 15
4. Single operation or section | 1 to 5

Ingenuity |
--- | ---
1. Very resourceful | 11 to 25
2. Average | 6 to 10
3. Uninventive | 1 to 5

Cost of Adoption |
--- | ---
1. Less than $25 | 0
2. $25 to $100 | −5
3. Over $100 | −10

Effort Involved |
--- | ---
1. Considerable personal research | 11 to 15
2. Average substantiation | 1 to 10
3. No research at all | 0

Completeness of Proposal |
--- | ---
1. Facts clearly presented, so that little further effort is required to put idea into effect | 11 to 15
2. Basic facts are sound, but needs some refining to put into effect | 6 to 10
3. Not completely or clearly presented, thus requiring considerable clarification | 1 to 5

Total Points _____

Award Scale

Less than 25 points	$ 5	61 to 64 points	$ 55
25 to 28 points	$10	65 to 68 points	$ 60
29 to 32 points	$15	69 to 72 points	$ 65
33 to 36 points	$20	73 to 76 points	$ 70
37 to 40 points	$25	77 to 80 points	$ 75
41 to 44 points	$30	81 to 84 points	$ 80
45 to 48 points	$35	85 to 88 points	$ 85
49 to 52 points	$40	89 to 92 points	$ 90
53 to 56 points	$45	93 to 96 points	$ 95
57 to 60 points	$50	97 to 100 points	$100

Total $ _____

Figure 12–1. Typical Form for Evaluating Suggestions with Intangible Value

Aside from the attitudes of supervision, there are other factors associated with effectiveness. Most of these represent aspects of downward communication. The suggestion system should be actively promoted in the downward media. Information regarding awards should be publicized. Special attention should be given to particularly meritorious ideas. In this way, high quality participation can be stimulated. Also, management must take steps to ensure that employees feel entirely free to submit suggestions. An idea that would almost certainly leave a man without a job, result in layoffs for others, or reduce incentive payments is not likely to be submitted. There must be guarantees against negative consequences.

Suggestion systems, like all of the communications techniques mentioned in this chapter, do not operate in a vacuum. For internal communications devices of any kind to contribute maximally to goal attainment, there must be a constant downward-upward interaction. Initiation may come from any point in the system, toward the top or toward the bottom, but there must be some feedback to the source. This is what is actually meant by two-way communication. It is essential for continued organizational effectiveness, i.e., for integration of effort in pursuit of mutual goals.

REFERENCES

1. Bass, B. M., *Organizational Psychology*. Boston, Mass.: Allyn & Bacon, 1965.
2. Bureau of National Affairs, Inc., *Upward Communications*, Personnel Policies Forum Survey No. 76. Washington, D.C.: The Bureau, 1964.
3. Carlucci, C., and W. J. E. Crissy, "How Readable Are Employee Handbooks?" *Personnel Psychology*, Vol. 4 (1951), 383–395.
4. Dahle, T. L., "An Objective and Comparative Study of Five Methods of Transmitting Information to Business and Industrial Employees," *Speech Monographs*, Vol. 21 (1954), 21–28.
5. Davis, K., "Management Communication and the Grapevine," *Harvard Business Review*, Vol. 31 (1953), No. 1, 43–49.
6. Habbe, S., "Does Communication Make a Difference?" *Management Record*, Vol. 14 (1952), 414–416, 442–444.
7. Hardin, E., "Characteristics of Participants in an Employee Suggestion Plan," *Personnel Psychology*, Vol. 17 (1964), 289–303.
8. Henderson, C. O., *The Company Magazine as a Medium for Communicating Persuasive, Management Oriented Subject Matter*. Eugene, Ore.: DBA Thesis, University of Oregon, 1964.
9. Hershey, R., "The Grapevine—Here to Stay But Not Beyond Control," *Personnel*, Vol. 43 (1966), No. 1, 62–66.
10. Katz, D., and R. L. Kahn, *The Social Psychology of Organizations*. New York: Wiley, 1966.
11. Katz, D., N. Maccoby, and N. C. Morse, *Productivity, Supervision, and Morale in an Office Situation*. Ann Arbor, Mich.: Institute for Social Research, University of Michigan, 1950.
12. Martin, N. H., and J. H. Sims, "Thinking Ahead: Power Tactics," *Harvard Business Review*, Vol. 34 (1956), No. 6, 25.
13. Miner, J. B., and E. E. Heaton, "Company Orientation as a Factor in the Readership of Employee Publications," *Personnel Psychology*, Vol. 12 (1959), 607–618.
14. Perry, D., and T. A. Mahoney, "In-Plant Communications and Employee Morale," *Personnel Psychology*, Vol. 8 (1955), 339–346.

15. Read, W. H., "Upward Communication in Industrial Hierarchies," *Human Relations*, Vol. 15 (1962), 3–15.
16. Redding, W. C., and G. A. Sanborn, *Business and Industrial Communication: A Source Book*. New York: Harper & Row, 1964.
17. Sutton, H., and L. W. Porter, "A Study of the Grapevine in a Governmental Organization," *Personnel Psychology*, Vol. 21 (1968), 223–230.
18. Walton, E., "Communicating Down the Line: How They Really Get the Word," *Personnel*, Vol. 36 (1959), No. 1, 78–82.
19. Walton, E., "Project Office Communications," *Administrative Management*, Vol. 23 (1962), No. 8, 22–24.

QUESTIONS

1. What types of communications media, utilized in what ways and under what circumstances, are most likely to be effective input-output mediators?
2. What is a readership survey, and how is it conducted? Why is it important for a company to conduct readership surveys periodically?
3. What is the readability problem? Why does it occur, and what are its consequences? What appears to be the future of the problem?
4. What are the upward communications techniques in widespread use? What special problems plague the use of upward communication channels? How successful are the various techniques in overcoming these difficulties?

13

Personnel Psychology and Labor Economics

The discussions in Chapters 8 through 12 by no means exhaust the variety of input-output mediators that exist. But they do provide fairly complete coverage of the types of mediators that have been of concern to psychologists.

Over the years, psychologists also have made contributions on a relatively small scale to those areas within the personnel process that have been the primary domain of the economists. Recently, there has been some acceleration, both in the number and in the significance of these contributions. From the following review of relevant psychological theory and research dealing with payment systems, employee benefits, and labor relations it is apparent that such matters have nowhere near the status of psychological testing or management development within personnel psychology. It is also clear that the opportunity for a worthwhile contribution from psychology to the resolution of problems in the general area of labor economics is considerable.

Payment Systems

The primary intent in developing different types of monetary payment programs for employees is to introduce an input-output mediator to maximize motivation to contribute to company goals, in particular productivity. Payment systems, like management development and training, are input-improving mediators; the objective is to maximize output contribution rather than merely to sustain it at the level of input potential, or to correct a negative deviation. Whereas training and management development are directed toward *changing* people to make them more effective, payment programs are instituted to induce individuals to make the best use of their *existing* capabilities. Pay, of course, also is used to induce people to join a firm, and to contribute to its goal attainment.

Within this broad area, psychologists have, not unexpectedly, been most concerned with the reward value of money. They have also conducted research dealing with employee preferences for salary vs. hourly wage payment and with problems associated with direct incentive payment plans.

THE REWARD VALUE OF MONEY

Although it is clear that money has reward value in a purely economic sense and can directly influence job behavior, its impact can also be largely symbolic (8). People will work harder and in a manner more consistent with role prescriptions not only to gain the things that money can buy, but to obtain the esteem and status that money represents. One study of a managerial group found that although greater pay produced more satisfaction insofar as the desire for security was concerned, its reward value in the areas of esteem and autonomy was even more pronounced. Money clearly provided feelings of importance and freedom (15).

Whatever its specific meaning to the individual, it seems safe to assume that money normally will be desired. As a result, it can be used to induce a maximal contribution to the company. Considerable research evidence indicates that people can achieve higher levels of task performance when there is the prospect of achieving a monetary reward commensurate with their efforts (24). Unfortunately this evidence derives from somewhat artificial laboratory situations. Research on the effectiveness of existing monetary compensation programs in the business world is almost entirely lacking. Although we know that money potentially can serve as an effective input-output mediator, we are much less certain that it does achieve this result in most cases.

What is needed is a series of studies evaluating the various types of payment programs currently in use. Research of this kind would utilize the evaluation models discussed in Chapter 8 to determine whether shifts in motivation and role behavior result from the use of a given compensation procedure. Because such studies are rare, any evaluation of various payment procedures must rely on what is known about the subject of motivation generally. Even from this limited perspective it seems clear that many people are paid in a way that does little to arouse motivation. As a result, the potential value of the payment process as a mediator is often lost (10).

It is apparent also that the motivational potential of money is conditioned by considerations other than the amount involved. There is ample evidence that satisfaction with pay is dependent on relative rather than absolute wage levels (20). Although comparisons with other individuals in the same firm have a strong impact on feelings of equity as regards pay, outside comparisons are also made—either with individual and average rates in the local area, or with information regarding the industry or profession. Research data indicate that such outside comparisons are particularly prevalent among lower-middle management, those with more education, and the youngest employees (1). In view of this tendency on the part of employees to use outside comparisons to determine whether pay is equitable, it is apparent that such considerations should have a strong impact when pay levels are established. Whether or not a given payment is viewed as a reward depends in large part on the payments received by others.

WAGES VS. SALARIES

A second topic of psychological concern has been the selection of a particular type of payment system. Although the term *wage* is often used to include all monetary payment based on time worked, there is a more limited definition that equates wages with an hourly rate. Such hourly wages have been the tradition in factory employment, in contrast to the weekly or monthly salary characteristic in the office situation. Where employment is intermittent and layoffs are frequent, there probably is good reason to maintain an hourly rate. But under more stable conditions, the use of a regular salary seems to offer a number of advantages.

Because of its association with certain high status managerial and professional positions, the salary approach appeals to employees at all levels. Carefully conducted research studies indicate that factory employees consistently prefer a weekly salary to an hourly wage (12). In addition, the evidence indicates that the introduction of salary payment for factory workers does not yield an increase in absenteeism and tardiness. If anything, the trend is the reverse, and, at the same time, the costs of administering the payment process are reduced (13). Taken together, these considerations yield a strong case in favor of salaried payment, rather than an hourly rate.

PROBLEMS ASSOCIATED WITH INCENTIVE PAYMENT

The essential characteristic of incentive payment is that earnings are related directly to output. A standard performance is established for each job in the case of individual incentives, or an interlocking group of jobs in the case of group incentives. The employee's earnings are then promptly and automatically varied in accordance with some established formula that relates either individual or group performance to the standard (27).

Research indicates that, taken as a whole, such incentive plans have resulted in increased output and reduced costs (19). Such plans can operate effectively as input-output mediators, above and beyond what the usual time-payment procedures achieve. Apparently, however, they do so less frequently when the work is extremely repetitive, or boring, and definitely disliked.

There are certainly many instances where the full motivational potential of the incentive is not obtained. This occurs largely as a result of a quite conscious restriction of output by the workers themselves. Many work groups establish a group production norm that sets a very effective lid on output (26). Any worker who produces above this norm is likely to become the object of considerable group pressure and, as a result, will hold back on his output. The desire to maintain the respect and acceptance of the group appears to be stronger than the desire for increased earnings.

Five different types of motivation have been identified behind this restriction of output phenomenon, which serves effectively to hamstring many incentive plans (11). For one thing, there may be a widespread belief that if incentive earnings, and production, were allowed to move up to the level possible, the job would be restudied and the standard set higher. Earnings would not increase for long, and all employees would have to work much harder to maintain the same income level. Second, workers assume that if the more competent individuals went all out in accord with the intent of the incentive system, a number of less capable workers would be fired. In this sense, restriction protects the ineffective members of the group. Third, if members compete for earnings, as the incentive approach implies, the social structure of the group will be disrupted. Restriction maintains the social ties. Competition would lead to distrust and individual isolation.

The other two types of motivation are more positive. The very process of establishing restrictive norms produces a sense of "groupness" with its consequent social satisfactions. In addition, restriction provides a feeling of control over one's own behavior, a sense of freedom from the manipulations of management. This final point may be particularly important in explaining why a group norm is often maintained long after any real threat of revised standards has disappeared.

Difficulties in the use of incentive plans are not limited to group output restriction. Another major problem is that workers generally will devote considerable effort to getting a low standard established, if this seems at all possible. When time and motion studies are conducted, workers may make the job appear more difficult and time-consuming than it is. The lower standards are not only a means to increased earnings; they are also viewed as a protection against layoffs. Under such conditions, it is very hard to set truly appropriate standards, and controversy between management and industrial engineers, on the one side, and workers and the union, on the other, may become intense.

It seems inherent in the very nature of incentive payment that although the approach contributes to the goal it is directed to, namely productivity, it does so at some cost to organizational maintenance. Disputes and grievances related to inequitable standards are common in nearly every case where incentive systems have been installed. Perhaps, if a system could be devised that would reward an appropriate balance between productivity and maintenance considerations, this problem could be overcome. To date, however, little has been done in this area.

Employee Benefits

The number and variety of benefits and services provided by companies for their employees have grown rapidly in recent years, to the point where such items are a major factor in total compensation. The so-called fringe benefits range from costly insurance and retirement programs to the use of company facilities in connection with the activities of various employee groups. They may be provided by the company on an entirely unilateral basis, or they may emerge out of extended bargaining with a union. They may have as their immediate goal the improvement of working conditions (music in the plant), the provision of more leisure time (vacations and holidays), or the guaranteeing of security in times of personal adversity (group hospitalization insurance and supplemental unemployment pay).

Although part of the total compensation package, these items are not intended to encourage task motivation. Little effort has been made to use fringe benefits as inducements or rewards, with a view to maximizing the effectiveness of role behavior. Differentials related to merit or productivity, therefore, are not a characteristic aspect of their application. The ultimate goal of employee benefits and services is to further organizational maintenance by contributing to high morale, a sense of security, and general job satisfaction. In this way, internal stress within the organization is minimized, but there is no reason to believe that productivity necessarily will be fostered as a result (3). In addition, benefits may be used as an inducement to continued organizational membership. A further objective, which is often noted, is that such benefits are a valuable asset in recruiting potentially effective employees.

EMPLOYEE ATTITUDES TOWARD VARIOUS BENEFITS

The field of benefit planning and administration has received even less attention from psychologists than have payment systems. The question of whether one approach or another will contribute most to organizational goal attainment is susceptible to psychological study, and research recently has begun to appear in this area.

Company benefit programs are often criticized for including items that fulfill no real employee need and that accomplish little in terms of goal attainment. A number of benefits that were initiated as legitimate motive-satisfiers have now become standard in most firms. Against the background of current practice, liberalizing them further has very little appeal for employees. Once benefits reach a certain level, wage increases are preferred to more benefits (9). Union leaders, on occasion, have had to sell the membership on the value of a particular fringe item, particularly where there is some feeling that a wage increase has been traded for a benefit that might well not be realized personally, i.e., higher retirement pay. Benefit plans that require employee contributions may, in fact, have a negative impact on employee attitudes. It is not particularly pleasant to find money deducted from one's pay check for benefits that are not desired, even if, under a certain amount of social pressure, one has signed an authorization form.

Nevertheless, it can be assumed that many benefits are considered important by the majority of employees. This is illustrated in Table 13–1.

TABLE 13–1. Employee Preferences for Selected Employee Benefits

Benefits	Employee rank	Employees in 111 firms indicating that the benefit was of great importance, %	Total firms providing the benefit, %
Insurance benefits			
Hospitalization	1	79.6	93.2
Doctor bill	2	73.9	94.4
Major medical	3	64.8	45.7
Retirement plan (other than Social Security)	4	63.5	70.4
Disability income	5	61.3	53.7
Accidental death and dismemberment	6	58.8	53.1
Group life	7	55.9	70.4
Noninsurance benefits			
Paid vacation	1	87.0	81.5
Paid holidays	2	81.0	98.1
Paid sick leave	3	54.1	25.9
Profit-sharing plan	4	42.2	15.4
Credit unions	5	38.7	24.1
Paid rest periods, lunch	6	38.2	71.0
Other paid leaves	7	38.0	46.9
Free medical exams	8	31.0	30.2
Layoff allowances, SUB	9	28.0	11.1
Stock options	10	20.6	8.6
Merchandise discounts	11	18.0	55.6
Free or low-cost meals on premises	12	14.5	n.a.

Source: M. R. Greene, *The Role of Employee Benefit Structures in Manufacturing Industry.* Eugene, Oregon: School of Business Administration, Univ. of Oregon, 1964, pp. 24–25.

In a few instances, such as major medical insurance, there is apparently a strong motive that is not being met on a widespread basis. On the other hand, group life insurance is ranked at the very bottom of the various insurance benefits even though 70 per cent of the firms provide it. From this and other studies, it is apparent that the various types of medical insurance are of considerable importance to employees (18).

Among the noninsurance benefits, there are also some discrepancies. One of the most notable is profit-sharing, which is ranked fourth by the employees, but is provided by only 15 per cent of the firms included in the study. There is some reason to believe that this may be an area of major concern to unions in the future. The Automobile Workers have recently indicated considerable interest in the idea of automatic wage supplements, to be granted whenever a company's profits rise above a specified level. In effect, this would suggest less emphasis on the usual fringe items in future bargaining, and more concern with increasing basic compensation.

The significance of various work-force characteristics is stressed in another study (18), which dealt with the preferences of over 1,000 members of a union local (International Brotherhood of Electrical Workers). Over all, hospital insurance was most preferred of the six items considered. But, as Figure 13–1 indicates, there were sharp differences associated with age. Pension preference progressively rose in each group aged thirty and over, although pensions were not clearly favored over hospital insurance until the fifties. Sex differences could not be studied in this instance, because only males were included. It can be presumed, however, that variations would emerge on this basis also. Young, predominantly female, office workers probably prefer more vacation benefits to most types of insurance.

Irrespective of what benefits and services a firm provides, they can have little value as a means to encouraging pride in the organization, loyalty, and satisfaction unless employees know about and understand them. Many workers are entirely unaware that the company pays for unemployment compensation and contributes sizably to Social Security. A large number appear to have little knowledge of the private benefits available to them through the company (9).

Labor Relations

The various approaches developed to deal with company problems in the labor relations area may be viewed as input-output mediators that have as their goal the reduction of employee dissatisfaction and the minimization of conflict. They are much more closely related to the organizational maintenance goal than to productivity and profit.

The use of these labor relations approaches is conditioned by several

Mean
preferance

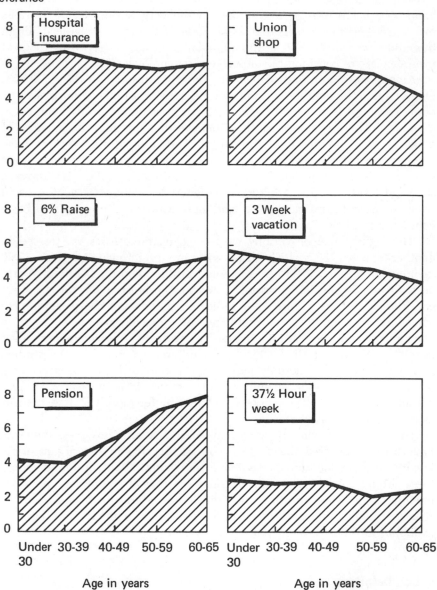

Source: Nealy, S. M., "Determining Worker Preferences Among Employee Benefit Pro-
           grams," *Journal of Applied Psychology,* Vol. 48 (1964), p. 8.

Figure 13–1. Benefit Preference by Age

considerations. For one thing, the goal in this area has normally been not
so much to maximize maintenance aspects as to achieve a suitable level
while pursuing productivity and profit to the maximum degree. This

means that companies do not normally devote their energies to conflict reduction at all costs. It is important, for instance, that management not sign a contract with a union that would impose internal constraints making it impossible to remain competitive in the industry, even if by doing so, continuing labor peace and high levels of employee satisfaction could be guaranteed. The primary objective, then, in using the approaches to be discussed is to attain the least internal conflict and stress possible while maintaining maximum control over all aspects of human resources utilization and productivity. Firms that have devoted themselves to internal conflict reduction, without adequate concern for the external realities of the marketplace and a competitive economy, have often made continued survival impossible.

MOTIVES IN UNION MEMBERSHIP

A large proportion of new members presently join unions automatically, because it is required under a union shop contract. Undoubtedly, many of these workers give relatively little thought to this action, especially if they were raised in a pro-union environment. In the past, however, such automatic membership was uncommon, and it is not always the case today, especially where employees select a new union as their bargaining agent. Under such voluntary conditions, union membership can provide for the satisfaction of important motives.

Over the years, scholars have advanced numerous theories of union membership. The earlier theories were predicated primarily on economic grounds. The assumption was that, as individuals, workers are at the mercy of their employers, particularly in times of job scarcity. Only by joining forces and forming a union can workers force an employer to provide fair wages and adequate working conditions. Furthermore, under prosperous economic conditions, when profits are high, the union's power in collective bargaining can ensure the workers a fair share.

More recently, however, investigators have found that the desire for economic gain may not be the primary factor in union membership. A variety of social and psychological needs are satisfied as well. The union can provide a worker with a sense of security, perhaps some status, a feeling of independence in relation to his employer, and the satisfactions of group membership. Even in a well-managed firm that pays good wages and offers ideal working conditions, union membership may have considerable appeal, solely because it frees the employees from dependency on their employer.

Furthermore, that employees join a union does not necessarily mean that they dislike the company or intend in any sense to be disloyal to it. A survey of attitudes in the meatpacking industry indicated that nearly three fourths of the workers were favorably disposed to both the company *and* the union. A dual allegiance was demonstrated among the rank-and-file union members (21).

It is generally conceded that dissatisfied employees are most likely to be susceptible to union organizing appeals. This dissatisfaction may relate to wage rates, to the lack of available channels for complaints regarding unfair treatment, and to many other things (7). Dissatisfaction may be primarily economic in nature, but it may also be associated with a variety of social or psychological considerations. In many instances, employees are not really aware of the true sources of their dissatisfaction.

In any event, if through appropriate personnel policies and procedures, a company can keep its employees satisfied with their jobs and with management's actions, a union will find it much more difficult to become established. On the other hand, union leaders will almost certainly attempt to capitalize on any signs of dissatisfaction within an employee group they are attempting to organize. For this reason, many companies conduct attitude surveys to ascertain the extent and sources of employee discontent, whenever they believe a threat of unionization exists. With such knowledge it is often possible to blunt the appeals of the union.

THE NATURE OF THE BARGAINING RELATIONSHIP

Although the factors associated with union membership have probably attracted more psychological attention than other aspects of labor relations, there recently has been an increasing interest in various approaches to collective bargaining and grievance handling. A number of studies deal with various kinds of bargaining relationships (4,5,6,14). In general, the emphasis has been on the identification of relationships that are and are not conducive to industrial peace. Several of the more frequently noted types are discussed below.

Open Conflict. Open conflict arises where management does not accept the union and refuses to deal with it on other than a "minimal compliance" basis. Relationships of this kind are unlikely to be effective from a management viewpoint, once a union has been certified. Not only do legal difficulties frequently result, but pro-union employees often become so disruptive that there is a major threat to both organizational maintenance and productivity.

Containment. The "armed truce" relationship, containment, is probably the most common type. It is based on the premise that management and the union have inherently conflicting interests. The company deals with the union only to the extent required by legal constraints, although it is careful not to violate the law. Every effort is made to contain the union's power and preserve the rights of management.

Accommodation. In the accommodation relationship, the parties recognize some common goals and therefore work together through information-sharing, problem-solving, and other techniques to achieve joint solutions to bargaining problems. The result is likely to be a minimum of conflict, but there may be other less desirable consequences. The Studebaker Company, for example, apparently had an extremely harmonious relationship involving considerable discussion of problems with the union. Nevertheless, very few real solutions evolved. In general, management acquiesced to the union arguments, with the result that little was done to control excess manpower. The consequent rise in production costs was a major factor in the company's being forced out of the automobile business (25).

Cooperation. The cooperative relationship usually involves an extension of the bargaining relationship under a formal plan for joint consultation and action on matters ordinarily handled by management alone. It tends to emerge because of some major problem facing the firm, or the entire industry; a new approach is clearly needed. There have been several dramatic examples of such cooperative efforts in recent years resulting from problems created by automation.

The Deal. One further relationship that has existed in the past and that no doubt still exists in some localities is where management makes certain special arrangements with the union leaders, usually without membership knowledge or approval. The leaders may agree to forego a wage increase in return for a union shop. Where racketeering elements are present, a small employer may agree to sign a contract under threat of being forced out of business.

Irrespective of the over-all relationship between a company and a union, it is almost inevitable that conflict will arise during the collective bargaining process itself, simply because the parties have different desires and expectations as regards the final solution. This concept is illustrated in Figure 13–2.

In most negotiations, each party begins by listing its demands for contract changes. These constitute the desired solution. The demands are normally accompanied by supporting facts and figures. The primary task becomes one of determining the tolerance limits of the respective parties, thus establishing the bargaining zone (23).

There are a number of problems that characteristically arise and contribute to conflict. Primarily, these are communications problems resulting from faulty perceptions and differences in the personalities, backgrounds, and motives of the management and union negotiators. Other sources of difficulty are the ritualistic formality of the bargaining situation, which tends to thwart new approaches, the needs of the negotiators to convey a favorable impression to their respective constituencies, and the lack of appropriate support, which may arise on either the management or the union side (7,25).

A number of approaches have been used to minimize bargaining conflicts. Sometimes, training programs designed to produce awareness of communications problems can have a positive effect. For example, if company negotiators can recognize when the union leaders are pressing a demand merely to placate the national officers, the vehemence of their counter-response may be reduced considerably. In several cases where outside consultants have had an opportunity to work with both parties

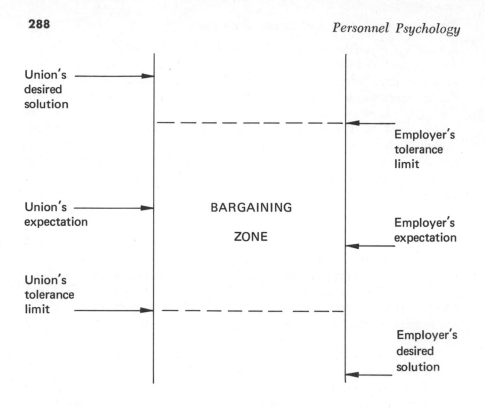

Union's desired solution

Employer's tolerance limit

Union's expectation

BARGAINING

ZONE

Employer's expectation

Union's tolerance limit

Employer's desired solution

Source: R. Stagner and H. Rosen. *Psychology of Union-Management Relations,* p. 96. Copyright 1965 by Wadsworth Publishing Company, Inc., Belmont, California. Used by permission.

Figure 13–2. Desires, Expectations, and Tolerance Limits That Determine the Bargaining Zone

along these lines, the incidence of conflict has been markedly reduced (2,17).

Similarly, some newer, essentially psychological approaches to grievance handling also reportedly have achieved major reductions in conflict. In one instance, the formal writing up of grievances was suspended; union and management representatives were encouraged to settle employee complaints orally and on the spot. The result: The number of grievances submitted for arbitration was reduced substantially (16). Other companies have resorted to what amount to group therapy sessions where supervisors discuss their grievance-handling methods and the reasons behind them. This approach has also been reported to be successful (22). Clearly, unique aspects of each situation contribute to the effectiveness of these approaches. What makes the grievance process function more efficiently as a means to organizational maintenance in one firm may not achieve the same result in another.

REFERENCES

1. Andrews, I. R., and M. M. Henry, "Management Attitudes Toward Pay," *Industrial Relations,* Vol. 3 (1963), 29–39.
2. Blake, R. R., H. A. Shepard, and J. S. Mouton, *Managing Intergroup Conflict in Industry.* Houston, Tex.: Gulf, 1964.
3. Brayfield, A. H., and W. H. Crockett, "Employee Attitudes and Employee Performance," *Psychological Bulletin,* Vol. 52 (1955), 396–424.
4. Derber, M., W. E. Chalmers, and R. Stagner, *The Local Union-Management Relationship.* Urbana, Ill.: Institute of Labor and Industrial Relations, Univ. of Illinois, 1960.
5. Dubin, R., "A Theory of Conflict and Power in Union-Management Relations," *Industrial and Labor Relations Review,* Vol. 13 (1960), 501–518.
6. Dubin, R., "Leadership in Union-Management Relations as an Intergroup System," in M. Sherif, *Intergroup Relations and Leadership.* New York: Wiley, 1962, pp. 70–91.
7. Dunnette, M. D., and W. K. Kirchner, *Psychology Applied to Industry,* New York: Appleton-Century-Crofts, 1965.
8. Gellerman, S. W., *Motivation and Productivity.* New York: American Management Association, 1963.
9. Greene, M. R., *The Role of Employee Benefit Structures in Manufacturing Industry.* Eugene, Ore.: School of Business Administration, Univ. of Oregon, 1964.
10. Haire, M., E. E. Ghiselli, and M. E. Gordon, "A Psychological Study of Pay," *Journal of Applied Psychology Monograph,* Vol. 51 (1967), No. 4, 1–24.
11. Hickson, D. J., "Motives of People Who Restrict Their Output," *Occupational Psychology,* Vol. 35 (1961), 110–121.
12. Jones, L. V., and T. E. Jeffrey, "A Quantitative Analysis of Expressed Preferences for Compensation Plans," *Journal of Applied Psychology,* Vol. 48 (1964), 201–210.
13. Kaponya, P. G., "Salaries for All Workers," *Harvard Business Review,* Vol. 40 (1962), No. 3, 49–57.
14. Kornhauser, A., R. Dubin, and A. M. Ross, *Industrial Conflict.* New York: McGraw-Hill, 1954.
15. Lawler, E. E., and L. W. Porter, "Perceptions Regarding Management Compensation," *Industrial Relations,* Vol. 3 (1963), 41–49.
16. McKersie, R. B., "Avoiding Written Grievances by Problem-Solving: An Outside View," *Personnel Psychology,* Vol. 17 (1964), 367–379.
17. Muench, G. A., "A Clinical Psychologist's Treatment of Labor-Management Conflicts," *Personnel Psychology,* Vol. 13 (1960), 165–172.
18. Nealey, S. M., "Determining Worker Preferences Among Employee Benefit Programs," *Journal of Applied Psychology,* Vol. 48 (1964), 7–12.
19. Opsahl, R. L., and M. D. Dunnette, "The Role of Financial Compensation in Industrial Motivation," *Psychological Bulletin,* Vol. 63 (1966), 94–118.
20. Patchen, M., *The Choice of Wage Comparisons.* Englewood Cliffs, N.J.: Prentice-Hall, 1961.
21. Purcell, T. V., *Blue Collar Man.* Cambridge, Mass.: Harvard Univ. Press, 1960.
22. Speroff, B. J., "Group Psychology in Labor Relations," *Personnel Journal,* Vol. 39 (1960), 14–17.
23. Stagner, R., and H. Rosen, *Psychology of Union-Management Relations.* Belmont, Cal.: Wadsworth, 1965.

24. Vroom, V. H., *Work and Motivation*. New York: Wiley, 1964.
25. Walton, R. E., and R. B. McKersie, *A Behavioral Theory of Labor Negotiations*. New York: McGraw-Hill, 1965.
26. Whyte, W. F., *et al.*, *Money and Motivation*. New York: Harper & Row, 1955.
27. Wolf, W. B., *Wage Incentives as a Managerial Tool*. New York: Columbia Univ. Press, 1957.

QUESTIONS

1. In what ways do payment systems, employee benefits, and approaches in labor relations differ insofar as their role as input-output mediators is concerned? How effective is each of the three types of mediator, typically, in contributing to goal attainment?
2. What is known about the relative merits of hourly wages, salary, and direct incentives? Do they appear to have the same reward value?
3. What are some of the newer approaches to collective bargaining and grievance-handling? Why does each of these approaches appear to have positive value as a means to organizational maintenance?
4. Why do workers join unions? What factors may keep workers from joining unions? How do you believe these factors will influence the growth or decline of unionism in the future?

14

The Input-Output Model for Human Resources Utilization

In bits and pieces, the preceding chapters present a comprehensive model of the personnel process. This model follows the conceptual approach of the input-output system, an approach that appears to be winning considerable acceptance in organization theory generally (2,3,4,5,6).

Until now, however, the various elements of this conceptual framework for a company's utilization of human resources have not been brought together in a unified presentation. It seemed more appropriate to develop the various aspects of the theory as they were needed. It is now time to pull together the threads of theory running through the earlier chapters. What follows, then, represents an integration and recapitulation. Little new is added. Yet, when the various fragments are joined into the whole, each may take on new meaning.

Goals and Constraints

The theory posits that organizations have certain goals that provide a focus for their activities. These goals tend to be established, not so much by the members of the organizations themselves, as by the next larger social unit, the society. In a sense, company goals are the role prescriptions established for organizations of this type within the framework of the total social structure. They define what the organization is expected to contribute. Although society tends to specify goals for its organizations, indicating how necessary functions are to be allocated among the various societal sectors, it also establishes restrictions on the means used to reach these objectives. Society both sets the goals of business firms and constrains the paths to goal attainment.

COMPANY GOALS

Business organizations, comprising the economic sector, operate with two primary types of goals under a capitalistic system. To the extent a firm is attaining both of these, it may be presumed to justify its creation and existence within society. These goals serve to guide all facets of organizational activity. As such, they are relevant for personnel, just as they are for marketing, manufacturing, accounting, and other functions.

The Productivity Goal. All organizations have one or more task objectives. In the United States, the economic sector of society is expected to operate in accordance with the capitalistic system. Thus, the task objective of business organizations is closely allied not only to the production of goods and services, but to the maximization of long-term net profit as well. Society expects business firms to produce as much as possible and make as much profit as possible within the limitations imposed by existing constraints and the organizational maintenance goal.

The Organizational Maintenance Goal. At the same time that companies are productive, they must also take steps to ensure survival on other grounds. The organization must be maintained as an ongoing social unit in the face of both internal and external pressures and stresses. Internal stress derives from intergroup conflict, low morale, and widespread dissatisfaction. Under extreme circumstances it may result in a total disintegration of the organization, as members leave and subunits split off. Such matters have been the special concern of psychologists and sociologists. External stress, on the other hand, derives from the pressures imposed by governments, public opinion, and other economic organizations. Here economists and political scientists have been particularly concerned.

In a historical sense, one major problem of the personnel field, and one factor accounting for its occasional low status, has been that a large number of its representatives have emphasized the maintenance goal at a time when the great majority of managers were almost exclusively concerned with productivity and profit. There was a time when many personnel people seemed much more concerned with matters of employee happiness than with corporate profitability. At present, the personnel field seems to have lined up more solidly behind *both* goals. As a result, current detractors no longer appear to be emphasizing these goal considerations in their attacks (1).

CONSTRAINTS ON PERSONNEL DECISIONS

Decisions made to implement the attainment of company goals are restricted by a whole host of constraints. There are a number of things that, at a given point in space and time, personnel people cannot do. Either they are physically impossible or the consequences are such as to make them distinctly unattractive. These constraint systems, which impinge on decision-making in the personnel area, are of two kinds.

Internal Constraints. The major internal factors that limit personnel decisions are the characteristics of the company's labor force, the existing structure of role prescriptions, and the union contract currently in effect. Individual differences, as they are reflected in a particular work force, in all probability have the most pronounced impact. At a particular point in time, a company's employees are characterized by specific distributions of abilities and personalities. These distributions limit personnel action although, with time, these internal constraints can be overcome through the hiring of new employees, training, and other procedures. Many companies have experienced serious difficulties because the constraints imposed by the existing work force have not been fully recognized. Accordingly, they have committed themselves too rapidly to major product diversification, office and plant automation, or a strong research orientation. Consequently they have failed, because their employees did not have the required capabilities, and thus could not adapt to the new mold.

Restrictions are also imposed by the existing procedures for segmenting the total work effort, as a result of organization planning and job analysis. When a particular structure has been developed, with prescribed lines of authority, status, and communications, limitations are imposed automatically on personnel decisions. These limitations can be overcome through a restructuring of the organization or through job redesign, but at a point in time they represent a clear-cut constraint system. Similarly, the union contract specifies what can and cannot be done in certain areas, with regard to the utilization of human resources. It, too, can be changed. But rarely with ease, and then only when the next occasion for collective bargaining presents itself.

External Constraints. Constraints imposed from outside the organization are even more resistant to change than internal ones. This is particularly true of external constraints introduced by the culture. Thus, in Japan discharging a man for incompetence has long been considered reprehensible, and the particular equalitarian value system of the communist countries has barred almost all psychological testing. Similarly, the high incidence of illiteracy in many underdeveloped countries severely restricts company training efforts.

Within a country, geographical differences also may introduce significant constraints. Existing attitudes may place major barriers in the way of hiring particular groups of individuals for certain types of jobs. Differences in the educational, intellectual, and other characteristics of regional populations may force much more intensive recruiting efforts, expanded training, or even a curtailment of expansion plans.

Similar constraint systems may characterize entire industries. Differences in the propensity to strike impose limitations on the extent to which organizational maintenance considerations can be ignored. In past years, in industries such as mining and lumber, it was essential to devote considerable effort to such matters; in agriculture and the utilities, much less so. Again, in fields such as petroleum refining, where advancing technology has markedly reduced manpower needs, selection is not available in most cases as a means of upgrading a labor force; new refinery workers are rarely hired. Industry constraints of much the same kind operate in other sectors of the economy.

Finally, there are the great variety of legal constraints that restrict personnel actions. Perhaps most widely known are the federal labor laws, the Wagner Act and Taft-Hartley. But there are also numerous state laws in the labor relations area, as well as laws that limit employment decisions, at all levels of government. The Fair Labor Standards Act, fair employment practices legislation, the Social Security Act, Workmen's Compensation, and so on, in addition to various court and commission rulings, can be cited as examples. These laws and rulings constrain the payment of wages, working hours, selection procedures, separations, safety procedures, the utilization of older workers, and employment in a research capacity.

Inputs and Outputs

Internal and external constraints operate on an organization, which may be most appropriately viewed as a behavioral system, performing in accordance with the input-output model. Insofar as the personnel function is concerned, the input side deals primarily with people, although for other purposes, financial resources, materials, facilities, and technology may also be treated as inputs. People become available to the organization as a result of the employment process. They enter the firm with abilities, skills, personality characteristics, cultural values, and so on that, as previously noted, operate to constrain personnel decisions. But individual differences are also the raw materials, in a human resources sense, through which productivity and maintenance goals are achieved.

On the output side, the major consideration insofar as the personnel process is concerned is the behavior of employed individuals as organization members. The latter involves three aspects: (1) the things that people who work for the company say and do, (2) the things that people who work for the company are expected to say and do, and (3) the relationships between expectations and what members of the organization actually say and do.

ROLE PRESCRIPTIONS

The things that people who work for a company are expected to do may be labeled role prescriptions. These are developed to contribute the most effectively to goal attainment. At least this is the intent. Unhappily, exact methods of determining whether a given structure of organizational roles is maximally supportive of productivity and maintenance goals are not generally available. Thus, there is usually considerable guesswork involved, even though experience can be a useful guide.

Once such role prescriptions are established, they become internal constraints on related decisions. They limit personnel actions, just as individual differences do. At the managerial level, a major contributor in introducing role expectations is organization planning. At lower levels in the company, some form of job analysis is used to perform this function, although on occasion aspects of a formal job analysis program are extended upward into the ranks of management.

At all levels, it is important that the role prescriptions established be clear and that they be accepted within the organization as legitimate. In part this is a necessary means to gaining the full advantages of division of labor in the pursuit of maximal productivity. But clear-cut jurisdictions, with little overlap and widespread acceptance, are also an important means to internal conflict reduction. Thus, the process of setting role prescriptions can make a sizable contribution to both major types of organizational goals.

ROLE BEHAVIOR

The things people are expected to do on the job are role prescriptions; the things they actually do are role behaviors. To the extent these role behaviors approximate a perfect match with the appropriate role prescriptions, an individual is effective or successful. It is assumed that he is contributing to company goal achievement.

Performance evaluation is essentially a matter of determining the degree of this matching. It is an attempt to take organizational goal attainment down to the level of the individual contribution. Or, put somewhat differently, it represents an evaluation of the behavioral output in terms of its contribution to the total firm. What is really important, insofar as an organization is concerned, is not how much an individual does, but how much that is organizationally relevant as determined by his role.

As with the establishing of role expectations, the evaluation of role behaviors tends to be differentiated on a vertical scale. Management appraisal techniques are utilized at the upper levels; employee evaluation at the submanagerial levels. In the former instance, considerable emphasis usually is placed on the performance of the group managed as well as on the performance of the manager himself; below the ranks of management only the performance or role behavior of the individual is of concern.

In presenting this theoretical model, the output side is discussed first because the selection of individual inputs must be carried out with a view to maximizing future role prescription-role behavior matching. An organization should select those individuals who subsequently will be most effective on the job. In order to fully understand personnel selection, then, one must be aware of what the concept of effective performance implies.

Studies should be conducted, using longitudinal and concurrent selection models as appropriate, to establish procedures that will identify those individuals within an applicant group who are most likely to succeed. Unfortunately, some firms are using cumbersome and often very expensive selection apparatuses, which fall far short of accomplishing this objective. In such cases, the selection process may contribute only very minimally to goal attainment. Certainly, there is little point in extensive recruiting if a company does not select from among those recruited those individuals who will contribute most on an organizationally relevant basis.

The requirement that selection techniques be evaluated in terms of their contribution to the company holds for all approaches. Such techniques for the evaluation of individual inputs to an organization are of two types. First, there are those that utilize information on past behavior to predict future behavior. Among these are most selection interviews, application blanks, biographical inventories, reference checks, and the more comprehensive background investigations. Second, there are the techniques that utilitize information on current behavior and functioning to predict future behavior. Among these are physical examinations, ability testing, personality testing, and skill or achievement testing.

The Input-Output Mediators

A final aspect of the model, perhaps most important in that it encompasses many types of personnel activities, is the input-output mediator. These mediators are used to sustain or improve on the original input so that the output is maximized. They may be grouped in several ways.

STRUCTURAL AND FUNCTIONAL MEDIATORS

One basis for grouping is in terms of structural and functional characteristics. The structural mediators are the techniques for establishing role requirements discussed previously. These techniques provide a basis for evaluating role behaviors, but only the role behaviors themselves represent actual organizational outputs. The structural mediators are procedures for grouping organizational tasks and establishing role requirements so as to channel the behaviors of organization members in the direction of goal attainment. This is accomplished through organization planning and job analysis. Once these role prescriptions are set, they represent internal constraints.

The functional mediators influence organization members through procedures that impinge on the individual directly, rather than through role prescriptions. Included in this category are management development, training, safety procedures, counseling, discipline, medical treatment, labor relations activities, fringe benefits, payment procedures, and employee communications. All the techniques used to influence organizational input discussed in this book, with the exception of organization planning and job analysis, are functional in character, but the current listing is not meant to be definitive. Fifty years from now, approaches at present not even under consideration may well have achieved widespread acceptance.

PRODUCTIVITY-ORIENTED AND MAINTENANCE-ORIENTED MEDIATORS

As previously indicated, the structural mediators normally serve both types of organization goals. They segment work, permitting specialization and thus more efficient productivity, at the same time establishing jurisdictions that limit internal conflict. Although, in any given firm, the major emphasis in developing role prescriptions may be on productivity or on maintenance considerations, both factors are likely to receive some recognition.

The functional mediators, on the other hand, appear to be much more susceptible to differentiation in terms of the type of organizational goal fostered. Even here there may be some overlap. Although management development techniques generally appear to be strongly oriented toward productivity, certain human relations programs and sensitivity training are clearly directed toward organizational maintenance. This suggests that, at least potentially, many of the functional mediators could be focused on either type of goal or on both. In actual practice, however, there has been a tendency to use a particular type of mediator primarily for one purpose or the other.

Management development, training, safety procedures, medical procedures, counseling, discipline, and payment procedures, tend to be applied most frequently toward increasing productivity. The various approaches in the labor relations area, employee benefits and services, and communications procedures are characteristically maintenance oriented.

INPUT-IMPROVING, INPUT-SUSTAINING, AND CONTROL MEDIATORS

In many of its applications, the input-output model has included a feedback or control procedure. When the operation of part or all of the system drops below a certain level, or deviates too much from certain predetermined standards, corrective forces are activated in much the same way that a thermostat activates a heating system when the temperature falls below a preset level.

Although this feedback or control concept is useful in understanding the functioning of some input-output mediators, it is not adequate to the task of explaining the whole gamut of techniques. At least two other types of mediators must be considered. These two categories, along with the control concept, provide a way of viewing mediators as they relate to the input side of the system.

One group of mediators is oriented toward the improvement of inputs so that role behavior eventually exceeds the level that could have been anticipated merely from a knowledge of the original input. The objective is to improve performance above and beyond what was manifest at the time of hiring. The structural mediators certainly contribute to this process, because in channeling effort and motivating individuals, they attempt to maximize output in the form of role behavior. The most obvious examples of input-improving mediators, however, are management development and training. Here an effort is made to change the individual in some way so that he now either is more capable of performing effectively or has a greater desire to do so. Various payment plans are also initiated with a view to mobilizing individual motivation behind organizational goal attainment. In these instances, the primary stress is not so much on correcting deviations from a pre-established standard, as on actually making the individual more effective than he was when he entered the organization.

Second, there is a group of mediators that serves primarily to sustain the behavior potential existing in the input. Such approaches are essentially preventive. They attempt to keep the situation from getting worse, rather than to make it better. Most of what is done in the organizational maintenance area is basically of this kind. Approaches in labor relations, employee benefit programs, and communications efforts tend to focus on protecting the organization against stresses that might threaten its survival. Few firms are concerned with totally eradicating internal conflict or maximizing employee satisfaction. It is sufficient to establish conditions and utilize procedures that prevent such internal stresses from becoming disruptive and that keep people at least as satisfied as they were when they joined the company. Similarly, activities in the areas of safety and preventive medicine are of an input-sustaining nature. The objective is to maintain the individual in the same state, insofar as his performance potential is concerned, that existed at the time of hiring.

Finally, there are mediators that operate selectively to control negatively deviant cases. In these instances, the feedback concept is adequate to explain what occurs. Individuals whose behavior departs from role requirements so markedly as to fall below a pre-established standard are identified, the sources of the failure are determined, and an appropriate corrective process is set in motion. Medical treatment, discipline, much reassignment, and employee counseling operate in this manner. On occasion, mediators that are more commonly applied in an input-improving or input-sustaining context may also be utilized in a corrective sense, and thus fulfill a control function. Thus, job redesign, training, payment procedures, and the like may be used at times for purposes of performance control.

The various elements of the total model are presented in Figure 14–1.

Personnel Psychology and the Solution of Personnel Problems

The model developed implies a problem-solving approach to the personnel process. Specific strategies must be designed depending on the particular task objectives and constraint structures of a given organization. The input processes, mediators, and output processes that maximize goal-attainment in one situation are unlikely to do so in another. Thus, each organization requires its own set of solutions. No one combination is universally applicable.

Personnel psychology has been responsible for the development of a number of techniques that are widely used to solve problems in the human resources area. In terms of the model of Figure 14–1, it has concentrated heavily on both input and output processes as well as on certain selected kinds of mediators, particularly management development, training, safety procedures, performance control techniques, internal communications, and job analysis.

There is at the present time a great need for new types of mediators that will serve to control, sustain and improve the human input to an organization. Hopefully, in years to come, psychologists will make increasing contributions not only in such areas as payment programs, preventive medicine (particularly the psychiatric aspects), labor relations, employee benefits, and organization planning, where they have been relatively inactive, but will create wholly new types of mediators as well.

At the same time, there is a continuing need for evaluation of techniques in terms of their contribution to organizational goals. Personnel research of this kind is largely a psychological task. We must clearly specify what input procedures, output procedures, and mediators are appropriate to the solution of what personnel problems under what conditions of constraint and goal demand.

It is unfortunate that the personnel field has attracted a number of individuals strongly committed to particular techniques rather than to developing over-all strategies for problem-solving. The result is often an attempt to find as many applications as possible for a specific technique, rather than starting with a problem and selecting or developing a tech-

EXTERNAL CONSTRAINTS

Cultural, geographical,
and industry characteristics
Labor relations laws
Employment laws

INTERNAL CONSTRAINTS

Individual differences
Existing role prescriptions
Union contracts

**INPUT
PROCESSES**

Recruiting
Selection
  • Techniques stressing
    past behavior
    (Interview, etc.)
  • Techniques stressing
    current behavior
    (Testing, etc.)

	Functional
	Primarily Productivity-Oriented
INPUT — IMPROVING	Management development Training Payment programs
INPUT — SUSTAINING	Safety management Preventive medicine
CONTROL	Performance control techniques (Discipline, counseling, etc.)

Figure 14–1. **The Model of the Personnel Process**

nique appropriate to it. This emphasis, where solutions are more important
than problems, creates a situation in which techniques are often applied
indiscriminately, with little attention to whether they are appropriate to
the need. In addition, particular approaches may be belabored long after
they have outlived their usefulness. Once a given technique has been
introduced in a firm and has gained acceptance, there is little incentive
to find new solutions in that particular problem area or to adopt other

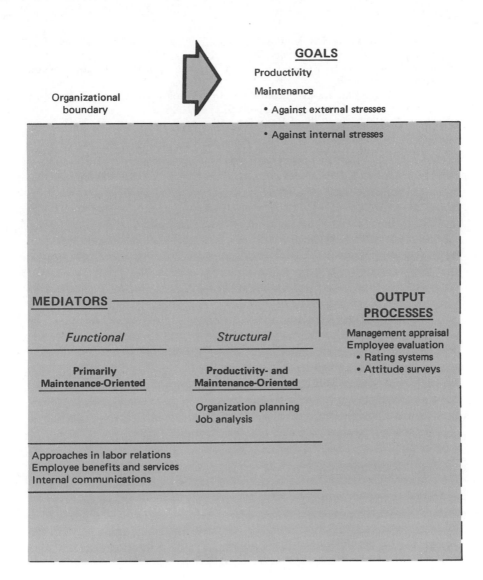

GOALS

Productivity

Maintenance

• Against external stresses

• Against internal stresses

Organizational
boundary

MEDIATORS

Functional

Structural

Primarily
Maintenance-Oriented

Productivity- and
Maintenance-Oriented

Organization planning
Job analysis

Approaches in labor relations
Employee benefits and services
Internal communications

OUTPUT
PROCESSES

Management appraisal
Employee evaluation
• Rating systems
• Attitude surveys

techniques. A problem-oriented approach, on the other hand, can provide protection against becoming technique-bound in this sense, and thus can serve to foster creative thinking with regard to human resources utilization, as well as to promote the adoption of new and more appropriate techniques of personnel management.

REFERENCES

1. Dunnette, M. D., and B. M. Bass, "Behavioral Scientists and Personnel Management," *Industrial Relations,* Vol. 2 (1963), 115–130.
2. Katz, D., and R. L. Kahn, *The Social Psychology of Organizations.* New York: Wiley, 1966.
3. Robin, D. P., "An Input-Output Model of Employee Behavior," *Academy of Management Journal,* Vol. 10 (1967), 257–268.
4. Stogdill, R. M., *Individual Behavior and Group Achievement.* New York: Oxford Univ. Press, 1959.
5. Stogdill, R. M., "Basic Concepts for a Theory of Organization," *Management Science,* Vol. 13 (1967), 666–676.
6. Thompson, J. D., *Approaches to Organizational Design.* Pittsburgh, Pa.: Univ. of Pittsburgh Press, 1966.

INDEX OF AUTHORS
OR SOURCES CITED

SUBJECT INDEX